# The First and Last Englishmen

# BRIAN BELTON

# The First and Last Englishmen

Foreword by Martin Peters MBE

Breedon Books
Publishing Company
Derby

First published in Great Britain by
The Breedon Books Publishing Company Limited
Breedon House, 44 Friar Gate, Derby, DE1 1DA.
1998

## This book is dedicated to memory of:

*Alan Sealey*
*1942-1996*

*(God bless you Sammy)*

ISBN 1 85983 115 X

Printed and bound by Butler & Tanner Ltd., Selwood Printing Works, Caxton Road, Frome, Somerset.

Colour separations by Freelance Repro, Leicester.

Jackets printed by Lawrence-Allen, Avon.

# Contents

# Foreword

**The Player**

IN 1959 I became a ground staff boy at Upton Park after the then manager, Ted Fenton, had convinced my father that West Ham United was the right club for me to join. Also joining the club at about the same time were Brian Dear, Dave Bickles, Ronnie Boyce and Roger Hugo. John Sissons was to follow. Bobby Moore, Geoff Hurst, Joe Kirkup and Jackie Burkett had already made their mark at the club.

My early memories were playing in the 'A' team under Ernie Gregory with Harry Cripps our captain. Following this, I turned out for the Reserves before making my debut in the first team at the Boleyn Ground against Cardiff City. It was Good Friday 1962. Ron Greenwood had dropped six players for that game, including Phil Woosnam, John Bond and Geoff Hurst. Bobby Moore was given the job of captain. Alan Sealey scored our second goal in the 4-1 victory.

These were great times for me, playing in Division One until the infamous match against Blackburn at Upton Park in December 1963. We lost 8-2 and I was replaced by Eddie Bovington. West Ham went on to win the FA Cup in 1964 with Eddie doing a great job.

In the 1964-65 season I claimed my place back in the first team, playing at centre-half. We had made great progress in the European Cup-winners' Cup and played the Final at Wembley. Our opponents were TSV Munich 1860. What a thrill for me after missing out the previous year. It was a wonderful match that was finally won by the player Ron Greenwood had bought from Leyton Orient, Alan Sealey. Two goals from Alan sealed the game on an evening at Wembley that we still talk about today.

Most of the boys who played in both Cup Finals came through the great West Ham youth scheme, being brought to the club by scout Wally St Pier.

These were wonderful times for West Ham fans to remember, and I shall never forget the smile on the face of Alan Sealey (God bless).

Martin Peters MBE

# Foreword

**The Supporter**

I ATTENDED my first match at Upton Park on 28 August 1954. It was the first home game of the season, the visitors were Notts County. West Ham had lost their first two games away from the Boleyn Ground, but on that bright day Jimmy Andrews and John Dick each got their third goal of that term. Harry Hooper (son of the West Ham trainer) made it a 3-0 victory for the Hammers. From that day, I rarely missed a West Ham game. It was the ill-conceived Bond Scheme, which was an insult to the intelligence of the loyal supporters, that condemned me to the role of armchair supporter. Only once since giving up my three season tickets, have I paid to watch a game at Upton Park.

The 1960s was the most evocative decade in the history of West Ham United. It was the club's finest period. During those years there were victories in both the FA Cup and European Cup-winners' Cup. We also reached the League Cup Final and two semi-finals of the same competition. We made the semi-final of the European Cup-winners' Cup in 1966 and, of course, England won the World Cup later that same year with three West Ham players in key roles.

In this era of success the club had four truly great players: the mercurial Budgie Byrne; the seemingly tireless goal machine, Geoff Hurst; the elegant, yet steely Martin Peters; and the imperious Bobby Moore. But there was also Alan Sealey. Perhaps he was not as glamorous as his four team-mates, but he was, like them, an Upton Park legend in his own right. Alan was a real local hero, who after supporting West Ham as a boy, was to score two goals in a couple of glorious minutes in the most momentous game in the annals of the club. These were the goals that defeated TSV Munich 1860 in the European Cup-winners' Cup Final, on a warm spring evening, below the awesome twin towers of Wembley stadium, the Mecca of world football.

This vintage performance would establish Alan's place in the history of West Ham United. It also gave him, and the Hammers, an unequalled record in English football. When Bobby Moore lifted the Cup-winners' Cup, West Ham had used 16 players to contest the nine games it took to win the competition. Those young Irons were all English. As such, they were the first and last team made up entirely of Englishmen (mostly Londoners and mainly East Enders) to win a European trophy.

The previous season had also been an historic one. The same 11 lads that had played in each round and eventually won the FA Cup in 1964 were all Englishmen. They were the last all-English FA Cup-winning side. When West Ham won the Cup again in 1975, an all-English XI took the field at Wembley, but Clyde Best, the Bermudan international, had played in the fourth-round tie and replay against Swindon. The feat of the 1964 side was again very nearly repeated in 1980, when we beat Arsenal, only Ray Stewart, being a Scot, was born beyond the English borders.

So, over two years in the 1960s, West Ham had become *The First and Last Englishmen.*

Years after his greatest triumph, Alan became a close friend of mine. As such, I was deeply saddened when, on 4 February 1996, he prematurely passed on, at the age of 53. Alan was a modest, unassuming man who rarely spoke about his achievements in football, or the most unfortunate of the injuries that shattered his blossoming career only three months after his epic feat at Wembley. He was only 23 years old.

That one occasion I paid to watch West Ham after the Bond Scheme was the match against Grimsby Town in the FA Cup, shortly after Alan's death. Along with thousands of others I went to pay my respects to one of our own. During the minute's silence, which was wonderfully observed, a recording of his Wembley triumph was shown on the big screens. A deeply proud and poignant moment for anyone who has ever given allegiance to the claret and blue of West Ham United.

A few days later it was touching to see so many of his former colleagues and personalities from the game attend his funeral. It was a wonderful tribute to him as a man.

Personally, I will always remember his humility. An example of this was when I once asked to take a look at some photographs taken during his playing days. He called to his wife Barbara, asking where they were. After rummaging in a cupboard for a while, he pulled out an old plastic bag, stuffed full of a visual record of his career in football. As I was going through them later, I came across one that was signed by all the Beatles and Yoko Ono. I subsequently placed the photographs in a claret red album, backing each one with blue card. I will always remember Alan's response. He said, "Thanks for the thought, Terry. I would never have done that myself. It's something for Anthony to show his kids." (Anthony is Alan's son, a teenager at the time). This sentiment and unassuming attitude was typical of the man.

A while later, just before going away for a few days, I visited Alan at his home. I thought that he wasn't looking well and asked him a couple of times if he was okay. He replied, "Thanks for your concern mate, but I am all right, honest." A week later he was gone.

I will never forget Alan's great sense of humour, gap-toothed smile, the somersault of delight after his opening goal in the Cup-winners' Cup Final of 1965 and the love he had for his family.

Alan, thanks for all the memories.

Terry Connelly

# Introduction

ON 7 FEBRUARY 1996, before the start of the fourth round FA Cup tie at Upton Park against Grimsby Town, over 22,000 supporters stood with the players for a silent 60 seconds. The footballing home of winger Alan Sealey was hushed in memory of one of their own. West Ham United and tens of thousands of fans who supported the club during the golden period of the 1960s were saddened and shocked by the tragically premature death, just three days earlier, of one of the club's most famous players. He was 53 years of age. West Ham manager and Alan's long-time friend Harry Redknapp (who brought Alan's goalkeeping cousin Les to Upton Park) summed up the feelings of many when he expressed his condolences to Alan's wife Barbara, son Anthony and mother Elsie, for the untimely passing of his friend.

Mention West Ham's triumph in Europe in 1965 to the players who knew Alan Sealey and the first response you will get will not be too far from the following:

Malcolm Musgrove, an established and distinguished professional with the club at the time when Alan joined West Ham: "Under Ron Greenwood's guidance Alan played for the Hammers in the European Cup-winners' Cup against TSV Munich, scoring two goals in West Ham's victory."

Ronnie Boyce, the engine room of the great West Ham teams: "My most powerful footballing memory of Alan is, of course, his goals against Munich in the Cup-winners' Cup Final."

Martin Peters, who played 79 games alongside Alan in the Hammers colours: "We played together in the 1965 European Cup-winners' Cup Final at Wembley, where, of course, Alan scored twice."

Bobby Howe, with the Hammers throughout most of the 1960s: "Undoubtedly, the European Cup-winners' Cup Final was Alan's 'finest hour' as a player."

Trevor Hartley, with the Irons as a professional between 1965 and 1969: "The European Cup-winners' Cup Final at Wembley was Alan's finest match-winning performance."

As such, the career and life of the man affectionately known as 'Sammy' by his team-mates, is forever intertwined with the history of West Ham United in the 1960s. Alan Sealey symbolises how those of us who give part of ourselves to a football club, both create its identity and, to some extent, are identified by it. But Alan was more than this. He was 'every-man'. When you looked at him, as a supporter, he could have been you. He came from the same place as you, he spoke like you, he thought like you and, as such, he exemplified West Ham in the 1960s. Alan was 'one of us'. He represented the ultimate link between the fans and the players; he was a supporter who had become a player. As John Lyall, who gave 33 years of his life to the Hammers as a player, office worker first-team coach and successful manager, put it: "The people of the West Ham area are tough, enthusiastic, loyal and value comradeship and Alan had all the qualities of an East End boy."

When Alan stopped being a player he was still 'West Ham', so much so that his brief encounters with other clubs just could not work. As a faithful supporter, I for one, can understand and appreciate this. Fidelity is sacred in the East End. The Hammers emerged from, and are an extension of, the same. This should be no surprise. Loyalty is ingrained in the institutions and movements of the working class. Notions of 'family', the network of blood loyalty, the traditional bastion in the face of grinding need, are important around the West Ham heartlands. Alan Sealey was connected to such feelings. The *First and Last Englishmen* is a celebration of him and this, through the voices of fans, including the author, and players.

Alan had close friends among the players, Budgie Byrne, Peter Brabrook and Eddie Bovington, but he was liked by everyone. This is confirmed by the words of his former team-mates. John Sissons, one of the most feared wingers in England during his years with Irons between 1962 and 1970, recalled that: "Alan had a wonderful sense of fun and humour and was able to lift his teammates, particularly when we were playing away."

Martin Peters underlined this feeling: "Alan was always fun to be around. I don't think he had a bad bone in his body. He was a lovely man."

Brian Dear, a Hammer throughout West Ham's golden decade, knew Alan as well as anybody "My mum and Sammy's mum went to the same school and, coming from the same area, Canning Town, I knew Alan before he came to West Ham. Sammy was a good bloke. There's nothing bad to say about him. Everybody liked and got on well with him."

But more than this, Alan was family.

Alan established himself in Ron Greenwood's first full season in charge at Upton Park (1961-62), appearing in 32 First Division games and two League Cup ties. He scored 13 goals in those matches, including a celebrated strike in a 2-1 Boleyn victory over Double winners Spurs. The 1960s was a good decade to be involved with West Ham, according to Ronnie Boyce, and Alan played his part:

"It was a good time to be at the club. After games the team would go and have a meal with our wives and girlfriends at the Moby Dick in Romford. Alan was always a lively part of this."

Alan Dickie, the reliable and competent goalkeeper who travelled as 12th man during the victorious European Cup-winners' Cup campaign, recalls: "After games we would often have a meal in Ilford with girlfriends and wives. This ritual was moved to above the Co-op in Stratford after a time. Alan was always involved in this type of thing and a real live wire. For me he epitomised the East End. He was chatty, always had a lot to say. If anything was going on, he was in on it."

According to John Lyall: "At that time the club was all about being gentlemanly and considerate; a wonderful place to work. You used to look forward to turning up in the morning."

For Bobby Howe: "It was an honour and a privilege to be playing at West Ham United during the 1960s. Not only was this one of the most successful decades in the history of the club, but also the quality of the players was first class. While I did not play in the successful FA Cup and European Cup-winners' Cup teams, it was a great thrill to be caught up in the excitement of those events.

"The entertaining, attacking style of play produced by West Ham at that time has to be attributed to Ron Greenwood, whose progressive coaching ideas were way ahead of his counterparts and have formed the basis of a philosophy of his former players who are still involved in coaching for many years."

Alan Sealey was pivotal throughout the whole campaign that took the Irons to the European Cup-winners' Cup Final in 1965. He played in the first leg of the preliminary round match against La Gantoise of Ghent. The next hurdle for the Hammers came against a side from behind the Iron curtain, Spartak Sokolovo of Prague. West Ham won 2-0 at Upton Park, a fine performance. It was Alan's pass from which John Bond scored the first goal. Sealey got the valuable second eight minutes from time. West Ham played chessboard soccer in that match, but they needed Alan's instinct for the goal that helped to clinch the tie. They lost the second leg 2-1, but Ron Greenwood was not too far wrong when he said of his team, that included Alan: "I honestly believe no other side in England could have done so well here today."

'Sammy' turned out for the Irons in both legs of the quarter-final, playing a crucial part in West Ham's first goal in the 4-3 home win against the Swiss club, Lausanne. He was also in the side that gained the invaluable draw with Real Zaragoza in the second leg of the semi-final in Spain. Then there was the Final – very much Alan's story.

However, Alan Sealey always kept his feet firmly on the ground. Unlike today's rather pampered élite of professional footballers, the number of games he played was not really an issue, enthusiasm seemed to take over. Brian Dear elaborates:

"We loved a game and would often turn out down at the Co-op club in Epping on a Sunday. Jimmy Greaves used to play in goal."

The 1964 FA Cup winners were the last all-English side to win the FA Cup. The same 11 men played throughout the seven-game campaign. West Ham nearly did it again in 1975 and 1980. Among the 15 players who took the Hammers to the 1975 Final was the North Bank favourite, Bermudan Clyde Best. Clyde, a fine and powerful striker, played in the fourth-round draw and replay against Swindon. He used to coach at my school, so from real close up I can say Clyde was a great player, but he was a good bloke too. In 1979-80, the ten-times Scottish International Ray Stewart turned out in the defence for all eight matches that ended with the Irons' 1-0 victory over Arsenal.

In 1965, the 16 men who together won the European Cup-winners' Cup were the first and last all English team to win a European trophy. Again, West Ham nearly repeated the feat in 1976, but lost in the Final to Anderlecht. However, there are always problems when one tries to make such an analysis, as Stan, son of a Polish 'Free Army' soldier and a supporter of West Ham for 50 years, reflects:

"What does it mean to be 'English', though? Both Johnny Byrne's parents were Irish. In another era Budgie might well have been a paratrooper in Jack Charlton's Irish Air Force. Was he any more 'English' than, say, Clyde Best or Ray Stewart? Likewise, the 'English' that watch West Ham, being Londoners, are the product not of a country, but a former centre of the largest empire in history, and one of the great cities of the world. Most of them, if their family goes back a couple generations or more in the area, are descendants of people who lived in the biggest docks complex the world had ever seen. People arrived in East London from every corner of the globe and many communities have been transplanted in the district. That is why there is no such thing as a 'pure East Londoner'. Myths about 'English stock' or 'blood' are just as vulnerable."

Alan Sealey's two goals against TSV Munich 1860 in the 1965 European Cup-winners' Cup Final at Wembley ensured him immortality and established West Ham as a force to be reckoned with in Europe following the 2-0 victory over the Germans. Sammy, characteristically, underplayed his part in both the goals, but they made history, not only in terms of West Ham United Football Club, but within the annals of English soccer. It was a new era, a time of change.

Following injury, Alan had just a handful of games for West Ham before moving to Plymouth. But his playing days as a professional were nearly over. He had a couple of goes at management, including the post of assistant to Cardiff City manager Jimmy Andrews, the former Hammers winger. Following this he came back to 'the Smoke' to coach young players at Charlton Athletic where Paul Walsh was one of his progeny. In 1980 he was given the number-two job at The Valley under the managership of Mike Bailey.

However, Alan was always an Irons man. He once said that the Hammers were 'unbelievable' and that West Ham were 'a club that has to be seen to be believed'. He said, "Players with West Ham don't know how well off they are. They don't know what life is like on the other side of the fence."

In later years Alan was beset by illness in the form of a liver complaint. Doctors diagnosed cirrhosis, but this was odd as Alan had never been more than a very moderate drinker. He later recalled: "Doctors asked me how much I drank. I did enjoy a pint, but I wasn't a day-after-day, pint-after-pint sort of drinker." It was thought that he may have contracted an infection whilst overseas. For all this, Alan never drank again. He said, "I wouldn't touch a drop, I couldn't chance it."

Alan seemed to have got over his health difficulties and had returned to football, scouting for West Ham and carrying out opposition assessment, when his illness suddenly returned.

Alan left a wife and son. Barbara, Alan's second wife, had know him for nearly 35 years, since she was just 11, when he was like a big brother to her. When Alan married his first wife Janice, they had remained the best of friends. As Barbara recalled: "I knew him as a brother, best mate, boyfriend and husband."

Anthony, 18 at the time of Alan's death, watched as the fans showed their respect for his father's memory before the Grimsby game. It was a minute of perfect silence inside the Boleyn Ground. The video screens poignantly depicted Alan's Wembley goals.

Alan's funeral took place at the City of London cemetery, Manor Park, at 3.45pm on Monday, 12 February 1995. It was just three months short of the 30-year anniversary of his Wembley triumph. The service, which was taken by the West Ham United club chaplain, the Revd Elwyn Cockett, was attended by a veritable West Ham hall of fame, including Geoff Hurst, Martin Peters, Jimmy Greaves, Brian Dear, Trevor Brooking, Eddie Bovington, Joe Kirkup, John Charles, Peter Brabrook, Ronnie Boyce, Frank Lampard, Billy Bonds, Harry Redknapp and Tony Carr. A claret and blue rainbow arched over the East End that afternoon as generations of West Ham fans welcomed Alan on to the verdant green of the celestial pitch, to line up along the likes of Len Goulden, Bobby Moore and Vic Watson. "We'll support you ever more."

On the evening following Alan's funeral, the West Ham team, most of whom had attended the ceremony earlier that day, beat Tottenham 1-0 at Upton Park. A young man from Portugal, Dani, scored. Croatian Slavan Bilic made his debut for the club.

West Ham could only get a 1-1 draw with Grimsby on that other night in 1996. The Hammers were still in mourning when they lost the replay 3-0. It was Grimsby's first home Cup win against a top division team since 1936. But the Irons had defeated them 1-0 at the same venue on the eve of Alan's ninth birthday.

Just three days after Alan was born, West Ham beat Reading 2-1 at Upton Park in the last game of the London War League season. Eddie Chapman and Mahon got the goals for the Hammers. On his fourth birthday, the Irons beat Swansea 3-0 at the Boleyn in the League South, and on the same day that Alan celebrated his 15th birthday, his team were again at home, winning the match against Bristol City 3-1, John Dick, Harry Lewis and Billy Dare scoring the goals. Just before Alan turned the corner for 44, West Ham defeated Newcastle 8-1 at Upton Park, Alvin Martin got a hat-trick. The Hammers celebrated Sammy's 47th with a 3-0 win over visitors Millwall, and as Alan made 50, the Irons were on their way to beating Manchester City by the only goal of the game.

Alan would consistently instruct young players when coaching to 'let it run'. He was asking them to allow the ball to do the work, a bit like Trevor Brooking used to do when he dropped a shoulder and let the ball move. Shortly before he slipped into a coma in hospital, his last words were, "Let it run." The tale of Alan Sealey, the local boy whose two goals made West Ham the stuff of front-page adulation on the morning of 20 May 1965, and a club that football fans all over Europe would now respect, will, like the ball, run and run.

# INTRODUCTION

**Author's note**: The statements, actions and views concerning Alan Sealey and other former West Ham United players in this book have been drawn from information found in literature, gleaned from interviews with Alan (radio, press and books) or are the product of material provided via letters from, and interviews (undertaken by the author) with Alan's family, friends, supporters and former colleagues. Every effort has been made to reflect Alan's upstanding character, kind nature, distinguished good will, and general affability.

This book makes no claim to be an exhaustive biography. It is a work that looks at West Ham United in the 1960s through the eyes of supporters and players. It features Alan Sealey's part as a major contributor to the club's fortunes during those years.

Alan's wife, Barbara, gave her blessing to this project on its inception. I would like to express my thanks to her and all Alan's friends, team-mates, the supporters and others connected with his time at West Ham United, including Ernie Gregory and Ron Greenwood, for all the help they gave me in the writing of this book. All these people have been kind enough to contribute to the development of the work in a genuine and generous manner. A number of supporters requested that their identity or at least full names would not be used. This being the case, when using the contribution of fans, I have stuck to the use of first names only. Some of these have been changed, respecting the wishes of those concerned.

Finally, the views expressed in what follows do not necessarily reflect the views of the author or any other person, organisation or group connected with the book.

# The Football Culture of West Ham United

**W**EST Ham United Football club started life as an entertainment or distraction for the working men of East London's riverside community in the wake of the 1889 dock strike. Their first manager was the consummate showman Syd King. Syd was behind 'the electric tram' that toured East London lit up by a constellation of light bulbs celebrating the Hammers' achievement of reaching the 1923 FA Cup Final. If you look at the original architecture of the Hammers' first home, the Memorial Ground and later Upton Park, you will see certain echoes in the structures, reminiscent of a showground, a hybrid of the racecourse, the fairground and the circus. The enclosures and stands which housed the supporters were close to the pitch, painted in loud claret and blue. The football produced by King and his progeny and his successor, Charlie Paynter, was dynamic and muscular. Paynter also introduced the Cockney patrons of the Boleyn Ground to teams from mainland Europe and even more exotic climbs. He also organised European tours like the one of Norway in 1927.

Ted Fenton continued the tradition of inventiveness. With the encouragement and motivation of Malcolm Allison, Fenton continued to bring the best of European sides to Upton Park and a few good South American teams. He created a modern youth policy and opened the team's horizon's in terms of foreign innovation, which influenced the team's shirts, boots and tactics. Gradually the effort to entertain incorporated the search for success through the adaptation of science, logic and mathematics to the requirements of football excellence.

With the arrival of Ron Greenwood at the club, a moral and ethical philosophy, which at times became close to being a religion, was added to the social make-up of West Ham. Greenwood, although not too far from Fenton in terms of his intellectual response to the game, was part of a modern European 'church' of football, which included the likes of England managers Walter Winterbottom and Alf Ramsey. Greenwood himself had been the England Under-23 coach before joining the Hammers.

As such, Greenwood's effort to take the traditional physical strengths of English football and merge these with the best of continental and South American ideas were soon taken up at national level. West Ham thus became a kind of laboratory of football in the early to mid-1960s, an 'academy' of soccer development.

This being the case, the England team that won the 1966 World Cup was a new model football team, representing a unique technology. This is why Ramsey wasn't taking as much of a chance as everyone thought when he predicted prior to the finals in England, that his side would win the Jules Rimet Trophy. The team that contested the Final, with three West Ham players in its ranks, was made up of players with a range of gifts and qualities that represented a mix of technical knowledge/ability, traditional English physicality and natural genius. Just looking at the players involved demonstrates this:

| Genius | Physicality | Technical |
|---|---|---|
| Banks | Charlton, J. | Moore |
| Charlton, B. | Cohen | Hurst |
| Peters | Wilson | Hunt |
| Stiles | Ball | |

Of course, there are overlaps. Martin Peters was technically perfect and could be quite physical. Alan Ball and Bobby Moore had huge elements of genius. But the point is that the England team, like the West Ham side of the mid-1960s, was something quite unusual. Indeed, study of the 'English system' – how it used flexible positioning in the 4-2-4 formation – provoked the Dutch 'Total Football' sides of later decades, the Danish European champions and even the successful German teams. All this can be traced back to Upton Park in the late 1950s and the fruit of this period was the West Ham Cup winners of the 1960s.

What happened? Well, the genius factor is important, but there is always a point where innovation becomes convention. This is why there is not much to choose between most Premier League sides and good First Division teams. It is why, in the 1998 World Cup, teams like Japan and Nigeria could come out with good results against traditionally powerful nations like Spain; everyone is catching up with everyone else. The focus of effort has been placed on the genius factor, hence the price of this in the market. But as exemplified by the likes of Brazil and Argentina in France 98, this is not enough. The next team to dominate world football is the team that can do what England did in 1966. Another West Ham is needed. Or are we doomed to watch various versions of the rootless, mercenary armies currently 'finessing' their way round the soulless, monolithic edifices of Stamford Bridge, Old Trafford and Highbury? This, of course, will all be our decision; us, the supporters. You see, it is only clubs like West Ham in the 1960s that will take a chance and experiment, to create something novel, because they have to. Manchester United, Liverpool, Arsenal and the like are too big to innovate. They will always play it safe, for the sake of shareholder dividends. If we support these clubs rather than our local sides, what we will get is bland homogeneity. This is already happening. Apart from the shirts, what is the difference between the group of players who turn out for Chelsea or Aston Villa or Inter Milan? Who would come out on top among this lot on the field of play? Take your pick; it's a lottery.

This is why I think we need to look back at the Irons of the 1960s. To understand where we are, post-France 98, we need to have some idea of where we have come from. This is also helpful in terms of getting where we want to go.

# Local Boy Makes Good

ALAN Sealey was a true East Ender, despite being born in Hampton, Middlesex (Alan's mum had been evacuated during the Blitz). He lived in Ernest Road, Canning Town when he was a kid and went to Pretoria Road School. His dad used to deliver fruit and veg for a living and his mum was a machinist.

To keep the family going, little Alan's parents were obliged to work full time, so he was often looked after by a downstairs neighbour. Her name was Liz but everyone knew her as 'Nan'. Liz had left school by the time she was 13 and worked at Keelers, the jam factory in Silver Town. Nan was a good old girl, and was always kind to Alan. She was a great cook, but he was easy to please (Alan would eat anything, although crab never agreed with him). Nan liked a drink. Nothing over the top, just sociable. Right into her late 90s, come hell or high water, she would have her rum and bitter in the Ordinance Arms in Rathbone Street market. In those days it was quite something for a woman to go into a pub on her own, it took some front, but Nan had plenty of that. All her brothers and sisters had been in service, but that was not something Nan would have taken to easily. Towards the end she had to be carried from her flat to the pub by the landlord, but she hardly ever missed a session. She smoked like a chimney too, but having a sing-song and a good time was her secret for a long life. Some of that 'lust for life' may have influenced Alan's approach to living. Alan enjoyed life but he didn't need drink to help him with this, never wanting more than the odd pint. He was a non-smoker apart from the occasional cigar on special occasions, but no more than the one.

If you go in the Ordinance today, you will see a plaque dedicated to the memory of Nan on the seat where she used to perch herself. She was a fighter and a survivor; a real character. She would hardly ever let anything get her down. And in many ways this is typical of the people of the area Alan came from. You often notice the same spirit in West Ham supporters. They might 'eff and jeff' a little when the team are not at their best – and, true, they gave Alan a bad time every now and then – but even after the worst defeats they sing. They seem to see what has happened as an opportunity to show their true strengths, to stand up together, stare into the face of adversity and stay loyal. It's a type of defiance.

George, who followed the Hammers to Spain for the team's semi-final second-leg game against Real Zaragoza in 1965 found a simile: "When I was in Spain with West Ham I came across something of the same thing when I saw a bit of flamenco dancing. The dancers appeared to disdain fate and relish who they were."

There's a deal of talk about feminism and the independence of women these days, but Nan did more than talk the talk, she walked the walk; she lived it. At the same time she was honest, kind and fun. Alan was out of the same mould.

A lot of kids dream of playing football for a living. It is certainly true that for the ordinary supporter, who never gets nearer to the game than watching from the stands, to be involved on the field of play would be as likely as sprouting wings and flying out of the stadium. But when it happens to you, as part of the stream of life, it is hard to see things through the eyes of others. Alan Sealey wouldn't have gone so far as to say that being a professional footballer in the First Division was ordinary, but he really didn't want to do anything but play sport for a living. In many ways he couldn't do anything else. Perhaps most professional players would say the same thing. Maybe that is why many ex-pros find it so hard to fit into 'normal' life once they hang up their boots. They are always an 'ex-player'. When Alan retired from the game he was 'the former

West Ham striker' before he was Alan Sealey. The player becomes the game; it is woven into his identity.

Like most people in football, Alan was an ordinary person. In the right place at the right time? Lucky? Perhaps. There's no doubt that there are hundreds of talented players making a living as cab drivers, factory hands or painter and decorators. They just never got the breaks. They played in the wrong game, on the wrong day, in front of the wrong scout or they turned up for a trial on a morning when the manager was hung over. We can do our share to help ourselves, but in the end fate selects us for what we do, whatever our place in life. That's how Alan felt about football, it chose him. For him, joining West Ham was just like this. The first he knew of it was when he was told by Orient that he was on his way to Upton Park. It just happened!

However, when Alan Sealey left school, things didn't look that certain. He started a plumbing apprenticeship at Harland and Wolfe in Silver Town, but lasted only a couple of weeks. He was never very practical, apart from pumping up and lacing footballs. Alan's first sporting love was cricket. His father supported Surrey, but Sealey junior followed and played at schoolboy level for Essex. He also turned out for his local boys' club cricket team. Fairbairn House Boys' Club was in Canning Town, about a 15-minute walk from the Boleyn Ground. Alan was selected for the London Federation of Boys' Clubs and was good enough to play against England Young Professionals at Lords. The LFBC's skipper that day was a lad called Alan Mullery. 'Mullers' was also a fair footballer. He took up with a little North London side called Spurs eventually. Sealey got the best score in both innings (26 and 36), and won a Pepsi Cola for his efforts.

Alan was one of the last of a breed of footballing cricketers, but there were quite a few at West Ham at that time. Eddie Presland, who played a consistent role in West Ham's good and well-supported reserve team, and was a constant member of the first-team squad, was also a fine cricketer himself, elaborates:

"Bobby Moore and Alan were also good cricketers and, as we were all East London boys, I knew them well through this side of things. Later on, with the likes of Geoff Hurst and Jim Standen, we had a fine cricketing side at West Ham. We would take on the best of the top amateur sides, like Ilford from the Essex League, and beat them with ease. We would play the Tate and Lyle team on their riverside pitch. We used to try to hit the ships that were moored nearby, towering over the field. Alan was a brilliant fielder. I only realised this as I ran past him. I was out again.

"As teenagers Bobby, Alan and I played cricket in the same side in regular games against the three big public schools, Eton, Harrow and Winchester. We were as different as chalk and cheese, but we got on well with these lads. Bob and Alan would have a good time teaching them the rhyming slang and so on. Even then Alan was a turn and half.

"I would often travel to cricket matches with Bob. As I was a bit younger I would get the half-fares for us both (Bob, at 14, would have been obliged to pay full adult price). Whenever I met Bob later on he would ask me if I was still getting halves."

Ron Penn, was a business partner of Jimmy Greaves (who was a close friend of Alan's) and Sealey's frequent comrade on the cricket pitch. He recalls the lighter side of Alan's cricketing career: "I played cricket against Alan when he was with Lennox – that was Eddie Baily's and John Walsh's team. We eventually played together for Walthamstow. In one game we had the Essex and England captain to-be, a young Keith Fletcher, in our side. He made a double century that day. Alan spent a good three to four hours padded up, waiting for his innings. When the time came for him to take the field he was in the lav, someone else had to move up the order and Alan had to sit it out a bit longer.

"In another game Alan was up against a good spin bowler and playing him very defensively. An old chap, Monty Ward, was shouting from the stands, "Hit it. Hit it out of the ground!" After a while, this got to Alan and he did hit it, only to find himself dismissed. He went straight into the pavilion and came out with a huge Elastoplast which he stuck right across Monty's mouth.

"Once a handbag got snatched and the bloke who nicked it made off across the pitch. We had a copper in our side at that time and he gave chase. Alan took off behind the policeman shouting, "Nee, nor, nee nor," like a patrol car siren.

Alan had a strong throwing arm. He'd throw as hard as anyone I've known. He would send the ball back to me behind the stumps whether there was a chance of a run out or not. He knew when I didn't have any inners on, but I think this made him chuck it all the harder. It did sting."

Long-serving goalkeeper Alan Dickie played in the West Ham cricketing side and his enthusiasm has endured: "This is the first year [1998] I haven't played football, but I still play cricket, although, as we are in the same team, I try to get my son not to call me dad on the pitch." Cricket played a part in 'Spider' leaving the professional ranks, he broke his nose playing the game whilst at Aldershot.

For what ever reason, though, Alan Sealey never broke into the professional side of the leather-on-willow game. However, in his late teenage years, his football was drawing attention. He could cover the ground pretty sharpish, and was able to take a football along with him. Alan also carried a bit of a shot if he caught it right, although he always had some skill. He played football for Fairbairn, the club had given a start to many top players. It was while playing for the boys' club on Hackney Marshes that Alan was spotted by Eddie Heath. The tall youth-team scout had been around the London football scene for some time with Orient, Chelsea and eventually Spurs. At that time Eddie ran the Leyton youth side that was used by Orient as a grooming ground. He invited Alan to play for his team as an amateur. So, one night Sealey turned up at the Orient ground expecting to take part in a training session. Instead he found that they were staging trails for players under the age of 21. Eddie asked Alan to join in. He was 17 at the time and, as such, the opposition was much older than him. Alan had a good game, managing to score five good goals. Les Gore, then the manager at Orient, approached Alan after the game and asked: "How would you like to be a pro footballer?"

The young man didn't need much persuading. Alan had a little motor scooter at the time and Les and Eddie followed him home to talk things over with his parents. It was a rush, but young Alan didn't need time to think. The next day Alan Sealey went off with the Fairbairn club side to play in a competition in Sandwich, Kent. Orient were so impressed, and anxious to avoid a slip-up, they recalled him to London by telegram for the signing formalities. After that he went back to Kent. Alan had become a £10-a-week professional player. He started in the Os' 'A' team and met Eddie Baily for the first time. Baily was the assistant manager at Orient. Eddie is recognised within the game as a ground-breaking coach of the 1950s and 1960s. He recalls: "Alan was discovered playing on the Marshes by Eddie Heath who worked for me at Orient. I got him to train with the youth team."

Eddie Baily had been a striker with Spurs and Forest. He later became the chief scout at West Ham and the assistant manager at Tottenham. Alan always felt indebted to him, seeing Eddie as a good man. Eddie would pick him up from home, and for a long time, he and his wife treated Alan like one of the family. Eddie reminisced: "Alan became part of the family for a few years. Me and my wife would pick him up and take him to games and training. We got involved with him as a young lad growing up."

Eddie Baily recruited Alan to play for his cricket team, Lennox, on Sundays: "I took him along to play cricket with the club I was involved with at the time and it was there that he met the lads who were playing for the Tottenham side of that era, Ted Ditchburn and so on."

The Lennox cricketers included many of the big names from the Spurs team of the time.

Eddie Baily's knowledge of football was vast. He knew how to play, but he could also watch a game well; he could see what was going on, even say what was going to happen before a move was made. Perhaps some of this rubbed off on and motivated players like Martin Peters and Bobby Moore. It is this gift of insight that turns capable players into great performers. Alan Sealey, at his best, was capable of this, but he was generally more intuitive. He wasn't gifted in the same sense as Peters, who was a phenomenon, born to play the game. Alan once said that Peters was the best player he had seen. Sealey never had the same type of discipline and control as Moore – who did? – that enabled Bobby to make himself into a great player. But, at times, Alan could move at exactly the right moment. He understood; everything seemed laid out before it happened and all that was required was that he just place himself. Moments such as these are euphoric, happening on days always remembered. They are given to few of us, and then only for a short period in our lives. You can see when others are having experiences of this kind, but, like so many things in life, you cannot appreciate them until they have gone from you forever.

Eddie Baily coached and taught Alan Sealey into the Orient Reserves and finally to the League side. In those days the Os had a reputation as a footballing club and it rubbed off on Alan. As he himself said: "I was a youth-team player some Saturday mornings and a League player some Saturday afternoons."

Alan turned out only four times for the Os' first team. His debut, a match against Rotherham, was followed by consecutive games against Swansea, Plymouth and Luton. Alan's first and last goal for the senior side was the winner in his last match for Orient, a confrontation with the Hatters. He then found himself transferred to his local team.

# The Beginning

## 1959-60

A T THE end of the 1958-59 season, West Ham finished in sixth place, this in their first term back to Division One since 1932. They had also been Finalists in the FA Youth Cup for the third time in three years. The Hammers were very much a local club. As Eddie Presland, who was part of the West Ham first-team squad for seven years from 1960, remembers: "In the 1960s the players were assimilated with the supporters. We would use the same pubs and cafes. Most of us lived in the same sort of area. We were doing a bit better than them, of course. After a raise in 1964, we got around £40 a week. That was much better than our predecessors. The likes of Malcolm Allison and Noel Cantwell were paid around £7 a week.

"The 1960s was the time to be at West Ham. They were 'infectious' years. I was picked for one home game and as I got to the ground it was already full. The gates had been closed at 1.30pm. That wouldn't happen now. We used to get eight or nine thousand turn up for reserve games. People didn't go to away matches you see, unless they were big cup matches."

At that time supporters were capable of turning games. Presland gives an example:

"We went to Sunderland once. When Charlie Hurley headed in the winning goal for them, the crowd behind the goal made such a roar. It was like they sucked the ball into the net. I looked at Joe Kirkup and he looked at me. After the game he said to me, 'Was that a noise or what?' It was overpowering."

In those days most kids started with their local clubs. Eddie continues: "Alan, Bobby, Ronnie Boyce and I had a lot of contact through our interest in football even before we were together at West Ham. Allison and Cantwell used to get an extra 30 shillings for training the local school boys – I was one of them – on Tuesday and Thursday evenings."

Alan Dickie (who was to be nick-named 'Spider') was a typical recruit: "I just wrote in for a trail, I wasn't even playing for my school side at the time. With a few others I was asked to go down to Grange Farm. Next time there were fewer kids and then I was invited to come to Tuesday and Thursday training sessions. I put much of my ability down to my aptitude for basketball."

Dickie was the part of the life-blood of the team that came into the 1960s: "I was tall, thin and sluggish. In training runs I was always at the back with Bondy and Cantwell. We had this thing called Pudding Lane. You were turfed out of the coach and told to run the length of the Lane. It was six miles or so, unless you could get a lift from a lorry or something. Bondy always told us to take some money with us so we could get a bus. Ted Fenton would take a shooting stick and binoculars. Ted was very much a country gent – tweed jacket and cap. It was rumoured that he would watch out to see if the players were shirking. Every now and then you'd hear someone say, 'Watch out, Ted's watching.'"

West Ham won their opening game of the football decade by 3-0 at Upton Park. Leicester were the victims. One Hammers supporter, Harry, was in the Army in Aden at the time: "I was away from England for the first time. It's hard to tell anyone who hasn't been to Aden quite what it's like. It's a remote place, locked in an atmosphere so far from the East End that you might as well be on another planet. We got British newspapers, even if they were a bit dated by the time we got them, and we had the BBC World Service, so you could keep in touch with events back home, including the football. There were also letters."

Fenton had his worries. Vic Keeble and Phil Woosnam were recovering from cartilage trouble and he also had his doubts about the age of his squad, who were getting on a bit. However, the victory against Leicester was followed by a draw at Preston and a 3-1 win at Turf Moor, despite allowing Burnley to open the scoring. This was a good result against the champions-to-be.

At the end of August, Preston, with Tom Finney in his final season as a player, were beaten at Upton Park. The Hammers were off to a respectable start and their supporters were entitled to some hope for the season.

Harry again: "News of football was regular, routine. Most of it you could expect, but between the lines there are always surprises. Kind of comforting really, especially when you are far away from all that you have known. Keeble, Woosnam and Ted Fenton, their small adventures, victories and disappointments. Their positions, right-half, centre-forward, left-back, felt familiar. One point for a draw, two for a win. Two clubs go down, the winner goes through to the next round. It gives a sense of continuity and security. This was particularly precious in Aden. Europeans were a constant target. Snipers, knife attacks, explosions, these were everyday events. As the results were read, it reminded you of home. The kettle singing, dinner on the table, Mum checking the pools and Dad whistling gently as he cared for his canaries in the back yard."

The first set-back came at the start of September when the Irons were beaten 2-1 at home by Leeds. The next week, following a brilliant display by the West Ham goalkeeper, Noel Dwyer, in a 2-2 thriller at Spurs, this seemed to be no more than a hiccup. However, in the return at Upton Park just a few days later, the Hammers were defeated in front of almost 38,000 fans. In between the two matches against Tottenham, West Ham had been beaten 5-1 at Burnden Park.

There was a race against time to get John Dick – injured since the second game of the season, at Preston – fit for the next game, at Chelsea. But the race was won, West Ham prevailed 4-2 before a 54,000 crowd at Stamford Bridge – and Dick scored two of them. Then Fenton took the Hammers back to Upton Park for a 4-1 victory against West Bromwich Albion. There was a creditable goalless draw at St James's Park. John Bond moved up to centre-forward during that game but Jimmy Scoular was the Magpies' centre-half that day; just the sort of player to encourage 'Bondy' to rethink any ideas he might have had about leading the attack being a soft option compared to full-back.

When winger Mike Grice was injured, Fenton threw young Derek Woodley into the home game against Luton Town. It paid off. Woodley scored twice on his League debut, in a 3-1 win. But it wasn't enough to retain his place and for the following game at Goodison Park, Grice returned. Maybe Fenton saw a need for some experience in the side, as he was obliged to bring in two 17-year-olds, John Cartwright and Andy Smillie, for Woosnam and Dick. Again, the use of youth paid off, although it was the experienced Malcolm Musgrove that got the only goal of the game. That same day, Bobby Moore made his sixth League appearance for the Hammers.

Just prior the game at Everton, Ted Fenton had been informed that Noel Dwyer had been chosen to play for the Republic of Ireland. Fenton believed that psychology played a large part in the football manager's life, and as such delayed telling Dwyer about his selection. Before the game he told him that he had heard that the lad was in the running for a cap, and reminded him that John Carey, the Everton boss, was the Eire team manager. Dwyer played out of his skin. So Fenton's tactics seemed to be effective, even if they were deceptive.

Back at Upton Park, Malcolm Musgrove scored again in West Ham's second consecutive single-goal game. It was a tight match against Blackpool. This was followed by a 1-0 defeat at Craven Cottage, a game that marked the beginning of the end of Vic Keeble's career, he played only one more game. Keeble was a determined character. He travelled 40 miles a day from his home in Colchester for extra training in an effort to get back into the squad. Often he was the only player at the club on Thursdays, then the team's one day off. He was subsequently forced to give up playing with persistent back trouble.

Fenton decided to move Harry Obeney from wing-half to centre-forward (apparently on the suggestion of club chairman Reg Pratt). Obeney played a Keeble-type game on the first Saturday in November, a 4-1 trouncing of Manchester City at the Boleyn Ground. Now the mighty Arsenal were waiting. But the Hammers were near the top of the First Division and looking confident. The feeling spread as far as Aden and Harry: "This really helped. It's peculiar how your team doing well can colour your life. Looking down from the top of the League the world looks …more manageable, and it's true that I became more comfortable in my posting as West Ham climbed up the table."

To combat the awe of playing at Highbury, the West Ham players were sent out in new lightweight shirts. This was not Fenton's idea. Malcolm Allison had been pestering him for some time before he left the club about the lightweight boots and kits used in Europe. That day in North London was the first small act of the hidden revolution in English football. This was the tiny starting point of the modern game in Britain. The ground was light and West Ham were playing fluently. The Irons won well, 3-1.

By mid-November West Ham had deposed Spurs as League leaders. Then it was the League champions, Wolverhampton Wanderers, at Upton Park. At one point The Hammers were 3-0 up. John Dick, whose strong shot and aerial power had gained recognition in his selection for the Scottish side to play England at Wembley, scored all the goals. However, late into the game Wolves came storming back, but the Irons were fit and confident and hung on to win 3-2. Young Brian Rhodes, who took Dwyer's place in goal when the Irishman was on international duty, did more than well, blotting out attack after attack with energy and courage.

November also saw Ken Brown selected for the England team to play Ireland at Wembley. John Smith was to be 12th man. The youth policy Fenton had initiated at West Ham was proving to be a good investment. However, at Hillsborough, on the final Saturday of that month, John Fantham scored twice as Sheffield Wednesday lashed the table toppers 7-0. This equalled West Ham's record away defeat, set against Everton in 1927. Although the Hammers seemed to recover by their next outing, beating Forest 4-1 at Upton Park, this was followed by a 6-2 thumping at Blackburn (Derek Dougan put four past his fellow countryman Dwyer). Two defeats in the Midlands, at the hands of Leicester and Birmingham (on Boxing Day), were succeeded by a win at home against the Brummie Blues, but then Burnley avenged their early-season defeat by winning 5-2 at Upton Park in January, and a trip to Elland Road was literally pointless. Three days earlier, on a freezing Thursday afternoon, Ted Fenton's lads were tipped out of the Cup in a replay at Upton Park by a Denis Law-inspired Second Division Huddersfield Town. Law was one of the youngest players ever to take the field for a League side. The final score was 5-1 to the Yorkshiremen. It was also West Ham's biggest-ever home defeat in the Cup.

Only three wins in the final 16 games of the season saw the Hammers slide down the table. For the most part the problem seemed to be in the players' minds. Danny, a supporter at the time, tells a familiar story:

"When things went well, the Irons could take on anybody, but they lacked the killer instinct needed to win the championship. This is what makes players want to beat the bottom clubs as well as the big outfits. Any team can get excited about a big match in front of a packed ground. The side that wins the title is the team that gets worked up about a League match against a struggling side in front of 10,000 spectators on a cold, wet afternoon in January."

West Ham put up one or two good shows during the rest of the season. Vic Keeble's absence forced Fenton to indulge in some experimentation. One of the most successful was playing John Bond at centre-forward. He made six appearances in attack in that period, scoring six times and netting a hat-trick in the 4-2 defeat of Chelsea at Upton Park in February. Terry Venables made his debut for the Pensioners that day, while the prolific Jimmy Greaves was marked out of the game by Andy Malcolm, a remarkable feat for any defender.

Not long after this there were newspaper reports suggesting that the result of West Ham's 5-3 home defeat against Newcastle had been 'fixed', but the rumours never came to anything. In later years there was a notorious bribes and betting case involving several Football League players, although no one who was remotely connected with West Ham.

West Ham and the East End in general were entering a period of transition. It was at about this time that Reggie Kray was accidentally caught backing up a demand for protection money and was sentenced to 18 months in Wandsworth Prison. This signalled the beginning of the end of the gang system that had ruled East London for the best part of 100 years. At the same time, it was clear that traditions at West Ham had to change. The old way and routine were clearly out-of-date. The good results were the product of determination and not a little skill, but the lack of a modern system for their game meant that the Hammers ran the tank dry. When the natural qualities of the players were tempered as the grounds hardened or turned to mud, their reserves of strength and their fitness diminished and there was no deep tactical structure to fall back on.

David Dunmore came from Tottenham in a deal that sent John Smith to White Hart Lane (as cover for Danny Blanchflower, Smith became one of the most expensive reserves in football). Dunmore, brought in as a replacement for Keeble, scored twice in his nine games for the Hammers at the end of that season, but what West Ham really needed was a Denis Law. Law, however, went to Manchester City and became the first player transferred between two British clubs for more than £50,000. The gap at wing-half left by Smith was filled by Geoff Hurst, but he made way for Bobby Moore.

Towards the end of the season West Ham were playing some good football, but were just not getting the breaks. However, over the season, 91 goals were scored against them. They lost 16 games after November, finishing in 14th place in that 1959-60 season, only four points clear of relegated Leeds. Aston Villa and Cardiff moved up to Division One replacing Leeds and bottom club, Luton.

Anthony Newley was at number one in the charts with *Do You Mind?* He had knocked Lonnie Donnegan's *My Old Man's a Dustman* from the top spot, and Adam Faith had come straight in at number three with *Someone Else's Baby* (even if Londoners couldn't win anything at football, they could at least sing everyone to death). The world held its breath as an American U-2 spy aircraft was shot down over the Soviet Union (who had won the European Championship, 2-1 against Yugoslavia). Wolves won the FA Cup, beating ten-men Blackburn in a boring Final.

Bobby Moore had played in the final seven games of the season after proving himself to be a more than competent replacement for Smith when the stocky wing-half was called up for the England squad to play Wales at Ninian Park, and again when Smith was selected for the FA team to play the RAF. It was on this occasion that Moore turned out against FK Austria in a friendly at Upton Park. The Austrians included most of their national team in the side that lost 2-0 to West Ham. Moore was a physical sign of change at Upton Park. The old days were almost over. Something was stirring down in the East End.

# 1960-61

IN March 1961, Alan Sealey arrived at Upton Park in a straight swap for David Dunmore, who went back to Orient after only one season with the Hammers. Dunmore scored 16 goals in 30 games for the Irons in the 1960-61 season, not a bad record, so the Irons hierarchy must have rated Alan Sealey pretty highly to accept the exchange.

THE BEGINNING

The move was particularly convenient for Sealey as a couple of years earlier his family had moved to Walton Road, not too far from the Boleyn Ground.

Following West Ham's plummet down the table late in the 1959-60 season, Ted Fenton decided to adopt the 4-2-4 system used by the Brazilian World Cup winners of 1958. To claim that Fenton made the decision alone is not quite accurate. For some time the senior players had been having a big say in how the team played. From the mid-1950s, Malcolm Allison had been as good as in charge of training and match tactics. These were hatched in an upstairs room of a local cafe with other senior members of the side. Eddie Presland recalls: "Malcolm brought a lot of new ideas to the club. He used to cut down the high leather boots they used to wear to resemble the modern/continental boot more closely. Bobby Moore was way ahead of his time in terms of thinking about the game. When we were eating everything that was bad for us in the cafe, he would be drinking carrot juice. It was odd to us, but he had read about it somewhere. He was so fit."

When Allison left, the likes of Noel Cantwell, Malcolm Musgrove and John Bond were working things out. This group, along with the developing Moore, were won over by the Latin American system following an early summer friendly game under the lights at Upton Park against the Brazilians, Fluminese.

The adoption of the 4-2-4 formation and associated tactics amounted to an incredibly bold experiment for the time, something totally new in British football. No one had tried this type of thing before, so there was little understanding of just how it would work in the English game. Nobody was aware of the intricate workings of the system. It was as much. 'suck it and see', 'trial and error' as anything else.

In the match against Fluminese, Noel Cantwell played left-back while Moore went to left-half. They decided they would have to change their tactics radically during the game because the visiting right-winger played a retractable role in a 4-3-3 formation, with the inside-right keeping well upfield as a free striker. Consequently, Moore marked the winger playing wide and Cantwell gave his attentions to the inside-right. The more they talked about it afterwards, the more the whole team became convinced that this was an effective way of organising play. By bringing one half-back into defence, the team were given a lot more defensive power, but didn't lose any attacking strength. So, from early on in the new 1960-61 season, this strategy was adopted at West Ham. At first, though, it didn't work well away from the Boleyn Ground.

John Dick for Andy Smillie was Ted Fenton's only change from the final line-up of 1959-60 as the Irons were beaten at Molineux, 4-2 in the opening game. This result had more to do with the quality shooting of Ron Flowers, who scored twice, than the formation adopted by the Hammers. With the season just eight games old, West Ham had a record of three wins and five losses – which included a 5-2 win at home to Villa and a 6-1 thrashing at Old Trafford. The experiment was ended following a 3-3 home draw with Blackpool. This match saw Bobby Moore, who in the 4-2-4 system was effectively playing at left-back, come face-to-face with his boyhood hero, Stanley Matthews. However, it was not a classic encounter. Matthews freely tormented Moore. As soon as he understood that the young man was going to stick close to him, trying to cut the great winger off from the supply of the ball, Matthews began to roam freely between all the attacking positions. Matthews, when playing for England against France a few years earlier, had done the very same thing to Roger Marche. This demonstrated how fixed English players were in their thinking. What was happening was not a lot different from the situation West Ham found themselves in when Milan had visited Upton Park for a friendly game some time before. In that match Brown, Bond and Malcolm played the very straightforward man-marking game.

Blackpool were one of the weaker sides in the First Division (they finished only one point clear of relegation) so a high-scoring draw, at home, was just not good enough. As such, Fenton felt obliged to reclaim the tactical decision-making. People in the game and the press took the opportunity to lambaste the 'new-fangled', 'Continental' ideas West Ham had embraced. The analysis of the Hammers as spineless theorists, who had abandoned traditional/cultural qualities for tricks and gimmicks, led to a demand for a return to the dashing, goalscoring wingers, and the 'W' forward line. Fenton ordered revision to the long-ball game and West Ham became one of the leading lights in the art of punting the ball into empty space beyond the halfway line. It was this tactic that they took with them into the new Football League Cup competition later that September. The Irons took part in one of the two ties which kicked-off the

League Cup, a competition which some other First Division clubs would have no truck with. The Hammers got a home win over Charlton Athletic in the first round but their next game in the competition ended in defeat at the hands of Darlington, a Fourth Division side.

Those looking to promote the 4-2-4 formation and way of playing at West Ham had hoped to use Moore, then a 19-year-old former youth international, in a critical role playing alongside Ken Brown in the middle. But getting used to the new situation was not easy, and for a time Moore lost form and so his confidence took a knock. This led to him taking up a less onerous role, that involved Noel Cantwell, who was the best attacking full-back in the country at that time, becoming a defensive unit as the auxiliary centre-half. Andy Malcolm, a faithful marker with a devastating tackle, but not the world's most able passer of the ball, became the attacking wing-half. To confuse things even more, the deep-lying forward Phil Woosnam was inside-right and so on the same side of the field as Malcolm. They ended up like this:

<pre>
                    Rhodes
    Bond        Brown        Cantwell      Moore
            Malcolm
            Woosnam
</pre>

In hindsight West Ham may have made better use of their personnel if they had lined up as follows:

<pre>
                    Rhodes
    Bond        Malcolm        Brown        Cantwell
                            Moore
        Woosnam
</pre>

This would have been a more balanced blend. Cantwell and Moore would have had more scope to use the quality of West Ham's attack, and Moore, being left-half, would have linked more efficiently with Woosnam at inside-right.

The Hammers made practical mistakes too. For example, in the game at

Villa Park, Bond shadowed Peter McParland wherever he went. This seems reasonable because McParland was a dangerous winger, but you cannot have zonal marking if someone leaves their zone. There were problems in attack as well. The four forwards in front of Woosnam were so worked up about their role, as the advanced component, they became immobile; they stayed in their set positions, failing to fully understand that if an attack is contained, the best solution is to come downfield to draw defenders with them. As a result, Woosnam was often left in possession in midfield, with his fellow forwards all tightly marked. The Hammers ended up losing 2-1 to Villa.

Real Madrid, who had won all the European Cups up to this time, used the 4-2-4 formation, but they played it subtly, as a very loose framework. If you stick too rigidly to any system, you get the mechanics, but lose the spirit. This is the same for anything really. Generally speaking, rules should only be regarded as a guide, a kind of catalogue of wise suggestions drawn from past experience. The acting out of any formula should leave room for creativity and innovation. However, people who can use systems and rules, but at the same time bring something new and developmental to a situation are rare. They are the few great players and managers who show up in any generation in football or those who make a difference in other professions. What makes a profession-al, footballer, lawyer, teacher is the ability to 'use' rules, rather than stick blind-ly to them. Innovation, and, if needed, departure from the regulations, is part of professional decision-making. To some extent, using judgement, one is making the rules as you go along – as anomalies and precedents present them-selves. This is how things are kept fluid and adaptation is made possible.

The Madrid team was full of players who were able to work with a refined fluidity, instinctively interchanging positions. Alfredo di Stefano, the heart of the team, might have been in his own penalty-area one minute and banging in a goal at the other end a moment later. But as he roamed around, the forma-tion stayed intact; someone else took his place as the link forward. In the Real side, not one forward saw himself as simply an attacker. At the same time, defenders were aware that they had attacking roles. Phil Woosnam understood this when England started to adopt the 4-2-4 system later in the season. When playing for Wales, he saw how Ron Flowers, who for Wolves was good at going forward and finishing with a powerful shot, was freed from his usual strictly defensive role as an international by the 4-2-4 formation. So much of what goes on in football is applicable to life in general. Watchful togetherness is often the key to situations.

The source of much of West Ham's trouble in 1960-61 was the lack of a reliable goalkeeper. Ernie Gregory, an England 'B' 'keeper, had made his final appearance for the club in the League game against Leeds on 5 September 1959. Dwyer and Rhodes both had spells between the sticks, but neither were consistent. The Hammers lost 22 goals in the 12 League and League Cup games following the draw against Blackpool. This encompassed a terrible string of away defeats and West Ham were beaten in each of their first seven games away from the Boleyn in 1960-61. Indeed, the Irons hadn't won an away match in the League since November 1959 (that victory at Highbury) and they had leaked goals in alarming fashion with fives, sixes and a seven being conceded.

That win at Arsenal was almost a year before their visit to Manchester City on 12 November 1960. For the whole game Fenton pulled everyone back except the wingers. The Maine Road connoisseurs pelted Rhodes with orange peel as West Ham held off Denis Law and managed to win the game 2-1 with goals from Dunmore and Grice.

Jim, who supported West Ham throughout the 1950s and the 1960s recalls: "All the best days that season seemed to be at Upton Park, where we scored five against Aston Villa (playing 4-2-4), Preston and Wolves. The 5-0 home win against the FA Cup holders, Wolves, was probably the best game West Ham were to play in the 1960-61 season. In the 50th minute of the match, Moore was advancing on the Wolverhampton goal, the 'keeper, Geoff Sidebottom, came out to dive at his feet, at the same moment that Bill Slater, the Wolves centre-half, attempted to slide tackle Moore as their left-back, Harris, was also piling in. Moore shot the ball into the net before any physical contact was made, but the three Wolves players crashed into each other as the ball crossed the line. The aftermath of the goal looked like a road accident. Eventually Sidebottom had to be carried off."

Wolves were in the middle of their campaign in the first European Cup-winners' Cup, the trophy for national cup winners. No one took a lot of notice of this competition at first, but some people in the game saw its potential in terms of bringing together clubs and players (like Alan Sealey) who thrived on the knockout excitement of cup football. The Cup-winners' Cup was the third major European tournament, following the European Cup and the Fairs Cup. It is intriguing that the tournament which was to mean so much for West Ham and Alan Sealey, was born the same season as player and club came together.

The Cup-winners' Cup suffered in its embryonic days through lack of support. Only in a few nations, notably England and Scotland, had domestic knockout cup competitions which were held in high regard. In some countries there was no such competition. In others, where cup competitions did exist, they lacked the magic associated with the knockout style in British football. Italy played such games in midweek, Spain contested their domestic cup at the end of the season. In France cup matches were played at neutral venues. Portugal employed a home-and-away system, while in Hungary and Belgium they revived their cup tournaments especially to provide qualifiers for the new European competition. As such, in the early days, only a handful of nations possessed the necessary qualifications or interest to take part in the new tournament.

It was in 1958 that UEFA first suggested the idea of a Cup-winners' Cup, but the notion did not have much appeal outside of half a dozen countries. This being the case, the plan was put on the back burner until 1960 when, with the Mitropa Cup out of action (the original 'European Cup' competition, for middle European countries) the number of possible entries rose to ten. The Mitropa Cup committee was given the task of organising the new tournament.

For most people involved in the game in England – fans, managers, administrators and players – the domestic competitions were the most important considerations. However, Eddie Baily's influence, and the traditional interest in foreign football at West Ham, would have had a great deal of impact on the young Sealey. Alan was quite a sentimental person and a sucker for anything with a slice of romance, so it would be surprising if the most romantic of European competitions would have escaped his notice.

The first series began with a preliminary round of two matches in order to reduce the entry to a manageable knockout competition involving eight clubs. In the first-ever match in the European Cup-winners' Cup competition, played in Berlin on 1 August 1960, ASK Vorwaerts of East Germany beat the

Czech Cup holders, Red Star Brno, 2-1. The Czechs won the return leg ten days later, 2-0. In the other preliminary tie, Rangers beat Ferencvaros of Hungary, 5-4 on aggregate. Rangers were out to justify their presence in European competition after their 12-4 aggregate thrashing at the hands of Eintracht Frankfurt in the previous season's European Cup. They found another West German club, Borussia Moenchengladbach, the ideal victims. After a 3-0 away win, the Scots scored eight without reply at Ibrox.

Rangers joined the Italians, Fiorentina, Dynamo Zagreb (Yugoslavia), and Wolverhampton Wanderers (who had beaten FK Austria 5-2 on aggregate) in the semi-finals. Fiorentina beat Dynamo and Rangers got the better of Wolves to win through to the Final, which was played on a home-and-away basis. Fiorentina took the first leg, winning 2-0 in Glasgow, both goals coming from Milan. In Florence, Milan and Hamrin scored to give the Italians victory. Scott got a consolation goal for Rangers.

However, at the start of the 1960s, the average British fan really didn't have time for all this. In London, the first Guy Fawkes' Night of the 1960s brought, for West Ham supporters, the most satisfying game of 1960-61. The Irons knocked six past Arsenal without reply. Dunmore, the man Sealey was to replace, got a hat-trick. Over 29,000 watched that game, but West Ham played before bigger attendances that season. One of the largest crowds, 46,000, saw Mike Beesley score in a losing debut at Goodison Park, but that figure was topped when West Ham visited Spurs on Christmas Eve and nearly 55,000 saw the home side win 2-0; two days later there were over 34,000 to see Tottenham complete the double, winning 3-0 at Upton Park. This was, of course, the season that Spurs won the biggest double of all – the Football League championship and the FA Cup.

As Sealey was injured at the time of signing, his first match as a Hammer was a reserve game, against Cardiff City. People hardly ever went to away games in those days and this meant that the Reserves had good support. It was not unusual for 6,000 to 8,000 people to turn up for those matches in the Football Combination. Sealey made his debut for the first team in April, against Leicester City at Filbert Street. In his own words he 'was a West Ham model mark one'. The Irons didn't do well. In fact they did very badly, going down 5-1. Joe Kirkup got the Hammers' goal. However, in his third game for the club, Alan Sealey got his first, and West Ham's only goal, in a draw against Manchester City at Upton Park. It was just a week before his 19th birthday and it was to be the only first-team goal of his first, six-game, season at Upton Park. All Sealey's outings took place in the last month of the League programme.

Alan Sealey got to the Boleyn at a peculiar time, between the departure of Ted Fenton and a week before the arrival of Ron Greenwood. Malcolm Musgrove remembers Alan's first days at the club: "Alan Sealey came to West Ham as a young, inexperienced centre-forward with a lot of potential. He was a good listener."

Sealey was signed by the chairman, Reg Pratt, who undertook all the negotiations with Orient. Alan described events leading up to his transfer: "I played a match for Orient against Plymouth on a Wednesday. The next day I went for treatment, although it was a day off. The injury was so bad that I couldn't get a shoe on and had to wear carpet slippers. I made my way home after treatment, then got a telephone call asking me to return to the ground. I went back, slippers and all, and found Reg Pratt waiting for me."

It was probable that Phil Woosnam had a lot to do with the deal. Although Woosnam had left Orient for West Ham before Alan arrived at the Os, he had got to know the young East Ender, and it is likely that the Welsh captain rated Sealey highly as a player. At that time Sealey was a centre-forward, a striker. He always played up front. West Ham fans may have raised their eyebrows on hearing that he was the replacement for David Dunmore, but he was more 'West Ham' than many of the lads who started their careers at Upton Park.

The players were using the period between Fenton leaving and Greenwood arriving to try out all sorts of things, and the level of innovation was high, even if the results were not all they might have been. Alan Sealey soon settled in. From the start he was a great admirer of Bobby Moore, who treated the new young recruit well. Moore showed him around the club on his first day and made young Alan feel very much at home.

Eddie Baily was doing work at Orient not too far removed from Ron Greenwood's style. So, when Greenwood came to Upton Park, Sealey just did the things he'd picked up from Eddie, the things Baily had drummed into him. This suited the type of game West Ham played. John Lyall, a member of the FA Youth Cup Final team of 1957, who played alongside Sealey between 1961 and

1962 recalls: "When he came from Orient he was bit younger than most of the established players, but he fitted in well."

The Hammers used someone up front, setting it up quickly. That was Alan's game. Eddie had taught him all about that. All Alan knew at that stage he had learned from Baily. Then Ron Greenwood took over as his mentor. Sealey, in common with many other players, consistently expressed his gratitude for, and appreciation of Greenwood's contribution to his development as a professional. Brian Dear, a great friend of Alan's, remembers: "Like the rest of us, Sam was a great admirer of Ron Greenwood. Ron was a purist and he liked Sammy."

Alan Dickie, who was with West Ham between 1962 and 1966: "Alan was a great admirer of Ron Greenwood, who brought many new ideas to Upton Park. Using the ball was central, though. There was a ball hanging up in the dressing-room, goalkeepers had to catch it, other players had to head it. In the players' lounge, where we'd have a drink with wives and girlfriends and opposition players after a game, there was a carpet and wicker chairs. Under the carpet was a mini-football pitch. Elastoplast tins were used as players. I think this came from the Fenton days. We would work out tactics with this. It was much better than a blackboard and chalk. However, Ron lost a few of us at times – 'put players in vacuums…'?"

Ron Boyce, who played 85 matches alongside Sealey, including Alan's first and last games with the club, reflects on this time in West Ham's history: "Alan came to the club as Ted Fenton, very much the last of the old school, was leaving and as Ron Greenwood, the first of a new breed of manager, was taking over. Ron broke it all down, lots of individual work. Nothing was rehearsed, free-kicks and so on. He did a bit on the near post, but Ron was a great one for keeping the ball moving. Alan worked hard for Ron and this was always appreciated, Alan, like the rest of us, had great respect for Ron as a coach. He was good at instilling technical ability into players. That's part of the reason why so many foreign players are coming into the British game now. It is harder to put technical ability into English players than it is for the continental players to pick up the pace of our game."

Alan Sealey became very much a Greenwood disciple. He once said that West Ham had a reputation as a 'nice-nice' side, and that, from a footballing point of view, there were things one would do for West Ham that would not be asked for elsewhere. According to Alan: "West Ham players didn't kick people." This attitude was confirmed by Brian Dear: "We didn't have the Vinnie Jones type down at Upton Park. We had some tough boys, but not hard players. Maybe that's why we didn't do as well as we might have done."

Alan looked like his dad, but he was probably more easy going, taking after his mum in the personality department. She was a thoughtful and kind person, not eager to push herself forward. Maybe he might have got on sooner if he had been a tad more pushy, but that was not Alan's way. He was a little nervous, and his stutter didn't help. He preferred to prove himself while having a bit of fun. He was always quite relaxed about his game as Brian Dear recalls: "Sammy was always the last to do everything. We'd be out on the pitch looking around for him and he'd still be on the lav."

But he had plenty of style. Brian Dear again: "He used to get around in a little Lotus Elan. Hardly room to get in."

Eddie Presland saw the influence of former mentors at work: "Malcolm Allison and Noel Cantwell were one step ahead in fashion in general and would always dress smartly, a bit like Bob and Alan really."

Although Presland made the point that not everyone was so inspired: "Peter Brabrook would turn up for training in his carpet slippers at times."

Alan Dickie recalled that Alan "was a smart fellow, always looked good in his gear".

Alan's interest in the greyhound racing helped him to integrate with a like-minded crowd including his best mate at the club, Budgie Byrne. They would go for a little flutter over at West Ham dog track and after a while Alan got into the ownership and breeding side of the sport. Although they were close as a team, West Ham players were always a certain type, there were definite social groups within the playing staff. No animosity, but certainly shared interests. It was one of these social groups who got to think of Alan as 'Sammy', and this was soon his 'Upton Park name'. According to Ron Greenwood: "He was known as 'Sammy' in the club. This was partly to do with his admiration for a particular foreign player, whose name he couldn't quite pronounce, so he called him 'Sammy'."

But most other people connected the title with 'Sammy the Seal', the kids cartoon character.

The 4-2 home defeat against Nottingham Forest in the League in November left West Ham looking like the very poor relations in London, with Spurs marching towards their League and Cup Double.

After the New Year, flame-throwers were used to make the third-round FA Cup replay at Stoke possible. But on the resulting gritty ice-rink, the Potters made it a hat-trick of first-game FA Cup exits for the sorry Irons. This, added to the departure of Cantwell to Manchester United for a record £30,000 fee for a full-back – an unpopular move, that was made in order to raise cash for new floodlights – was the scenario to the shock resignation of Ted Fenton in March. He was only the third manager in West Ham's history.

At first it was not clear if Fenton had resigned or if he had been sacked. He never commented on the affair, but it was rumoured that he had 'been allowed to resign'. Maybe he went because all the skill and promise at the club had failed to produce results. Fenton was the man responsible for bringing all of the great West Ham players of the 1960s to Upton Park. But he had been very distressed about the 'fixing' allegations of the previous season, and unhappy about the transfer request from John Smith.

Many thought that Fenton was a permanent fixture at the club. In his 11 years at West Ham, he had presided over the birth of a small revolution in British football at Upton Park (although this was instigated by the young Malcolm Allison). At the same time he was one of the 'old school'. He was a white-collar leader, wielding a pipe rather than wearing a track suit. He called a great deal on his military training. Perhaps in the end he knew what was needed and understood that he was not the man for the job. He was not a Brazilian, and although he brought something of the modern world to the club, particularly in terms of his relationship with the press and the fans, he was a man made in the English Second Division game of the 1930s and '40s. He moved on to Southend. His departure was part of the ushering in of the future. He had opened the door to progress, but quickly resisted it. Perhaps if he had embraced what was clearly 'the future', things would have been different. As it was, the need for the new was obvious; a 2-0 win at home to Cardiff was followed by an amazing 5-5 result at St James's Park and the five-goal Upton Park demolition of Wolves. In the next 20 games, though, West Ham failed to get a point in 11 outings. They won only three of these matches.

Long-serving goalkeeper and coach Ernie Gregory made the point: "Ted, Allison and the talent of scout Wally St Pier, brought the likes of Peters, Moore, Hurst and Boyce to the club. That had laid the basis for the future. Ron Greenwood built on these foundations." Eddie Presland remembered: "Wally was a gentleman. He was always an example to the kids and never forgot to ask how their parents were."

Fenton had cultivated a relatively warm relationship with the fans via the media, but the Ron Greenwood era was to be more reserved.

Malcolm Musgrove, who in 1959-60 had become the first winger to top the club's post-war scoring chart, repeated the feat in 1960-61. Just a single away win all term (a record 'feat' only equalled in 1922-23, 1932-33 and 1937-38) meant that in the first full season of the new decade, West Ham achieved a final position of 16th. Bobby Moore won the Hammer of the Year title for the first time.

Supporter Jim looked back at the summer of 1961: "During the break of 1961, Ron Greenwood must have wondered where he had ended up. London's biggest-ever manhunt took place in June, after two policemen had been shot in cold blood and a third was seriously wounded in Tennyson Road, West Ham. The final showdown between the cops and the gunman took place around a phone box in Lake House Road, Wanstead. Scores of policemen, in more than a dozen cars, in uniform and plain clothes, many of them armed, converged on the booth. As the cars screamed to a halt, the cops leapt out and encircled the telephone box. Two unarmed policemen from a patrol car approached the box, as they did so, a shot rang out and a man slumped against the door and fell on the pavement. He'd shot himself. One or two people thought he might have been a disgruntled West Ham supporter that finally had to face the reality of his situation. Folks can be so cruel!"

At the start of the new season, there were grounds for optimism. West Ham had a good manager and some decent players. But Alan Sealey always kept his feet firmly on the ground. For him "today's headlines are tomorrow's chip paper". Like everyone else in the game, he wanted success, but there were more important things going on. During his short time with the club, the Soviet Union had put the first man into space, Cuba had been invaded, Ernest Hemingway had committed suicide, and a wall had been built to divide Berlin.

At any moment the planet looked ready to blow itself to bits. For many people, at the start of the 1960s, it seemed more important to try to enjoy life. If scoring one or two goals could be part of this, that would be fine. At least it would put a smile on a few faces.

# 1961-62

MANY fans had been affronted that an 'Arsenal man' had been put in charge of the Irons. Before Greenwood's appointment, only 'dyed in the wool' West Ham men, who had played for the club, had been put in charge of the team. Greenwood was an outsider in more senses than one. He had been the assistant manager at Highbury and had been with the Chelsea side which won the championship in 1955. He was also a northerner, from the Lancashire cotton town of Burnley.

On his arrival Greenwood called all the players together and told them: "Let's face it, you are a team that is just like your theme song. You're always promising – and then the bubble gets burst before you win anything. That's what my job is – to stop the bubbles being burst."

Some of the lads had a little difficulty with this, not quite grasping exactly what he was talking about.

For all this, Greenwood had worked with the England youth and Under-23 teams and he had youth on his side. He was still in his 30s, just. This, together with the fact that he had been left a decent legacy in terms of the potential of the team, gave supporters cause to be optimistic about the coming season. However, doubts about Ron Greenwood were not helped by the fact that he missed the first game of the season, the 1-1 draw at Upton Park against Manchester United, because of a cold. Alan Sealey laid on the Hammers' equaliser for John Dick.

Sealey's connection to greyhound racing and the environment that surrounded 'the hounds' grew from the start of his time at Upton Park. As Martin Peters related: "Alan liked a gamble." Johnny Byrne, who played 205 times for the Irons between 1962 and 1967, and scored 107 goals, was a fellow dog racing enthusiast and a good friend and team-mate of Alan: "Sammy was a friend, colleague, gambling and social mate. Yes, we had a lot in common."

Ronnie Boyce, who gave nearly 40 years service to West Ham as a player, coach and, between the departure of Lou Macari and the appointment of Billy Bonds, manager, recalls: "He loved his dogs. He met Barbara [Alan's second wife] through that interest. Her dad had dogs in his back garden and, of course, that suited Sammy down to the ground."

His love for the dogs could even bridge the Atlantic Ocean, according to FA Cup and Cup-winners' Cup veteran Jack Burkett: "In America in 1963, I shared a room with him. He was constantly on the telephone speaking to everyone and ordering food for people. He was a racing man, so he was also getting back to England, finding out results and laying bets. He gave me a few winners too."

Johnny Byrne goes on: "I remember on one occasion we had been to Walthamstow dogs and unfortunately it was one of those days when we both backed too many 'also-rans'. We ended up going home with about two quid between us and decided to stop off for a drink, knowing full well that the couple of pounds we had would not get us very far, but I had been scheming and when we had knocked out the money we had, I 'went to work'. As we had some celebrity status, it didn't take long to get an audience. In those days I was pretty adept at lining up half a dozen tanners [sixpenny pieces] on my sweaty forehead. Yours truly managed to win 20 quid for us and off we went with a tenner each and a good laugh before I dropped Sammy off in Barking."

Greyhound racing was to be a lifelong passion for Alan. Jack Burkett continues: "After he had left West Ham, Alan would often come down to Chadwell Heath [the West Ham training ground]. He would walk his dogs, the greyhound kennels are not far from there."

Alan always enjoyed the big horse meetings too, especially the Cheltenham Festival. Johnny Byrne again: "I can remember an incident when we went to the Cheltenham Festival. Sammy and I were both very excited as neither of us had been to Cheltenham races before. Somehow we managed to get the day off training and we were soon speeding through the countryside towards Cheltenham. We had a marvellous day and we actually won money. The champagne flowed. The one thing that people hadn't warned us about was that getting out of Cheltenham was a nightmare. I think I must have tried four or five times and each time we finished up in the champagne bar. We eventually got home around 10pm that evening after spending a wonderful day together."

As might be guessed, Greenwood did not make wholesale changes in the first few games. Woosnam, Dick, Musgrove and the rest of the 'old guard' were all in the team. His bubble bursting prevention was taking time to get off the ground. A draw at Tottenham, where over 50,000 saw the game, was followed by a 3-2 defeat at Wolverhampton. That match wasn't the near-thing it sounds. It was only Alan Sealey's goal, three minutes from time, that made the score look respectable.

The first win of the season came against Spurs at Upton Park, under the new, £30,000 floodlights. Doris, one of the few women who regularly support-ed the Irons at that time, looks back at that day:

"It was very hot and humid. St John's were carrying out loads of people who had collapsed with the heat. Tony Scott put us one up late on in the first half. Halfway through the second, Allen equalised. Although West Ham were well on top, it looked like one of those, 'no matter what you do you're not going to score again today' draws, until Sealey, who had messed up a couple of easy chances, got the winner with a fantastic shot, with less than a quarter-of-an-hour to go. Before the end we were chanting, 'We want six, we want six!'

"In our next game, a 3-2 home win against Forest, Sammy got our second, just after half-time. He was a lad for those late goals. It wasn't a good game, full of mistakes, but it was Forest's first defeat that season. In our win at Villa he popped up in the 74th minute. We won 4-1 at Bramall Lane. Again Alan Sealey waited until the last couple of minutes to score."

Les, another supporter, casts his mind back to mid-September 1961: "Greenwood was a knowledgeable bloke. I went to the Chelsea game at the Boleyn. It was one of those days when Upton Park is bathed in sunshine and many of the spectators were in shirt sleeves. Tommy Docherty, his days as a player were nearly over, scythed Woosnam down. Eventually he had to leave the field with a knee injury. Bottles began to fly about and a number of fights broke out in the crowd.

"West Ham had a two-goal lead by the end of the first half, Dick and Musgrove did the honours. Chelsea, who'd lost Jimmy Greaves to AC Milan, had little in the way of an answer. In the second half Bobby Tambling collided with Leslie [the Hammers 'keeper] knocking him sideways and drawing blood. Barry Bridges tapped the ball into the undefended goal. The fighting started up again, but this time it was more concerted and widespread. Two fans came on to the pitch to have a go at the ref, a third was more physical, and was dragged off fighting with stewards and police. Woosnam staggered back, and Moore took over from Leslie in goal.

"Not long after the commotion, Sealey hit the crossbar. West Ham won in the end, but I couldn't remember seeing so much aggro in the crowd before. I can't think what set everyone off. The atmosphere felt quite different to what I'd been used to. The whole game felt very intense."

The most enduring effect of this match was the necessity for Greenwood to review his pool of players. This was to result in Geoff Hurst being moved from the a workhorse role at right-half and tried at inside-forward. In training Greenwood had worked hard with Hurst on the art of arriving late to shoot. Geoff had a deadly drive on both legs, but he was getting better and better all round. Not many people seemed to be noticing this and he was still not the most popular player with the supporters, but gone were the days when he'd be under a goal-kick and the ball would fall behind him.

West Ham crossed the first hurdle in the League Cup, beating Plymouth at Upton Park. The Irons lost only two of their first 11 League games and were unbeaten in four, winning three, when the previous season's FA Cup Finalists, Leicester, came to Upton Park. For the second match in succession the East Enders won 4-1. It was one of their best games of the season. Sealey got the first goal. Gordon Banks stopped Woosnam's shot with his legs but Alan banged home the rebound. That was the second time he had scored in consecutive matches. It brought his goal tally for the season to six.

Leicester, despite losing at Wembley in the FA Cup, were playing in the Cup-winners' Cup that year because Spurs, having won the League and FA Cup Double, had entered the European Cup. Fourteen other teams were in with Leicester at the start of the tournament. The Midlanders beat Glenavon of the Irish League, 7-2 on aggregate. Fiorentina, the holders, were excused the first round, as were eight teams who had drawn byes.

Sealey scored against Ipswich and West Brom. Ron Tindall, a 26-year-old, former Chelsea junior, and a professional cricketer with Surrey, arrived at the club, but did more to strengthen the burgeoning cricketing side at Upton Park than anything else, but overall, things were looking quite good in the last few days of 1961. Three straight wins in December – 1-0 at home to Bolton, 2-1 at Old Trafford (where only 29,000 turned up on a Saturday afternoon) and 4-2 against Wolves at Upton Park – left West Ham with the Christmas present of fourth place in the table. But they had been beaten six times in the first half of the League programme. In the home match against West Brom, the Irons threw away a three-goal lead, ending up with just a point for their trouble. Despite Sealey and Dick pounding the woodwork, they were ejected from the League Cup by the holders, Villa. Yet again, the club were dumped out of the FA Cup in the third round, Plymouth gaining revenge for their defeat in the League Cup.

All this was against a background of events that overshadowed the mere winning or losing of a football match. After building the Berlin Wall, the Soviet Union put even more pressure on the city, and the nerves of the Western Allies, by reserving the air corridors between West Germany and West Berlin for use by its own military planes only. They were harassing Western aircraft and the world held its breath yet again.

Bobby Moore scored the only goal of the game at Stamford Bridge in February. It was a beautiful thing to behold. When he picked up the ball from Woosnam, everyone expected him to pass. Instead he let loose a sweeter-than-sweet volley to leave Peter Bonetti nowhere.

In March, Johnny Byrne was brought to Upton Park from Crystal Palace for £65,000, an English record fee. He was bit on the short side for a centre-forward, but he was a sleek, artful player. However, he did not make too much impact during his first game, a goalless draw at Hillsborough. But in his third match at Upton Park he had a good game. Sealey got the rebound when Byrne hit the Cardiff bar in the 53rd minute. With just seven minutes to play, from a tight angle, Johnny scored his first goal as a Hammer.

On the other side of the coin, after 13 games, resulting in only three goals, Ron Tindall was on his way to Reading. Les reflected: "Apart from Byrne, all the other big names of the season were at the club when Ron Greenwood arrived. However, the purchase of Lawrie Leslie, the Scottish international from Airdrie, went some way towards solving the goalkeeping problems. He was voted the Hammer of the Year in 1961-62. The fans loved Leslie, he was a brave 'keeper, but also a real character. His performance against Arsenal at Upton Park late in the season was typical. Had Arsenal won, it would have lifted them above West Ham. Early on in the second half, Leslie's hand was stamped on, so the Hammers were obliged to put John Lyall in goal while Lawrie played the rest of the game on the right wing. At one point he tore past two Arsenal defenders and forced a corner and from it, Billy Lansdowne scored in the 84th minute. This made the score 3-3. Arsenal finished one point and two places behind West Ham.

"At the end of the season it was just as well that John Dick, rediscovered the target. He had scored 23 times and was leading scorer. Although Alan Sealey started well, the goals dried up after the start of the season. But he had shown himself to be a strong, skilful player, unafraid to run off the ball, and he opened up space for others. The more discerning fan saw that he was an unselfish, generous player, a good team man."

Greenwood had begun to use Martin Peters, Alan Dickie, England international Peter Brabrook from Chelsea, Jack Burkett and Ronnie Boyce, who, like Peters, was a local lad. Most of the side were East Enders, fellows who had grown up in the youth team together and who knew each other as well as anyone could.

Ronnie Boyce recalled: "Ron's coaching emphasised passing and holding the ball. However, this couldn't have been successful without players with the appropriate ability and insight. He liked to see players using space and moving off the ball."

But a former playing colleague of Boyce remembered: "West Ham players had been doing this for some time, on their own initiative, of course. In fact, all the skills that Greenwood was nurturing so well were being cultivated by Malcolm Allison and up-and-coming players like Moore and Peters prior to the arrival of Ron. But it was Greenwood who organised an emerging culture at Upton Park, lead by Moore on the field."

Indicative of this is the re-emergence of the 4-2-4 formation.

The possible impact of Greenwood's presence should not be underestimated. He was part of an international soccer network, and this, alongside the 'Allison effect', was transforming West Ham into a hothouse of football experimentation and innovation. To almost anyone who looked carefully at West Ham's play during that season, it was obvious how different their football was from other clubs. Not all the players were world beaters, but as a team their level of invention and adventure far surpassed their competitors. They certainly punched above their weight. This was also entertaining and good to watch. However, it must be said, although always capable of coping with the top sides, West Ham did fail at critical moments, often against inferior opponents, like Plymouth. The ideas were right, but there weren't enough quality players at Upton Park to make them work. This said, the team had finished in eighth place, only three points outside the top five. A big improvement on the previous term.

A former player said of Greenwood: "Ron never was short of respect from the players, but he did lack some ability as a 'man manager'. For example, he argued with Bobby Moore about a request for a two-pound-a-week pay rise. Mooro had great potential and was consistently turning out for his country. Greenwood told Moore that the club didn't have the cash. Another example of Ron's shortcomings was when Bobby was chosen to go to the World Cup with England in Chile. Ron broke this news to him in his typical fashion, first telling him sternly that he would not be going on the club's summer tour of Africa. Bob's initial response was to ask what he had done wrong. Moore's slight show of anger and resentment at this taunt made Ron smile. It was only then that he told him the good news: 'Walter wants you to go with him to Chile.'

"Ron didn't tell Bob 'well done' or anything. It may only have been Bobby's consummate professionalism and gentlemanly attitude that stood between Greenwood and a right-hander that day."

Although Greenwood often lacked important social skills, there is no doubt that he was a wise and knowledgeable manager. However, it must be remembered that the club had two or three 'thinking' players. And this mix had transformed West Ham into a kind of conduit of modern football in England.

In the Cup-winners' Cup, Fiorentina were shaken by Dynamo Zilina of Czechoslovakia in the quarter-finals, losing 3-2 at home. However, they reversed matters with a 2-0 win away. Atletico Madrid, who had knocked-out Leicester 3-1 on aggregate in the second round, disposed of the West German representatives, Werder Bremen, in the quarter-finals. Neither Fiorentina nor Atletico had a goal scored against them in the semi-finals, eliminating Ujpest Doza (Hungary) and Motor Jena (East Germany) respectively. The Final was played at Hampden Park, but it was an anticlimax. The teams drew 1-1 after extra-time, Peiro hitting the Madrid goal, Hamrin replied for the Italians. A replay had to be arranged and, remarkably, was held over until the following season because of the World Cup Finals that summer.

No analysis about West Ham in the 1960s would be complete without some consideration of the World Cup in Chile. Although not involved in any of the qualifying games, Bobby Moore played in all of his country's matches in South America. The games against Hungary and Argentina would have been an education, but the final match against the Brazilians must have been a revelation. They played the kind of football he had been striving for since his arrival at Upton Park, but to a standard only to be imagined before his encounter with the World champions. His young mind was ripe for such stimulation and he would take what he learned back to the Boleyn Ground.

England were based in Rancagau for the first-round group games. Rancagau is about 90 kilometres south of Santiago, on the north bank of the Rio Cachapoal. In truth, it was a seedy and broken-down place, dominated by the Braden Copper Company. The city is the capital of the sixth region and is relatively old, founded in 1743. It was a hotbed of the Chilean independence movement in 1814 when the Spanish crushed an uprising. The Chilean leader at the time was a chap by the splendid name of Bernardo O'Higgins. His statue, astride a horse, can be found in the centre of the city. Although Rancagua is run-down, the surrounding area is quite beautiful. Condors fly over its forests and there are dramatic mountains and lakes. Not far away is Pichilemu, with its beautiful Pacific beaches

The World Cup was the biggest thing to hit the Rancagau since O'Higgins, although the Campeonato Naçional de Rodeo (the national rodeo championship), an annual March/April event, probably brought more people to the area, as most of the local interest centred on Chile's group playing in Santiago.

Chile couldn't have been the ideal host for the World Cup. It's a string-bean of a country, stretching 3,000 miles from top to bottom. It is a place that is both squalid and sophisticated, backward and yet subtle. Recent earthquakes had ravaged the country, bringing down or damaging about half of the nations' buildings. Even as the first games were kicking-off in the World Cup, earthquake relief was still going on. However, the tournament had become connected with national recovery, which had been instigated by the president, Carlos Dittborn, when he made the case for Chile to host the competition. He said: "We *must* have the World Cup because we have nothing." Alas, he died just a month before the tournament started.

The three games that were taking place locally were to be staged in the Braden Stadium, which belonged to the copper company. England shared the group with Hungary, Argentina and Bulgaria.

At the time there was still tension in Berlin, and in the Congo bitter fighting was taking a heavy toll in human life. In Paris, an attempt on President de Gaulle's life was followed by gun battles in the streets. Adolf Eichmann was hanged in Jerusalem for war crimes. The head of the Jewish Affairs Department of the Gestapo in Nazi Germany, he had been kidnapped by the Israeli secret service in Argentina in 1960. His execution was carried out the same day as the England v Hungary match. The American astronaut, Scott Carpenter, orbited the earth three times, and despite losing contact with earth, got back safely. Elvis Presley was top of the charts with *Good Luck Charm*.

The Braden Stadium was set against the backdrop of the Andes and for the 8,000 spectators, it was a strange experience. The place was no more than a quarter full when the game kicked-off. It was a fairly cold day – in Rancagua it never gets up to more than eight or nine degrees centigrade in June – and the pitch was slippery after incessant drizzle. It was the middle of the rainy season.

During the game Moore never seemed to break sweat. He was majestic. For all this, England went a goal down before the 20-minute mark. Tichy let fly from over 20 yards. In the second half the English pulled level by way of a Flowers penalty. Just before that, Moore had hit the ball around 30 yards from the Hungarian goal only to see it turned over the bar by the 'keeper.

Most of the final period of the game was dominated by the Eastern Europeans, and it was they who ended up winning the match with a goal that had more to do with English players, including the goalkeeper, slipping on the wet surface. Albert got the Hungarians' second.

The next match, a couple of days later, had more local interest with the involvement of Argentina. The attendance was slightly increased, to just under 10,000, and English hopes lay primarily with Jimmy Greaves and Johnny Haynes. England had to win if they were to have any chance of progressing to the next stage of the tournament. The sun was shining brightly as the teams came out and from the start England ran rings around the Argentinians. England's first goal came from another penalty, following a hand-ball. Moore had a fine game. He was ahead of the Argentinean number-ten all the time. At the same time he initiated attack after attack. Even then it was clear that Moore was a philosopher of the game. There was not a dirty bone in his body. Every inch of him looked upright and honest. Every pass he made was done with thought. He tackled with care and precision, never harming an opponent, sending team-mates away with the ball.

England's second goal never looked far off, and just before the interval, after hitting a post, it came from a real thumper, delivered by Bobby Charlton.

In the second half the Argentineans claimed that Moore had handled the ball, but it was clear 'ball to hand'. The referee would have none of the Argentinean demands for a penalty. Greaves got the third for England. Argentina scored ten minutes before the end, but by then it was all over.

For the last group game, the attendance at the Braden Stadium was less than 6,000, even though a place in the quarter-finals was at stake. On paper it looked easy enough – Bulgaria had lost 1-0 to the Argentineans. The Hungarians had put six by them and they had been able to find only one goal in reply. Hungary, having drawn with Argentina, had already qualified as group champions.

England wore red shirts. The sky was grey and it was cold. Greaves missed a couple of chances and, in the end, it was down to Moore and the rest of the defence. The game ended without a goal, but that meant that England went through on goal average.

The quarter-final game was on the Thursday. Brazil had won their group and the match between them and England would take place at the Sausalito Stadium in Vina del Mar, the 'garden city', north-west of Santiago, over 200 kilometres away.

How did Bobby Moore, a lad from one of the poorest parts of London, find himself playing against the champions of the world? He was first brought to the notice of West Ham by scout Jack Turner and he became part of manager Ted Fenton's youth policy. In his first report about the young Moore, Turner described him as 'looking fairly useful, but not likely to set the world alight'. Moore made his first-team debut at Upton Park on 8 September 1958, against Manchester United, in front of nearly 36,000 spectators. West Ham won the game by the odd goal of five. Bobby Moore was 17 years old. He got four more games that season, but was unable to get a regular place until John Smith left the club.

Bobby Moore worked closely with Malcolm Allison in the late 1950s. He wasn't the most outstanding of the kids, but he would listen and was able to learn. His growing knowledge and ability to read the game meant that he was able to compensate for his lack of pace by placing himself well. From his first games with the senior team the young man showed an uncanny and powerful awareness of his team-mates' activity and the movement of opponents. Moore made his England youth debut at the end of 1957, against Holland in Amsterdam.

After gaining a record number of England youth caps, Bobby Moore was selected for the full England squad for the game in Lima, Peru, in May 1962. He became only the second Hammer since Len Goulden in 1939 to win a full England cap. He had a good game and England came away 4-0 winners, Jimmy Greaves getting a hat-trick. Later, Moore, who was making his debut alongside another player winning his first cap, Spurs' centre-half Maurice Norman, said: "I was surprised at being selected, but it was an absolute delight and a tremendous thrill."

The place where England were to face Brazil had some football history. Vina del Mar and, just a few kilometres down the road, Valparaiso, the former British port, were where football was introduced to Chile. Valparaiso FC were founded in 1889, just four years after nine clubs, mainly of British origin, formed the Football Association of Chile. The Thames Iron Works Football Club, that was to become West Ham United, were born during the same year.

Vina is a popular tourist resort, its manicured subtropical landscape of palms and banana trees contrasting sharply with the colourful disorder of its neighbourhood. Pelicans sit on the rocks around the place and many wealthy

Chileans, together with other well-off Latin Americans, own property there. It has beautiful beaches and many cool green places. The Sausalito, the stadium which would host the game the next day, was surrounded by pine and eucalyptus trees on two sides and the Pacific Ocean on the other two. The stadium was newly-built especially for the tournament. It was small, but quite exquisite in design.

Most people were preoccupied with the Chilean match against the Soviet Union, but the England-Brazil game would provide the semi-final opponents for the winners of that encounter and so there was a deal of interest in the outcome. Pele was out due to injury but, obviously, most of the 18,000 in the stadium were rooting for the South Americans.

It was the second time that England had been drawn against the holders in a World Cup quarter-finals. In 1954, they had been beaten by Uruguay. The last time England and Brazil had met, the South Americans had won 2-0 in Rio in May 1959.

Now, a sea mist blew over the pitch as the teams appeared, England wearing all white.

Not long after the start, England went close when Greaves shot over the bar from a Bobby Charlton cross. Charlton was playing brilliantly. There was a moment of light relief when a small dog got on to the field and ran amok before Greaves captured him.

Then Armfield – later voted full-back of the tournament – had to clear off the line and, although England had their chances, the match was just over half-an-hour old when Garrincha, running with his odd bow-legged gait, scored with his head, outjumping the bigger English defence. It looked as if Brazil were going to run riot after that, but before half-time England got a free-kick in Brazilian territory. Greaves headed the ball against the post and Hitchens banged it back in. England's jubilation was short-lived, though. Brazil regained the lead from the head of Vava, who picked up a rebound from goalkeeper Springett's chest following a Garrincha shot. Then Garrincha made it 3-1. He said later that his second goal came by way of his 'autumn leaf' shot, a powerful drive that dipped and at the same time swerved.

Despite the result, Moore and the rest of the England defence had done a terrific job against a wonderful attack. Indeed, Brazilian football was a culture, a way of life. To play that way, you had to live that way. It presented the likes of Moore with a new way of thinking. No matter how much he had gained, he must have known, even then, how hard it would be for his compatriots to take this 'way of being' on board, on the grey days and in the grey stadiums of the English game.

Ron Greenwood might take a lot of the credit for what happened at Upton Park after 1963. But it was Bobby Moore, the boy who played against Brazil, who saw how they could switch from 4-2-4 to 4-3-3 to create extra punch in midfield when necessary. It was Moore who would help enact, for the first time in England, the modern pattern of play as a flexible system rather than a rigid formation. The golden boy brought back Inca treasure to the East End from South America. The next few years would see him and his team perform the alchemy that would turn this into European silver.

# 1962-63

THE replay of the 1961-62 Cup-winners' Cup Final was not held until nearly four months after the first game. They played it in Stuttgart in early September when Atletico beat Fiorentina 3-0 with goals by Jones, Mendoca, and Peiro.

Returning from the World Cup in Chile, Bobby Moore was in the West Ham side which found itself 1-0 down to a Derek Dougan goal within a minute of the new season's first whistle at Villa Park. A couple of minutes later McEwan had Greenwood's boys chasing the game. Baker, Dougan and McEwan all hit the woodwork in the second half and West Ham lost 3-1, Byrne scoring for the Hammers.

Then Wolves won their first game in four visits to Upton Park, 4-1. This, alongside the opening match at Villa and, most disastrous of all, a 6-1 walloping from Spurs (John Lyall scored an own-goal) in front of over 30,000 disgruntled home fans, meant that the Hammers started the season with three straight defeats.

Brian Dear, made his debut in the fourth game of the season, at Wolverhampton where the slide was arrested with a goalless draw. 'Stag' was born in West Ham in 1943 and joined the club as a 15-year-old. He was a rumbustuous striker who went on to score 39 goals in only 85 senior appearances.

Jack Burkett also came into the side. He had made his debut in the last game of the previous season, at Upton Park against Fulham. Another local lad and a product of Ted Fenton's youth policy, Burkett, barely 20 and a former England youth international, would now stake a regular place in the first team. He was a left-back, tenacious, quick-tackling and not adverse to bucaneering forward on raids down the wing. Fans were no longer at risk from a heart attack if they saw a defender moving into the opponents' half, as long as team-mates were covering. Anyway, Burkett was speedy and could get back into defence pretty sharpish. When he turned professional in 1959, it must have been hard on his morale to see defensive players like John Bond, Noel Cantwell and Joe Kirkup ahead of him. This said, 5ft 9in Burkett was ready when Cantwell and Kirkup had gone. His style was never going to see him compete with the likes of Moore so far as the media went, but he was to be a key player for West Ham in the first part of the 1960s. Burkett came in as part of an effort to stop the awful early-season run.

After the point snatched from Wolves, the Irons lost to newly-promoted Orient, 2-0 at Brisbane Road. Dave Dunmore, the man West Ham had swapped for Alan Sealey, scored for Orient after only six minutes to help the Os on the way to their first win in the First Division. If Alan had been a spectator, this might have amused him.

People who knew Sealey understood that he would go a long way for a good laugh. He was something of a practical joker, well-known for his sense of humour. Martin Britt who was with West Ham between 1963 and 1965: "Alan will always be remembered in football for his two match-winning goals in the European Cup-winners' Cup Final in 1965. However, much more importantly, I remember Alan as a very happy person. He was always ready to help and advise the younger and less experienced players. Alan had a tremendous sense of fun and his laughter was infectious."

Ronnie Boyce, a West Ham first-teamer for over 13 years, recollected: "Alan had a dry sense of humour and you never quite knew when he was taking the mickey."

And the relatively reserved Martin Peters, confirmed: "Alan liked a joke."

Ken Brown, an Irons warhorse for 15 years up to 1967, remembered:

"Alan didn't like to be miserable. He was always happy-go-lucky and prepared to take the mickey."

John Lyall, who was at Upton Park throughout Sealey's claret and blue career, said: "Alan was a funny man. He had a bit of a stammer, but had the personality to laugh at it."

According to Ernie Gregory, the longest-serving member of the Upton Park staff:

"Sammy was always laughing and joking."

Ron Greenwood also said that Alan "had good sense of humour" and Johnny Byrne, scorer of 30 goals in the 43 matches he played alongside Alan, saw him as "a comedian".

For Jack Burkett, a pivotal component in the West Ham Cup sides of the 1960s: "Alan was always a jovial person. He had quite a dry sense of humour, but he was also up for a practical joke, like tying shoe laces together and so on. He was always up to something. He would make you laugh when you needed it, and he helped me keep my feet on the ground."

Bill Lansdowne senior, who was with the Irons from the mid-1950s well into the 1960s, and lined up with Alan between 1961 and 1963, said: "Alan had a great sense of humour. You were always assured of a laugh when he was around."

As a young professional, Trevor Hartley witnessed, first hand, some of Alan Sealey's greatest moments. He shared his lasting memory of Alan: "He was a live-wire, and humorous with it. He told Brian Dear off during a practice match. Brian had called me 'Milk bottle top' – I had lots of blond hair in those days! Alan thought I should be called, 'Johnny' for obvious surname reasons. I found it quite amusing that this argument should take place during a game, with Ron Greenwood looking on. Such was the spirit at the club at that time that you just accepted the nicknames given to you. Alan certainly contributed to that spirit during my years at West Ham."

Terry Connelly, a particular friend of Sealey, said: "Alan had a lovely, wicked sense of humour. My son played for the same junior team as Alan's son, Anthony, a team that Alan helped to train. I remember one occasion when Alan came out of the shower room with just a towel around his waist in front of the boys' mums. He had arranged for Anthony to come up behind him to pull the towel away – to reveal he was wearing pants underneath! He was a great practical joker and lethal with one-liner retorts."

Ron Penn, a close friend of Alan for many years, told how he and Sealey played football together for a Sunday side: "Harry Redknapp, Jimmy Greaves, Frank Lampard senior and Alan all used to turn out regularly. We hardly lost a game in years. We used to play on a pitch belonging to the brewers, Watney-Mann. They never charged us anything for the game – we'd give the grounds-man a fiver. One day it was arranged that we would play the company team. Our groundsman friend advised us not to rile them as they would be out to prove a point against so many professionals. But Alan did like to wind every-one up and walk away, and he spent most of the game needling the Watney-Mann players. It ended up with everyone fighting and us being banned from using the pitch.

"Alan was, without a doubt, the funniest man I have ever met. We were playing golf and I had lost a ball in the rough. As we were looking for it in the bushes, Alan asked me what kind of ball I was using. I replied that they were 'Dunlop 65' and he immediately held up a baked bean can and told me that he had found a 'Heinz 57'!"

The need for a sense of humour was an essential asset in the game at that time. West Ham first-teamer of the mid-1960s, Eddie Presland: "Alan was a funny man, but footballers had to be sharp, especially in London. We had this stuff for sweat rashes, 'Whitfields'. It worked, but it stank something awful. Dollops of that were often slapped in underpants. This was the source of a great deal of amusement as the recipient would start to discover and some-times try to hide his fate."

However, there was little to laugh about at Upton Park as winter drew on in 1962. West Ham's poor results were, in part, a reflection of the domestic life of the club. There had been constant bickering about pay between players and management and a number of the old hands were unsettled and this spread to other members of the team. In the last week of September, John Dick left for Brentford where he was to continue his good goalscoring record, playing a big part in the Bees becoming the champions of Division Four.

But things started to look up when the Hammers beat a strong Liverpool team at Upton Park. Then the first away win of the season came at Maine

Road. It pulled West Ham off the bottom of the table – and in remarkable fashion. With less than half-an-hour gone the score was 1-1, but goals from Scott, Budgie Byrne, Martin Peters, and a second from Malcolm Musgrove, slaughtered City. After Malcolm's second goal, City's goalkeeper, Bert Trautmann, was a little too eager in his accusation that the West Ham man was offside. He kicked the ball towards the ref. It hit Mr Stokes in the back and the big German was sent-off for only the second time in his career. Poor old Oakes had to keep goal for the last 20 minutes. He was no match for Geoff Hurst who made it six for the Irons.

On 6 October 1962, Ken Brown scored his first senior goal for the Hammers. It was part of West Ham's best-ever win over Birmingham City, a 5-0 thumping at Upton Park. Pushing aside Plymouth Argyle for the second season in succession in the League Cup – Byrne got a hat-trick in the 6-0 win – the Irons were yet again removed in ignominious fashion by Rotherham, who won 3-1 at Millmoor in the second round.

England international Peter Brabrook, a recent recruit from Chelsea, made his first appearance in a home draw against Burnley. A talented winger, tall and speedy, Brabrook had been wanted by Everton but expressed a preference for coming to Upton Park. He had slipped through the Upton Park scouting net, having been on the groundstaff in 1953, and was a West Ham supporter. He played schoolboy football for East Ham, Essex and London. At first Chelsea didn't want to sell, but in the end the cost of getting Brabrook back was £35,000. He'd scored 47 goals for the Blues in over 250 League outings, winning England youth, Under-23 and three full caps, going to the World Cup in Sweden in 1958. He made his debut against the Soviet Union in a group play-off and hit a post in England's 1-0 defeat.

There had been some allegations about West Ham illegally approaching Brabrook. Although he was hanging around the club before actually signing from Stamford Bridge, the transfer negotiations took months to complete. Chelsea reckoned that the winger refusing to sign a contract at Stamford Bridge was down to statements made by Ken Brown and Ron Greenwood, and that West Ham had not made a decent offer because they thought they could get Brabrook on the cheap. Around the same time the Professional Footballers' Association was threatening to go on strike. The charges were not well met at

Upton Park. The board said it could answer any charge Chelsea might bring. But the West London club were fond of picking up promising East End players, and they knew one or two tricks of their own to entice talent to Stamford Bridge. A League tribunal cleared West Ham of all charges.

Meanwhile, the Hammers' run of six games without a win was turned around at Hillsborough at the end of November. What started out as a Peter Brabrook cross put the Irons one up after only two minutes, following a shrewd dummy by Hurst. This was Jim Standen's debut. He had been signed by Greenwood for £7,000. Standen, who had been with Arsenal and Luton, was also playing first-class cricket for Worcestershire and had topped the county bowling averages. At Hillsborough, his opposite number, Ron Springett, brought Sealey down in the box with around half-an-hour gone and Martin Peters converted from the spot. Tony Scott made it 3-1 before half-time and that's how it finished. It was West Ham's fifth win of the season – not a great record in 19 games. By this time Phil Woosnam, perhaps understanding his lack of popularity at the Boleyn Ground, had moved to Aston Villa.

West Ham were holding up Division One when they began a fight back in the final weeks of the year. Just before Christmas they visited Spurs. Ex-Hammer John Smith opened the scoring, notching up Tottenham's first after just eight minutes. Things looked dire when Dave Mackay beat Standen to open up a seemingly unbeatable gap. But Martin Peters pulled one back in the first half and Joe Kirkup completed the claret and blue revival ten minutes after the break. However, almost straight away Mackay swooped in for his second. Boyce equalised and with little more than ten minutes left, Tony Scott put the Irons into the lead for the first time. Just when the West Ham supporters thought their side had done enough, Dave Mackay completed his hat-trick and the fighting Hammers were left to vent their frustration. Over 45,000 had been treated to a thriller.

This was the greatest Spurs side. Having retained the FA Cup the previous year, they went on to take the European Cup-winners' Cup that season. The competition was notable for a giantkilling act rarely seen in European circles. Bangor City, the Welsh non-League club, were drawn against Napoli. The Welshmen took a deserved two-goal lead to Italy and only late in the second leg did the Italians score to win 3-1. Had the away-goals rule been in operation, Bangor would have gone through, but Napoli came out on top in the replay, winning 2-1.

Atletico Madrid beat Hibernians (Malta) 5-0 on aggregate and were almost as convincing against the Bulgarians, Botev Plovdiv, winning 5-1 in the quarter-finals. In the semi-finals they found themselves 2-1 down to 1FC Nuremberg after the leg in Germany, but won the return 2-0. In the other semi-final Spurs, who had knocked out Glasgow Rangers with 5-2 and 3-2 results, and beaten Slovan with a fine 6-0 win in North London after losing 2-0 in Bratislava, accounted for OFK Belgrade, (Yugoslavia) winning both legs and making a convincing aggregate of 5-2. For Tottenham this meant a meeting with the holders in Rotterdam.

For the Final, Spurs were without Dave Mackay who had a severe stomach upset. Added to this worry, their captain, Danny Blanchflower, was not fully fit after sustaining a knee injury against Rangers. The Northern Ireland skipper was able to play only with the help of a pain-killing injection. The injury kept him out for 22 matches and, in effect, he had to play on one leg throughout the Final.

The loss of Mackay seemed to unnerve Bill Nicholson, the Tottenham manager. Instead of a rousing team talk before the game, he restricted himself to talking about the quality of the Atletico players. After Nicholson had left, Blanchflower went through the Spurs team player by player. He told them that they were world beaters, particularly Terry Dyson, a winger not noted for his match-winning qualities.

Spurs went out to display the type of football they had shown in winning the English League and Cup double two years earlier. Although they were now playing the runners-up in the Spanish League, they were two-up at the interval, through Jimmy Greaves and John White. The tide looked to be turning two minutes into the second half when Ron Henry conceded a penalty and Atletico pulled back a goal through a Collar conversion. For the next 20 minutes the Spaniards pressed hard for an equaliser.

Just after the hour, however, Spurs regained their rhythm, and in the 67th minute Dyson scored. The left-winger hit a high cross that floated close to the goalkeeper. Somehow the Spanish 'keeper misread the flight of the ball and it sailed over his head and into the back of the net (Dyson later stated that he had spotted the 'keeper off his line). Dyson now made this the game of his life. Less than a quarter-of-an-hour later, Greaves picked up his cross and made it 4-1. And with just over five minutes of the match remaining, Dyson started a 30-yard run, passing defenders all the way. The attack ended with his 25-yard shot smashing into the net.

As Tottenham left the field, their centre-forward, Bobby Smith, advised Dyson to retire on the spot as he would never have a better game. Spurs had achieved an impressive 5-1 victory and had became the first British side to win a European trophy. They were truly a United Kingdom team, with the Scot, Mackay, doing so much to get them to the Final and their Irish skipper, Blanchflower, being such a massive influence on the side.

West Ham did not play at all in January 1963 – nearly all the grounds in Britain had been put out of action for six weeks or more by the severe winter. Alan Sealey got his first goal of the season, a header, in February. It was part of a 2-0 win at Sheffield United and it was another late effort, coming with less than a quarter-of-an-hour to go. He got his second against Manchester United in a win at Upton Park, on 78 minutes this time, and two more came his way when Leicester visited the Boleyn Ground. West Ham ended their 16-game unbeaten run and knocked them off the top of the First Division on 13 April. At that late date there were still nine games to play, thanks to the weather.

The winter, though, was a good one for the Hammers as far as the FA Cup was concerned. In the third round, although taken to a replay at Craven Cottage, they got by Fulham and then beat Swansea Town to reach the last 16, where there was a great 1-0 result against the League champions-elect, Everton. West Ham had reached the quarter-finals for the first time since 1955 and now faced Liverpool at Anfield. Playing the 4-2-4 system, the Irons had the Merseysiders flummoxed for some time. Sealey got one brilliant header in, but Tommy Lawrence was standing in the right, or wrong place, depending on your loyalties. However, Roger Hunt, having hit the post earlier, put Liverpool through with just nine minutes left.

In the early spring of 1963, Ron Greenwood's old club, Arsenal, came to Upton Park. His new team froze and the Gunners strolled to a 4-0 victory. Despite the result, it was one of the best games Bobby Moore had played to date. But such was Greenwood's disappointment that all he could muster was a mumbled, "Well played," as he passed Moore. This was a shame. Players need to be acknowledged at times like that. Moore had given his all for Greenwood and the club that day. It's an art to put yourself and your own feelings aside at certain points, but that's what managers, at their best, can do for their players.

Although West Ham finished off the season with a 6-1 home win over Manchester City – remember they had also won 6-1 at Maine Road in September – and Sealey bagged a pair (the second eight minutes from time), the Boleyn club fell to 12th place. But the goal count showed that, for the first time in years, they had scored more than they had conceded. Sealey had scored only six League goals all season, but then again, leading scorer Geoff Hurst could only manage 13. This was not a particularly bad sign. West Ham were playing for each other and, this being the case, the goals were shared around. Bobby Moore won the Hammer of the Year award.

The season had had its dramatic moments, true, but there was still something missing from West Ham's performance. The team needed a collective experience near to that which Moore had been through in Chile nearly a year earlier, but it is doubtful that West Ham's trip to the USA in the summer of 1963 had been planned with this type of thing in mind. In the main, it started out as one of the many pilgrimages in football history that have attempted to popularise football (soccer) in North America.

West Ham went to the United States amid a deal of criticism because the club had committed the players to a summer of competitive football. The team had to play at least eight games in June; if they did enough to qualify for the later stages, they would have to come back in July for a semi-final and a Final over two legs.

The weekend before the Hammers left for New York, the young Irons won the FA Youth Cup. Greenwood was, would you believe, 'over the moon' about the youngsters' achievement of beating Liverpool 6-5 over two legs. He described the 5-2 win at Upton Park, that turned around a 3-1 defeat at Anfield, as 'wonderful'. Ten years of hard graft had brought the win that expunged the memory of two previous losses in the Final. Martin Britt sent home three superb headers after the Scousers had made the overall score 5-2. Nine of the youth side would still be available for the Youth Cup the following season; only captain John Charles and Dennis Burnett would be too old.

A few days later Bobby Moore, who was on tour with England, became the youngest captain his country had ever had. He led his side to a fantastic 4-2 victory over World Cup Finalists Czechoslovakia in Bratislava. Moore was the unanimous choice of the players and manager Alf Ramsey to take over as skipper from the injured Jimmy Armfield. It was his 12th cap. Within a few days he had also led his country to a 2-1 win over East Germany in Leipzig and an 8-1 thrashing of Switzerland in Basle.

When the Hammers got to the United States they were obliged to use Central Park for a training ground. One of the strangest sights was Jim Standen putting in some batting practice, following an invitation from a Somerset exile to play a game, on a coconut matting pitch (Standen had come on the trip in preference to turning out for Worcestershire). He got a better crowd than some of the tournament matches.

Byrne and Moore were in Europe with England when the tournament kicked-off and there is no doubt that there comrades missed them. The first game was against Kilmarnock, the Scottish League runners-up. The Hammers had shared the flight over with the Killies, having first gone up to Scotland to catch the plane across the Atlantic. The Rugby Park club were veterans of the 'International League Tournament'.

In the sun-drenched Randall's Island Stadium, a crowd of nearly 15,000 shirt-sleeved New Yorkers – the biggest attendance in the history of the series for the opening game – paid $2-50 each (about 18 shillings or 90p) to see West Ham and Kilmarnock. Lawrie Leslie played brilliantly, defying his countrymen time and again.

Leslie was in goal because Jim Standen had contracted enteritis, which was not much of a way to celebrate his 27th birthday, which fell on the day of the match. Leslie, who had almost miraculously recovered from a broken leg, sustained only the previous November, stood in. At the time he was the only Hammers player with the tour who had not re-signed for the next season, he was still in negotiations with Ron Greenwood. Ken Brown captained the team and the 19-year-old Dave Bickles made his debut for the Hammers.

Three goals in the last nine minutes of the game made for an exciting finish. Peter Brabrook, with his winding runs, impressed the crowd. Ernie Yard gave Kilmarnock the lead and Brabrook equalised. Bertie Black put the

Scottish side back in front. Geoff Hurst made it 2-2, and the see-saw stuff continued with a goal by Jim Richmond. With 87 minutes gone, Martin Peters came from nowhere to give West Ham the draw. But the Hammers had not adjusted to the surface. Cables had been dragged across the middle of the pitch, tearing up the turf badly. There was precious little grass in the centre, yet the goal-mouths looked like plush unripe cornfields.

The West Ham party was based in an hotel just off Fifth Avenue, less than a block from Central Park. The players were in $16-a-day rooms with kitchens, lounges and fridges. To make their allowances go further, they made tea and breakfast in their rooms. Ken Brown did most of the cooking for the squad. In contrast, Ron Greenwood and directors Brian and Will Cearns were in the 17th-storey penthouse suite, rumoured to cost $1,000 a month.

There was little time to take in the sights, but one afternoon Bill Jenkins, the West Ham physiotherapist, English referee Jim Finney and a few of the players went out to Coney Island. It was a hot day and some of the lads took off their shirts, as if they were walking along the prom at Southend. No sooner had they gone topless when three gun-toting, gum-chewing cops let them know, in no uncertain terms, that they were breaking the law. Everyone pleaded ignorance, and it was probably their Cockney accents that saved them. In the end the police seemed relieved to see the back of the strange crowd of gibbering Limeys.

The Hammers came up against the Italians, Mantova, in the next game. It took place in Chicago's 110,000-capacity Soldier Field. Jack Dempsey had fought in this sporting palace, but the pitch was no more than all right. Greenwood switched Ronnie Boyce to left-half for the match and also drafted in John Sissons at inside-left for his second first-team game. The young striker had made his debut against Blackburn in April.

The thickness of a post cost the Hammers the points. The uprights were square. If they had been rounded, the story could have been different. West Ham were two down after five minutes. Hurst pulled back one via the penalty spot, and just before half-time Tony Scott curled in a centre that fooled the 'keeper. The ball smacked the inside of the square post and cannoned out. It was 80 degrees in the stadium – Chicago was not a very windy city that day – and this, of course, suited the Italians better.

The Londoners were served tea during the break by their all-too-considerate hosts. In the second half, the Hammers managed to pull it back to 2-2, by way of the hard-working Alan Sealey, but in the last five minutes Mantova scored twice. After the 4-2 defeat Ron's analysis was that "We boobed." He went on: "You can't give a team like the Italians two goals start and hope to succeed." The wisdom of this statement was that you must try not to let the opposing team score against you too often. Kind of basic that, but well worth remembering.

Just one day before Byrne and Moore joined the team, the Irons were bottom of the table. Greenwood was grim, saying: "We stand little chance now after our bad start." This was either a very clever psychological ploy or he had dwelt a little too long on the Kilmarnock manager's statement at the start of the tournament. Willie Waddell had declared: "This will be a cut-throat competition and the team off to a good start stands the best chance." Whatever, one point from two games looked somewhat bleak, but on his arrival, Bobby Moore was more optimistic. He told journalists: "Turn the league table upside down – and you might see the winners of the competition." Bold words, but they came from no mean source.

West Ham now faced Oro of Mexico, just 24 hours after the arrival of Moore and Byrne. Although West Ham were a goal down at half-time, Greenwood had seen weaknesses in the Mexicans' pattern. These were conveyed to the players and the Irons broke through. Byrne, after being cut down in the box, put West Ham back in it with a penalty. Then Hurst got a couple more to give the Hammers their first win of the tournament.

In the next game the Hammers beat the fancied Preussen Munster of West Germany, a match which took place under floodlights in Detroit's University Stadium. It was a crunch game and the home city of the massive Ford empire advertised the match as 'England v Germany'. Detroit had a big German population and the crowd of over 10,000 were almost completely behind the Munich club.

For 70 minutes the game was balanced, with both sides playing well. But in the last quarter-of-an-hour, West Ham turned on the style. Goal-a-game Hurst got the first and Martin Peters made it two. Afterwards, Alec Cassidy, the biggest name in soccer in Detroit, said of West Ham: "They are the best thing that has happened to the game in these parts and they showed the American public how the game should be played."

The after-match reception took place at the Detroit headquarters of Post 84 of the Canadian Legion. The members who were mostly British, were delighted about beating the Germans. Brian Cearns, the West Ham managing director, who was about to make his way back to London, and Ron Greenwood made speeches, thanking Post 84 for the roast beef and strawberries. This was followed by rousing chorus of *Bubbles*, led by Bobby Moore. There were a good number of East Londoners present, including Maurice Allison, the younger brother of Malcolm, the former Hammers favourite, who had driven down from Canada for the game. The Motor City, birthplace of Tamala Motown and Soul, home of the likes of the Four Tops and Sam Cook, hadn't heard the likes before or since.

The Yanks loved Bobby Moore. His obvious athleticism and good looks appealed to them. The newspapers called him 'England's best'. He was featured on a number of radio programmes, fielding questions on football. Some of these were, predictably if understandably, incredibly inane, but Bobby responded to them all with respect, good humour and not a little compassion. He also turned up on *What's My Line* on the television; it needed only a couple of questions to identify him, by then he was so well known.

Back in New York the Hammers faced bottom team Valenciennes. It was near 100 degrees that evening, but it was fine game, and even though there were under 6,000 people in the stadium, the atmosphere was good. Geoff Hurst moved from wing-half to inside-left for this game and the Hammers used two main strikers, supported by an attacking defence. Byrne, who seemed to be working from the centre-circle, was on top form, creating movement and holding up the ball when needed. Hurst was the powerful front runner, but was also able to shield the ball if necessary, to hold on for reinforcements. He scored all three West Ham goals, which made him the top marksman in the competition with eight goals from five games.

A player with the tour recalled that: "By now Moore and Byrne were in the penthouse with Ron and the team had been using the roof to look after their tans, but some of the players were getting homesick, particularly John Sissons.

Peter Brabrook spent $40 on a phone call to his wife, Doreen, which was the equivalent of about £13 at the time, a week's wage for most supporters."

The Germans had lost their opportunity to finish top of the table, having lost their final game, and West Ham now needed a single point from their last game to give them the championship. The concluding match was against Recife from Brazil. The Randall's Island stadium was like an oven. It was 1-0 to West Ham at half-time, Johnny Byrne got the goal. Just after West Ham scored, there was some fighting in the crowd. Then 100 sailors from SS *Caronia* in the near-8,000 crowd started singing *Bubbles* and this was enough to keep the Brazilians quiet.

Before the game the teams had exchanged club pins as a gesture of goodwill, but it turned into an angry match. At one point Joe Kirkup was fouled three times in quick succession, while the ball was at the other end of the pitch. Jack Burkett was limping following a nasty knock, Byrne was shamelessly hacked about and Standen was kicked in the head as he made a save. Then Alan Sealey had a set-to with Adelmo Guimares and they were both sent-off.

It was rough justice for Sealey. Guimares, the best forward in the Brazilian side, had kicked him a couple of times, once badly enough to require treatment from the trainer. The referee ordered the Recife player off, but when he went to restart the game, the Brazilian inside-left picked up the ball, held it behind his back and wouldn't let the referee have it, instead gesticulating wildly. This caused a delay of some minutes and then, shocking everyone, the referee sent Sealey off as well. The referee and both linesmen were Brazilian.

However, Alan Sealey was no angel, as Ron Penn pointed out: "Alan did like to wind everyone up." Eddie Presland also remarked: "On the field he could be verbally aggressive, although Alan's bark was worse than his bite, being in reality a lovely man, always friendly and good humoured."

Brian Dear confesses: "There was a bit of rivalry between me and Sammy, though. Once we were playing head tennis with Geoff and Boycie and others. There were a lot of good one-touch players at West Ham then, and Sammy had a bit of a go at me. I had a go back and I ended up having to have five stitches in my finger and he got a fat lip. But it was nothing serious. We all got on and those days were a good laugh."

Alan's propensity to stammer when he got worked up may not have helped the situation either. As Ronnie Boyce, a fellow member of the successful Cup-winners' Cup team, recalls Sealey's slight speech impediment had its consequences throughout his career: "He had a bit of a stutter, but he was the first to see the funny side of it. I remember he would often try to call to me for the ball: 'Ba, Ba, Ba, Ba, Boycie!' By the time he'd got that out, the player I'd passed to had got rid of the ball."

And there were other 'mishaps' according to Eddie Presland: "He was always getting me run out. It was his stutter. I would say, 'Yes!' and start to run. Meanwhile Alan was saying, 'Na, Na, Na.' By the time he got 'No' out, I'd been stumped. He'd just shrug his shoulders in regret and apology. When we had both finished playing football we played cricket together for Romford. Once we agreed that he would say 'Yes' when he meant 'No' and 'No' when he wanted to say 'Yes,' thinking that this would be easier for him to get out, but he got excited and forgot. After that I told him that I would make all the calls."

However, Alan made his stutter into a kind of trade mark, in many ways using it as a means to enhance his personality. Brian Dear provides some examples of this: "West Ham started playing as a cricketing side after we turned out at Cranbrook Park against an Essex XI. A big crowd turned up. The county saw that it was a money maker, so a fixture was arranged at the start of every season. Sammy and I used to play cricket with East London Bakers. Greavesie was in that team too. I remember in one game at Mill Hill, I sent him back. He got run out and pulled a muscle. Everyone laughed as he passed me, and with his bit of a stutter said: 'F, F, Fanks a f, f, f***ing lot, Stag!'

"He got his own back though. We were playing in a reserve game at Gillingham and I got caught offside or something and had a word with the referee. I got booked. Anyway, Sam then started with his stutter and everything. In the end I got sent-off. I told the ref that I didn't have a stutter but he just said: 'You're off.' Sammy looked at me as if I was in the wrong and that was it."

And Martin Britt recalls: "His slight stutter when he got excited caused many a joke. Some of the players took the mick out of this, but he never stopped laughing and was always fun."

At half-time in Randall's Island, the Brazilian coach, Palmera Pessoa, threw the West Ham pins at an astonished Greenwood. Like the gentleman he was, Greenwood totally ignored this most unsporting gesture. He had played a slow game and made it frustrating for the South Americans. In the 50th minute, Jose Matos – 'little Garrincha' ('little small bird'?) – put things level. But West Ham held on to finish ahead of Mantova. Following the game, Greenwood said: "This could open a new era of winning for the club."

West Ham had mastered top club sides from six countries. Ron Greenwood, who did not count wild speculation among his weaknesses, predicted: "This could be a great team in two or three years time …it would have taken us three years at home to accomplish this experience." The New York triumph was to prove the stepping stone towards the realisation of an ideal of football thinking and coaching. The importance of this trip for Ron Greenwood and West Ham cannot be stressed too highly. They matured in a startling way in the course of only a few weeks. Young men developed character, playing against sides differing tremendously in styles and patterns of play.

The team flew back to London as International Soccer League champions but were back in town a few weeks later for the final stages of the American Challenge Cup. Everything now rested on a semi-final against Gornik Zabrze of Poland. In reality it was the Final of that year's national tournament. The Poles had won another league competition which was going on while the Hammers were playing in the first part of the series. What you might call the 'championship' would be contested by the winners of the Gornik-West Ham encounter and the previous year's winners.

Gornik were a strong side with the young Lubanski, the skilful World Cup player of the future, in their ranks. They had been good enough to beat Spurs 4-2 in their home leg of the European Cup, so they could not be taken lightly.

West Ham took 15 wives and girlfriends with the party when they returned to the United States. Unfortunately not all the women got on and there were some serious differences by the time they all got to America. This soon led to bad feeling between the players, a situation which did nothing to help match preparations.

The first part of the tournament had been taken seriously by all the teams taking part, but now it seemed that even greater prestige was at stake. Lawrie Leslie, having re-signed too late to be included in the West Ham party, the second goalkeeper was transfer-listed Brian Rhodes, who was awaiting a move to

Southend United. On his return, Bobby Moore was awarded the Eisenhower Trophy as the Player of the Series.

Byrne scored the goal which earned West Ham a 1-1 draw in the first leg at Randall's Island, but the pitch was showered with beer cans when Ray Morgan, the referee from Southampton, refused to award the Poles a penalty.

Inside a seven-minute spell in the second match, again at a baking-hot Randall's Island, Jim McLean, a 58-year-old Scottish exile, called two Gornik efforts offside. The Gornik players jostled and shoved the official. Beer cans again began to rain down and this heralded a pitch invasion by hundreds of spectators armed with Polish banners and flags. One of them hit a linesmen on the head. McLean took flight, getting battered and losing most of his kit as he fled. The West Ham players were interested spectators until Greenwood took them off.

After half-an-hour, the match was restarted although the referee was so badly shaken that one of the linesmen had to take over. The game took two and a half hours to complete. Geoff Hurst scored the only goal, after a move which was started by Standen. The win put the Hammers into the Final, to be played in Chicago, against Dukla Prague of Czechoslovakia, winners of the American Challenge Cup for the previous two years.

Dukla boasted half the Czech national side that had played in the World Cup Final the year before, among them Josef Masopust, European Footballer of the Year in 1962, and Svatopluk Pluskal, who had played in all six of his country's World Cup games in Chile.

A crowd of almost 11,000 saw Dukla throw up a blanket defence to win the first leg in Chicago 1-0. Some 15,000 spectators, in temperatures that hit the 80s, watched international goalkeeper Pavel Kouba put on a majestic performance in the second leg. He denied Hurst the hat-trick he would have got in almost any other game, and saved the Czechs. Peter Brabrook played his best game for the club since his move from Chelsea. Tony Scott put West Ham ahead, but Masopust, the man with 59 Czech caps, scored the equaliser and eventual aggregate winner, the game ending in a 1-1 draw.

Dukla took the trophy, but West Ham were cheered off the field in both games. The East Londoners were heralded as 'the finest British side to ever visit America'. Masopust predicted: "West Ham will be a top grade side in two years."

Greenwood saw the final two games in America as the best the Hammers had played since he took over. This tournament had opened the Irons to international play. Indeed he described West Ham's display in the Final as 'the most technically perfect display I have seen from a British team I have been connected with'. High praise from a man who was not prone to high praise and who had been around a few accomplished teams.

It was a different West Ham that came back to England for the 1963-64 season. The side had developed playing a modernist version of the game. Moore was voted Player of the Tournament. It was the dawn of a golden time for West Ham United. A team grew up in Manhattan, Chicago and Detroit that summer; boys became men. West Ham, an under-achieving club, with many players who had never even been abroad before, who, like their club, had stayed their spirit and soul in the footballing foundry of London's East End, had found its heart near to New York's glitzy Broadway.

# The Golden Years

## 1963-64

**B**UDGIE Byrne was beginning to shine, playing deep in the attack, Moore switched to sweeper, and together they inspired the whole side. In August, West Ham defeated Blackpool 3-1. It was the second game of the season, the first home match. Byrne played brilliantly. This game was seminal. It demonstrated that the 4-2-4 formation was light years ahead of the traditional British game that the Blackpool team of the time exemplified so well. They were outclassed and out-manoeuvred in every facet of play. West Ham were faster, but also much more intelligent than their opponents. This was the embryonic FA Cup-winning side: Standen, Kirkup, Burkett, Peters, Brown, Moore, Brabrook, Boyce, Byrne, Hurst, Scott. Byrne's dribble past four Blackpool defenders that evening was an astounding show of skill. Martin Peters opened the Hammers' account for the season with an almost mystical shot that mesmerised Waiters. West Ham were 'becoming'.

Peters, who had made his debut for West Ham on Good Friday 1962, against Cardiff City at the Boleyn Ground, was destined to play in every position, including goalkeeper for the Irons. It was already obvious to most Hammers supporters that Peters was someone quite special. No one had seen his like before and as such it took the fans time to understand him (if we ever did). Unlike Byrne, who had ability obvious to even the dimmest spectator, Martin's skills were set in a new approach to football. Subtle and thoughtful, sometimes subdued and covert, his game was not based on physical speed, but a swiftness of thought and eye. Like Bobby Moore, his perception and aware-ness were of an exceptional quality. He moved easily around the field with all the in-built confidence and stealth of a natural hunter. If ever a footballer was born, it was Martin Peters.

Spurs were back in the Cup-winners' Cup as holders and, like the previ-ous season, got a bye for the first set of games. However, England's advantage of having two teams in the 1963-64 tournament was devalued when Tottenham and the FA Cup winners Manchester United were drawn to play each other. United, who had beaten Willem II, Tilburg, of the Netherlands, 7-2 on aggregate in their opening tie, proved too good overall for the Londoners. After losing 2-0 at White Hart Lane, they turned the tables at Old Trafford to win 4-1. A similar victory at home against Sporting Club appeared to be enough to take United into the last four, even though the Portuguese had won the home leg of a previous tie against Apoel Nicosia of Cyprus by the remarkable margin of 16-1. Instead, United were trounced by five clear goals in Lisbon and rudely eliminated from their first venture in the Cup-winners' Cup.

Glasgow Celtic had a parallel shock in the semi-finals when their 3-0 lead over MTK Budapest vanished in a 4-0 massacre in Hungary. Sporting had come through against the French of Olympic Lyon, but only after a play-off in Madrid.

The Final in Brussels, watched by fewer than 10,000 people, was a high-scoring affair resulting in a 3-3 deadlock after extra-time. Two days later, in Antwerp, the replay ended in favour of Sporting, who won by the only goal of the match – coming direct from a Morais corner.

In September, West Ham had started a good run in the League Cup. They beat Leyton Orient at Upton Park, despite good form on the part of the Os who took charge of the middle of the park. Orient's Gordon Bolland ran rings around Dave Bickles. It was Bolland who rounded Jim Standen to put his side ahead before ten minutes were up. Scott drew the Hammers level less than a quarter of an hour later and Byrne, after three near misses, scored what turned out to be the winner just before half-time.

West Ham went on to beat Aston Villa 2-0 in Birmingham, John Bond and Martin Britt the scorers. Then the shock headlines of round four read:

SWINDON 3 WEST HAM 3. Swindon, although on their own County Ground, were from the lower half of the Second Division. The Hammers had been two goals up, from Hurst and Brabrook, when a 17-year-old winger, Don Rogers, had pulled the Wiltshire team back into it through the West Country mud. They got another three minutes later. Byrne seemed to have settled it but then the Swindon centre-half, McPherson, scored with less than ten minutes remaining and the Robins had forced a replay at Upton Park. Bobby Moore had not played in the first game because he was due to turn out for England the next day, but he returned for the replay.

At Upton Park, Woodruff fluffed a kick just 40 seconds into the game, Hurst made the most of the mistake and smashed the ball home. However, West Ham failed to capitalise on the good start and come half-time the game was still there for the taking by either side. Then, with five minutes of the second half gone, a Byrne header thumped the bar and Brabrook darted in to make the rebound count. Within 15 minutes Rogers got Swindon back into it, but with less than 15 minutes on the clock, Brabrook's cross was met by Byrne who made no mistake to score his team's third goal of the game. Scott finished off the brave lads from the West Country. West Ham went on to defeat Fourth Division Workington, 6-0, in the quarter-finals. Byrne got his first from a Hurst cross and went on to score a hat-trick. Boyce, Hurst and Scott also notched up one each, without reply from the Reds. West Ham were through to their first semi-final in 32 years.

Yet despite their League Cup success, the early part of the League season had not gone well for the Irons. And things didn't look set to improve late in October when they visited the League leaders and FA Cup holders at Old Trafford. West Ham had won four of their 14 games, and although this included a 2-1 victory at Anfield, they had lost half-a-dozen matches. In typical West Ham fashion, the team managed to beat United in Manchester. Martin Britt recalls the game:

"A game that lives in the memory was a late October match in 1963 against Manchester United at Old Trafford. United had a terrific home record, on the crest of a 100 per cent unbeaten run at home. For most of the game we had to play without Alan, with ten men, there were no substitutes at that time. He'd been hurt in a tackle from Noel Cantwell, a former West Ham player. I scored the only goal of the game, side-footing in a flick from Ronnie Boyce. Although we spent the best part of the match under siege, missing Alan's penetrative influence up front, we held on to end United's magnificent home run. The crowd applauded us off the park."

The winning margin could have been bigger but when an effort from Geoff Hurst hit the United bar, the ball bounced straight down into Harry Gregg's arms. As a result of that defeat at the hands of the Irons, United lost their top spot. It was quite a game for West Ham, especially as Sealey had to go off injured after only ten minutes.

On 22 November 1963, US president John F. Kennedy was assassinated in Dallas. The following day, West Ham drew 1-1 at Bolton.

On Boxing Day, The Hammers were up against Blackburn, who had come to the Boleyn Ground on top of Division One and without defeat in ten games. Bryan Douglas, the England winger, was on peak form and bamboozled the West Ham defence. The game was no more than five minutes old when Fred Pickering hit the ball from around 20 yards, sending it sailing passed Standen. Within ten minutes the equaliser came from Johnny Byrne. It was a terrific goal. Budgie twisted and connived passed three Blackburn defenders and 'passed' the ball beyond the Rovers 'keeper, Fred Else, and into the net.

The goal seemed to invigorate West Ham and soon afterwards Byrne made a sweet connection. The ball seemed to stick to his boot momentarily as he hit it. It smacked against the bar. Hurst was on the rebound like the predator he was, but in the rush he wasted the chance. However, Douglas had started to cause mayhem. All through the first half he pulled three defenders in his wake, put Blackburn back in front on the half-hour, made McEvoy's goal some five minutes later, and laid on the ball that allowed Ferguson to score after 40 minutes.

At the break, the sad Irons were 4-1 down. Douglas didn't lose any of his venom in the second half and was instrumental in McEvoy's second goal before helping Pickering complete his hat-trick. McEvoy finished off the Rovers' barrage with his third. Byrne did get a consolation goal just after the hour, but it was still 8-2, a record defeat for West Ham. It was also a record away win for Rovers, and the biggest away win in Division One for eight years. As Mr Osborne blew the final whistle, the stadium became a sea of claret and blue as, it seemed, every one of the 20,000 crowd 'upped scarves' and let out the melancholy yet gently defiant Hammers anthem: "I'm forever blowing bubbles, pretty bubbles in the air…" But if these Hammers could do nothing else, they could learn. Two days later, on a sodden pitch at Ewood Park, West Ham won 3-1. It was Blackburn's first defeat in 11 games. Bovington came in to replace Peters, in order to mark Douglas tightly. Sissons went wide and Budgie brought his personal account against Rovers to four. Geoff Hurst got the first goal.

Unfortunately, this was not to be the beginning of a revival for the Irons. By the start of the new year, things were not getting much better for them. The League Cup run was some consolation, but with only seven wins in a League programme that was more than half complete, their record was not impressive. For all this, they were playing some decent football, and the team was developing all the time. By the start of 1964, Bobby Moore had nearly 150 first-class games under his belt and 17 caps to his credit.

A good win in the FA Cup, over Second Division Charlton, helped morale though. Budgie, the man-of-the-match, set up Hurst for the first goal after ten minutes, and a quarter-of-an-hour later did it again for Peter Brabrook. Eddie Firmani had a couple of chances for Charlton, but when Sissons grabbed the last-minute goal for the Irons, the scoreline looked about right.

In the next round West Ham were drawn to meet Orient again, this time at Brisbane Road. The home side started well. Norman Deeley, of Wolves fame, nodded home Gregory's corner after only two minutes and they were all over the Irons for a while. But just before the break, Sissons dummied Charlton to set up Brabrook's equaliser. The replay was all over with just 15 minutes played. Hurst scored twice in the opening ten minutes and five minutes later, Johnny Byrne made it three. Hurst was upended by goalkeeper Mike Pinner just after half-time, but Hurst's penalty was well saved by the goalkeeper.

In February, West Ham went into the first leg of the League Cup semi-final against Leicester at Filbert Street. It was to be Alan Sealey's first game since injury the previous November.

By now many supporters understood Alan to be hard-working, unpredictable, fast and something of a fighter. His battle against his stuttering was an example of this. Alan started singing as a kid to help with his speech impediment. Eddie Presland recollects: "Alan could really sing and, along with Brian Dear, all but took over the entertainment at my wedding. It was his stuttering that started him singing. They used to get stutterers to sing sentences as a kind of speech therapy."

This is a fine example of how Alan Sealey had learnt to turn a seeming drawback into an advantage. He took something of this attitude into his football. His ability to knock out a tune stayed in the memory of Ken Brown: "I have fond memories of Alan singing *Bye-Bye Blackbird*. He had a tremendous voice."

Johnny Byrne said that Alan was "a very good singer".

Brian Dear, a close friend, was another songster: "Like me, Sammy liked a sing-song. We did a double act at Dennis Burnett's wedding and we had a good time at Sammy's wedding reception down at the Spotted Dog. He would sing a song, then I'd sing one. He used to lock himself in a room and practise in front of the mirror."

Alan's love for the great Tony Bennett numbers was confirmed by his friend and life-long Hammers supporter Terry Connelly: "He loved a sing-song, his favourite being *I Left My Heart in San Francisco*."

As we have just heard, at Dennis Burnett's wedding in the late 1960s, Alan and Brian Dear did a double act, a sort of Fred Astaire/Gene Kelly-type routine complete with straw boaters and walking canes. It brought the house down.

Alan Dickie also recalled the Dear/Sealey duo: "Alan would, at any opportunity, sing on the mike. He had a good voice. I remember him and Brian Dear doing a duet on one pre-season tour."

Alan also had an impact on future West Ham manager, John Lyall: "Apart from his football, he loved giving a song."

Even the youngsters at the club knew of Alan's vocal talents, as Bobby Howe explains: "His accomplished singing voice and lively spirit entertained all of us away from the field of play."

Older players were also impressed. Bill Lansdowne senior: "I remember him entertaining us with his singing after the Cup Final victories."

Defender Bill Kitchener: "I remember Alan having a good singing voice. He seemed to have a liking for Tony Bennett and could often be heard singing *I Left My Heart in San Francisco* when wandering into the showers."

However, Alan Sealey was keen to learn more contemporary material, at the same time using his interest in music to help and benefit his fellow players, as former West Ham centre-half Paul Heffer testifies: "Alan was a very friendly and amusing colleague. He always made a point of making the new and younger members of the squad feel welcome and comfortable when they were promoted and joined the first-team squad.

"In my particular case, I was 18 and he noticed that I knew all the words to the top hits of the time – they were printed in the *New Musical Express* which I read regularly. He liked to talk about the top songs although he was a bit older. He really liked *Hole in My Shoe* by Traffic (I think). He heard me singing the words and he asked me to teach him the lyrics so he could perform it and 'relax' us before the next game. He had immediately made me feel wanted. We met at various times during the week and I taught him the words. He loved showing off and performing, and before the next home game he 'starred' in the changing-room, amazing the senior players with his knowledge of the lyrics. The squad loved it. As he finished, he gave me a big grin and a wink."

But Sealey had little to sing about by half-time in the first leg of the 1964 League Cup semi-final. Before the first 20 minutes were up, West Ham had let in three goals without reply. Although Geoff Hurst pulled one back on the half-hour, with little more than 20 minutes to play the Hammers were trailing 4-1. But Hurst's sixth goal in three games, running right through King's challenge, gave the Irons hope, and Sealey was determined to improve their chances and managed to bang one home with just eight minutes remaining. Another late, late goal by Sammy. The result was disappointing, but it was the away leg.

Three days later West Ham faced Tottenham at the Boleyn Ground in a First Division game which ended in a 4-0 home victory. This meant that West Ham had done a double against England's two European Cup-winners' Cup entrants. Hurst, Sissons, Boyce and Byrne netted in front of nearly 37,000 spectators, mostly Hammers fans. Hurst's goal haul was again restricted by the woodwork.

Ronnie Boyce was the epi-central inside-forward of the side. He was known as 'Ticker' because he worked like clockwork. He was the heartbeat of the team, all over the field, prompting forwards and holding the midfield. He played the game simply, feeding the likes of Hurst, Byrne and Sissons with accurate passes. A push-and-run player if ever there was one. As such, Boyce was the ideal midfielder for the 4-2-4 system. He had made his League debut against Preston at Upton Park in 1960-61, when he was 17. That was the year after Fenton gave the East Ham Grammar School boy his first 'proper' game for the club in a Southern Junior Floodlit Cup tie against Millwall. Unselfish and hardworking, Ronnie also had suburb passing skill.

After beating Spurs, West Ham got a day off and then it was up to the Midlands on the Monday to face Wolves. Hurst's goal, his 20th of the season, was a second bite of the cherry after Davies, the Wolverhampton 'keeper, had parried the initial shot and it put him into double-figures over six games. Sissons set up Johnny Byrne for the second. The defence was really solid, playing with a 'funnel' system, and the talented strike force that Wolves put up against the Hammers, including Peter Knowles, was all but snuffed out. A win at Hillsborough the following Saturday was nearly thrown away. The Hammers were leading 4-1 going into the last quarter-of-an-hour, but by the end the match had turned into a seven-goal affair. All this set West Ham up for their seventh game in February, the FA Cup quarter-final against their first opponents in the competition from Division One, Burnley.

John Connelly dodged three challenges before putting Burnley in front after 13 minutes and the Irons were a goal behind for nearly half the game. Just before the hour, though, the worries of the Hammers faithful were eased when the Burnley defender, Alex Elder, could only help a John Sissons effort over the line. Then West Ham turned on the pressure and three minutes later Budgie hit a tasty volley to put his side in front. Burnley had hardly pulled themselves together when Byrne struck again. The Lancashire club's players went into a frenzy about this one. They really didn't think that the ball had crossed the line and in the fall-out, Gordon Harris chinned John Bond. For all that, it concentrated their minds brilliantly and Ray Pointer scored with ten minutes left, but Greenwood's men held on to go through.

A few days later, in the League game at Turf Moor, Burnley got some revenge. Although Hurst hit the post twice, Moore and company were well beaten. Burnley were two up at half-time and made it three just after the break before Byrne got one back late on. Harris went heavily into Bobby Moore, but

Martin Peters got him back. You wouldn't have thought it to look at him, but Peters was one of the hardest players of his era. He wasn't one for waving his fists about, but he knew how to put himself about if the need arose.

Born in Plaistow in 1943, Peters was a perceptive and complete midfielder. He was an excellent player with both feet, strong in the air, with an eye for a goal. He would prompt with delicate touches and beautiful clipped passes and then appear on the end of crosses with headers, finely-judged at the near post or crashed in from a distance. He could shoot, too. So many times Peters seemed to come from nowhere. He was difficult to mark, often arriving in the box late, on the blind side. He went to Fanshawe School in Dagenham and played for Dagenham Schools, London, Essex and England Schools (in the same team as Brian Dear) and then England youth after signing as an apprentice for West Ham in May 1959.

Early in March, West Ham lost their next home game, to Manchester United, not a good omen as United were to be the Hammers' FA Cup semifinal opponents. Before that, however, there was the second leg of the League Cup semi-final to contemplate. As it turned out, Leicester City plundered the Boleyn Ground. Gordon Banks, back in goal after five weeks out injured, had one of his inspired games and made all the difference for Leicester, who took the tie 2-0. Four days later, West Ham beat the other Finalists, Stoke City, 4-1 in the League at Upton Park. Leicester eventually took the trophy, 6-3 on aggregate over the two legs against the Potters.

Two Second Division teams had reached the last four of the FA Cup, but there was to be no prospect of an historic Final as Preston and Swansea were drawn against each other. West Ham were obliged to face the Cup holders and the eventual runners-up in Division One that season, so the Irons' chances of making the Final were completely written off by the press. No one gave them a chance at Hillsborough, where the likes of Law, Charlton and Crerand were returning to the United side.

The match, being played in Sheffield, perhaps gave the advantage to the northern team, but the pre-match entertainment was provided by the Dagenham Girl Pipers, so this more or less evened things up as far as some of the Cockney supporters were concerned. West Ham played above themselves, depriving the opposition of the ball. Jim Standen was solid in goal, particularly when Law piled into him feet first at one point. Byrne and Hurst worked well up front, adapting to the muddy conditions much better than their counterparts in the Manchester team. Bobby Moore was dominant that day, marshalling Bond, Burkett, Bovington and Brown to generate a resilient defence.

'Ticker' Boyce got the first two West Ham goals in a seven-minute period which started just over ten minutes into the second half. His opener was lofted in past the stranded the United 'keeper, David Gaskell, from just inside the United half. His second was nicely put away from a short corner. Ronnie didn't score often, he just seemed to save them for the big occasion. Denis Law pulled one back in the 78th minute, but just a moment later a Bobby Moore pass was picked up by Hurst and put away from the edge of the penalty-area.

Beating Manchester United is a big event in the history of any team, but to knock them out of the FA Cup at the semi-final stage is a rare achievement for an English club. Any United team is good, but this was one of the great sides to come out of Old Trafford. That semi-final will always stand as one of West Ham's finest 90 minutes.

On the way to the FA Cup Final, West Ham scored three goals against every team they came up against, Charlton, Orient (following the draw Brisbane Road), Swindon and Burnley. Hurst got a goal in every round apart from the sixth.

Just four days later, West Ham were pitted us against Leicester in the League. Jack Burkett got his first goal in Division One in a 2-2 draw at Filbert Street. Three days later the Irons held Arsenal 1-1 at Upton Park, Standen saving a George Eastman penalty. Ian Ure kicked Johnny Byrne all over the park, and once right out of it, over a barrier. It was a shame Peters wasn't playing.

West Ham had seven more games before Wembley. They won three and lost four to finish 14th in the table, just above Fulham. Liverpool, over whom the Hammers had done the double (3-1 over the two games), won the championship. Manchester United were runners-up and, of course, the Irons had beaten them two times out of three that season.

Alan Sealey had played 22 games during the season, none in the FA Cup, but the West Ham side, even in those days, were very much a squad team and most players felt part of the campaign that took the club to Wembley, being involved in preparation and training. Sealey obviously hoped to make the

Wembley team, but realistically, given the form of Hurst, Sissons, Byrne and Brabrook, he knew that he was unlikely to get the nod unless there was an injury.

West Ham were favourites for the Final. Preston, although they had only just missed out on promotion to the First Division, were, after all, a Second Division side. They had also suspended their left-half, Ian Davidson, for misconduct. As such, the Final seemed to be something of a formality, given the decisive 3-1 defeat of Manchester United at Hillsborough, Bobby Moore being voted Footballer of the Year (Johnny Byrne came fourth), and both Byrne and Moore being picked for England's match against the Scots at Hampden (Jack Tresadern and Vic Watson were the last two Hammers to play together for England at Hampden; that was in 1923).

For all this, Preston had done well to get to the Final, beating the First Division sides Nottingham Forest, and Bolton on the way, albeit Bolton were relegated at the season's end. Alex Dawson, a centre-forward of the English tradition, would be their main threat. He was a tall, strong man, made for aerial combat. Eddie Bovington would play deep, which would give West Ham an extra defensive option, with Moore starting the match as sweeper. Some had their doubts about this, given Dawson's ability in the air and Moore's lack of the same, but most supporters had every confidence that Bobby would do a job, and The Hammers were doing everything they could to prepare themselves.

Eddie Presland said: "In preparation for the Final, the Irons trained at West Ham dog track in Custom House. The pitch was nearly as big as Wembley."

Ron Greenwood chose to stage John Lyall's testimonial match on the Monday evening before the Final. It was a game against a London XI, a big crowd turned up and a deal of pride was at stake. John Lyall was a good player, cut down before his time by injury, but this was a chancy decision on Greenwood's part. It might have been a better bet to have played the game after the Final. Of course, it being a London thing, the players went for it. This made it very competitive and a good game, but it took its toll on the team. Some Hammers fans muttered the hope that the Final would not go to extra-time.

The youngest player on the Wembley pitch, the youngest ever to start an

FA Cup Final, was 17-year-old Howard Kendall, and it was he who began the move that led to Doug Holden giving Preston the lead. Jim Standen messed up Alex Dawson's drive and Holden, who had been to Wembley before with Bolton more than once, followed up.

West Ham then attacked in numbers and John Sissons made the most of a pass produced from Moore's advance upfield. Moore took the ball from a Preston attack and found Byrne. Budgie put Sissons, also 17 but some days older than Kendall, through and he levelled the score with a shot from a tight angle. Thus John Sissons became the youngest player to score in a Wembley Final.

Byrne came near to putting his side ahead about halfway through the half, but Preston regained the lead at half-time from a well-timed run that led to a goal, headed with strength and determination by Dawson from a Kendall corner.

The Alec Ashworth-Dawson pairing was looking to be a more powerful attack than the Hammers could muster. They were being given too much room in midfield and Preston's forward play was by-passing Moore. So, Greenwood decided to switch to a flat back four at the start of the second half. Brown and Moore moved in to mark the Preston strikers, and Bovington was pushed into midfield. Eddie Bovington was an Edmonton boy. He was 23 and had signed for the club five years earlier from the junior ranks. He was an abrasive, dependable wing-half who made his League debut against Manchester United at Old Trafford at the end of the 1959-60 season. His presence in the middle of the park made the game faster.

Early in the second half, the Irons won a corner and Hurst connected with it to send a header hard against the underside of the crossbar. The ball spun off the woodwork and swerved to the ground off Irish international goalkeeper Alan Kelly, then twisted slowly over the line and into the net.

The match was now being played at breakneck pace, back and forth. Chances came and went at either end. Although Preston had the majority of opportunities, it was anybody's game, and the 100,000 spectators moved with the action. With five minutes left, extra-time seemed inevitable. Exhausted West Ham legs were now feeling the cost of Lyall's testimonial which looked to threaten West Ham's chances of taking the trophy.

In the dying moments of the game, Geoff Hurst hurtled forward, breaking through a wall of challenges. He got a pass to Brabrook who swiftly sent the ball into the centre. Ronnie Boyce launched himself as Brabrook hit the cross. It was the very last minute of the Final, the second minute of injury time. The Preston defenders watched as Boyce came into contact with the ball near the goal-line. It glided just clear of Kelly. It was the third time the 22-year-old had scored in the Cup. It was his 11th goal of the season, and the 17th of his professional career.

Peter and Gordon were top of the charts with *World Without Love, Dr Strangelove* was fast becoming a cult film and, in the FA Cup Final, Preston North End, 'Proud Preston', had managed 23 attacks on West Ham United's goal. The East Londoners had answered with just 16 raids of their own ...and they had won the FA Cup for the first time.

## A Football Disaster

Just 19 days after the greatest moment in West Ham's history thus far, the worst disaster football had seen occurred in Peru's capital city, Lima.

What did this have to do with an East London club? Well, the people who died were supporters. That is what any football club 'is' – supporters. Those of us who stood on the terraces, who now fill the stadiums, are brothers and sisters in our passion. It is also 'to do with us' because as history shows, if nothing is said, it will eventually be our turn.

Lima is sprawled untidily on the edge of the coastal desert. Upon hearing the name, most people imagine it to be rather exotic, but it is, in the main, a modern city, although overcrowded, polluted and noisy. It is a place beset with problems and can be quite threatening to the first-time visitor. Almost one-third of Peru's near 20 million population live in Lima. The city is constantly expanding due to the very poor people moving in from the impoverished rural highlands. These people come seeking work and opportunities for their children. By the mid-1960s the colonial charm of the place had been overwhelmed. Unfortunately, for most the search for prosperity ends in the *pueblos jovenes*, (young towns). These shanty towns fringe Lima. They have no electricity, no water and inadequate sanitation. Work is hard to find. Most people coming to the city hopefully end up working as ambulates or street vendors, peddling anything from sweets to safety pins. They are lucky to scratch together enough to feed themselves.

Lima's climate is dismal. From April to December, the sea fog, the *garua*, blots out the sun, covering the city in a grey mist. Most of the buildings are not often painted. This, together with the pollution, means that the place is covered in a concrete-like layer of grey sludge. Downtown Lima is built in the Spanish Colonial style with streets in a checker-board pattern surrounding the Plaza de Armas. Although grand, the area is rundown.

The Alejandro Villanueva is the home of Alianza, in 1964 the national champions for the previous two seasons, and Sporting Cristal, the winners in 1961. The stadium is not quite as big as the Estadio Naçional, where, on 24 May, a qualifying game for the 1965 Olympic Soccer Finals in Tokyo, between Peru and Argentina, was taking place. The stadium is an awesome structure

Lima has a brief summer, but at this time the smog takes over from the mist, making being outside a sticky and uncomfortable experience. As the waste from the millions who populate Lima mostly ends up in the Pacific, the beaches are overcrowded cesspools. For all this, the people of the city are mostly good-hearted, jovial folk and the singing and general carnival-like atmosphere before the big match was not unusual.

When the game kicked-off, some 45,000 people were in the stadium, mostly supporters of Peru. The Argentineans took the lead and the score was still 1-0 with only minutes to play when Lobaton, a popular Peruvian winger, scored what everyone thought was the equalising goal. The crowd went wild with delight, but in a matter of seconds their cheers turned to howls of protest. The referee, Angel Eduardo Payos, a Uruguayan, had disallowed the goal for dangerous play, giving Argentina a free-kick.

The whole stadium was soon in an uproar. Fighting broke out on the terraces and missiles rained down on the pitch. The crowd's reaction was so terrifying that Payos, after being set about by a couple of supporters, ordered all the players off the field. The game simply could not continue in such an atmosphere, and it was clear that Payos was genuinely worried at the inadequacy of police protection for the two teams and himself. They all ran for shelter down a ramp that led out of the stadium.

Then the riot started in earnest. It was triggered by a well-known football fan, Matias Rojas, nicknamed 'The Bomb'. He was a thick-set local character, habitué of the stadium, and was one of those who rushed on to the pitch to attack the referee. All of 40 police and two dogs fell on him in front of the volatile crowd in the stands. He was dragged off. At this, the fans' indignation could contain itself no longer. With a mighty roar the spectators in the South Stand surged forward, leaning and heaving on the iron fence which separated them from the pitch. It gave way, spilling bodies all over the ground. A flood of humanity went tumbling down towards the pitch.

The few police on hand had already managed to barricade the players and referee behind the steel door of a locker room, and two hours later they were smuggled out of the city centre. However, innocent members of the football crowd had little chance to reach safety as easily. People were literally being trampled to death by the descending crowds.

As screams and cries filled the air, every window in the stadium was being smashed. Fires were shooting up in the stands, a common protest among Peruvian football supporters. The frightened police overreacted, adding to the pandemonium by lobbing tear gas at the crowd and shooting bullets over their heads. This created panic and a blind flight for the doors, which were all locked. The people at the front tried to shout, "There's no way out here – go back, go back!" but the mob, now with no rationality left, surged forward, so that many people were crushed to death or suffocated by the press of bodies against the stadium doors. The effect of the tear gas on those in the crowd was acutely painful. Many rushed up into the stands to get out of the mêlée, choking and coughing. The gas was so thick that it hung like a cloud over the lower part of the stadium.

Mounted police attempted to herd people towards the exits, unaware that they were locked. In desperation the crowd started pelting the police with whatever missiles they could find. One man, who seemed to be suffering from a rib injury, kept grabbing his side as he tried to save a tiny girl by holding her high above the terrified crowd. But he lost his balance and let her go. She was one of the victims crushed in the crowd against the corrugated iron doors. She was his 18-month-old daughter.

The events inside the stadium were not enough to exhaust the pent-up emotions of the crowd. Another mob marched on the Presidential Palace, tearing down flags from the Plaza San Martin on the way, waving them in the air and shouting: "Justice! Justice!" They wanted to protest to President Fernando Belaunde Terry at the police brutality and to have him intervene officially to have the match declared a draw. Both demands were ignored. Meanwhile, outside the stadium running battles between fans and police continued through the night.

The hospitals were overloaded with casualties. A temporary morgue was set up, and bodies were laid out on the lawn outside the hospital building.

Next day, feelings were still running so high that a third mob stormed the stadium once more, breaking in and stealing trophies and fencing swords from one of the practice rooms. At the university campus, another crowd of chanting students demonstrated, calling for the resignation of the entire cabinet. The students' union called a 24-hour strike.

It was sometime before an assessment of the tragedy could be made. The exact number of dead was never established, but according to official figures, 328 people perished. Most were crushed and trampled to death, but at least four were killed by police bullets. There were 500 seriously injured. The Peruvian Government, in the face of accusations of brutality and lack of control, declared a state of emergency or siege throughout Peru and suspended the constitution. At the same time it ordered a full investigation of the event, although the official line was that the riot was caused by the actions of 'left-wing extremists'. In effect, they were seeking to make political gain out of all that death. Legislation was rushed through Parliament to give financial assistance to widows and orphans and pay for the victims' funerals. Seven days of official mourning was announced. The hope here was that this would placate people and encourage a lull in the unrest out of respect for the dead.

The riot in the Estadio Naçional on 24 May 1964, was one of the most bizarre events in sporting history. It was violent, mass hysteria. Admittedly, football is a passionate interest among Latin Americans of all classes, but this riot has to be set against the high tension running through Peru's political environment as well as the sporting arena at that time.

The funerals began the following day at 9am. Each service was taken individually, unlike the more common practice in other countries of mass burials after such a disaster. The traffic jams created by the mourners stretched for several miles around the main Lima cemetery.

Almost at the same time, the Chamber of Deputies rejected a motion to censure Minister of the Interior, Juan Languasco, for alleged responsibility for 'police brutality'. And on 27 May, the police arrested more than 50 individuals. This group was charged with looting and incitement to violence. Some had callously robbed victims as they lay dying in the stadium.

A year later, an examining magistrate again called for the trial of the, by then, out-of-office Minister of the Interior and the chief of police officers on duty at the time of the riot. In a report submitted to the Peruvian Supreme Court, the magistrate, Dr Benjamin Castaneda, accused these individuals of having direct responsibility for the disorders that led to such a severe loss of life. But the Government had given its verdict at the time of the riot: 'left-wing extremists' were to blame for trying to organise demonstrations despite the state of siege (a modified form of martial law) that was in effect at the time.

In a report published in the *New York Times* just after the event, American journalist Robert Lipsyte commented: "In many countries where soccer is one of the few diversions and emotional releases for a poor and restless mass, the game takes on the proportion of a kind of controlled warfare."

There is much to this. When something is repressed in one sphere, what we know of our psyche and the universe in general, tells us that this energy will emerge in another place. So often, football has acted as a means of expressing frustration, anger and feelings arising out of injustice and oppression. Football violence tells us something about a society; like everything else, it has a history and a cause.

It would be wrong to think that the riot in Peru was a demonstration of a kind of passion found only in Latin countries or poorer nations. There were peculiar political tensions in Peru in 1964, but tensions created by a lack of money, few job opportunities or mishandled crowd control by police could cause mass violence anywhere.

Locked gates, barriers, crowd misbehaviour, and police incompetence. Shades of Hillsborough? Police over-reaction. In Rome? In France?

From the mid-1960s 'football hooliganism' has been the passion and obsession of the popular media. Maybe we need to rethink our definition of what 'a hooligan' is. When one looks at the figures it begs the question: is the violence by official negligence, incompetence or insensitivity worse than anything the fans could do to each other? Between the 1902 Ibrox disaster (the first of two at that stadium) and the 1989 Hillsborough disaster, a total of 1,256 people died and a further 4,785 were injured in 13 major disasters at football grounds. Seven of those games were in Britain, five in England.

It is interesting to note, incidentally, that between March 1963 and April 1965 there is no record of Peru having played international football. Argentina, meanwhile, went to the Tokyo Olympics in 1964. They lost both their games.

# 1964-65

THE new FA Cup holders opened their season well. A 2-2 draw in the Charity Shield against the champions, Liverpool, at Anfield meant that they shared the trophy, but as they had been obliged to play on their opponents' home ground a moral victory could be claimed.

The inaugural match of the season gave West Ham a good 2-1 win over Fulham, who would just escape relegation that term. Johnnys Haynes and Byrne each had a good match. Budgie started the move that got him and West Ham their first League goal of 1964-65. Dave Metchick grabbed the equaliser. Lashing hopefully at the ball, he was more surprised than anyone to see his effort go in off the post. The Hammers' winner came via Geoff Hurst's boot, Tony Macedo saved the first effort, but only managed to send it to John Sissons, who finished efficiently.

On the Monday, the Irons kept up their domination of Manchester United. In four games against them West Ham had come away with three victories. This time the Hammers were 2-0 ahead with about ten minutes to play at Upton Park. European Footballer of the Year, Denis Law, headed home to make it 2-1, just before Maurice Setters was carried off, leaving United a man short (Boyce had cut through one of Setters' boots with his studs). A frantic finale resulted in a goal by Hurst with five minutes remaining.

September brought West Ham's first-round, first-leg European Cup-winners' Cup match with the part-timers of La Gantoise, the first Belgian team to compete in the competition. Ron Greenwood had been based in Ghent in the RAF during the war, and so quite enjoyed the idea of going back. He and his team made their way by coach down to Dover and took the ferry to Ostend. Then it was back on the coach to Ghent. The Boleyn Boys loved it. Not everyone in the side was used to going abroad and two of them turned up without passports. Defender Eddie Presland, an East Ham lad, was due to play in this game, but as he was getting changed, Greenwood had to tell him that he had not been registered. This oversight almost certainly changed Presland's future because chances of getting into the side were to be few and far between.

In their first venture into Europe, West Ham learnt a few lessons from La Gantoise, who were a rugged side. Most importantly they discovered that nothing can be taken for granted on foreign fields. Tradition dictated that home sides attack and away teams defend at the difficult and complex level of the game that is European football; but in this tie, La Gantoise seemed committed to defence over both legs. The Belgium Cup winners, inevitably, were the side to suffer. They stuck to their 4-2-4 lines with almost military rigidity, defending in depth, tackling with gusto and covering like men possessed. The Irons countered with a method that amounted to 1-4-1-4. Brown came back as a centre-half, Moore acted as general caretaker and Peters played at left-back. His speed and instinct for an opening plagued the Belgian side.

The outcome of all this was that the Hammers asked most of the questions. They created five good chances in the first half while La Gantoise did not manage one. It was all too clear that sooner or later the Belgian team would come up with the wrong answer and they did so in the 52nd minute. Sealey took a corner on the right, Armand Seghers, the 40-year-old Belgium 'keeper, dithered and 'Ticker' got his head to the ball. It passed over Seghers' head so gently, almost in slow motion, that it seemed to give a little sigh of regret as it tucked itself into the net.

La Gantoise emerged from their shell a little in the second half. They owed no less to their now-despairing supporters; but they had neither the skill nor the method to break down a West Ham side playing well within itself. The time for them to profit by positive football had passed. Long before the final whistle the 11 Irons, and their following of 600 from East London, in a crowd of 18,000, were looking forward with relish to the second leg at the Boleyn Ground.

Just before the return leg, the Hammers were pitched out of the League

Cup by Sunderland. Moore was rested because of a forthcoming England game, but Sunderland played with ten men for almost half the game and even then West Ham managed to lose 4-1 in front of a crowd of nearly 23,000. Three days later the Hammers were facing the Belgians again at Upton Park. Alan Dickie played in goal, one of his rare first-team outings as Standen had been injured. However, the reserve 'keeper found out about his inclusion somewhat late in the day: "I didn't think I was in the team for the match against La Gantoise. I got held up in Blackwall Tunnel – it was murder in those days. We were told to get to the ground by 6.30pm at the latest. I didn't get there till 7.10pm, to be told that I would be playing. The kick-off was only 20 minutes away, so I had no time for butterflies."

Bond, Peters, Bovington, Moore and Brown were in front of 'Spider'. Brabrook and Boyce were behind Byrne, Hurst and Sissons. West Ham were fired by ambition and full of ideas, but their passing was erratic at vital points. Their finishing was also inaccurate and at times unbelievably poor. The boys from Ghent, as in the first leg, stuck solidly with their rigid 4-2-4 system, but a bit more aggressively than in Belgium. Again, though, they found it difficult to make the formation work. Their last line of four defended and the rest looked after themselves.

West Ham always appeared destined to move on to the next round, even if they made hard work of it. Indeed, the Hammers should have scored four in the first 20 minutes. The Belgians never fought less than bravely, within the limitations of their system and ability. Even when Denayer, his left thigh strapped, limped out to the wing, and Ghellynck and Lanbert dropped back, they kept on running and tackling with strength. However, a moment of outrageous confusion by the Hammers' defence gave La Gantoise a goal. Peters intercepted a through ball and turned to make a back-pass to Dickie. It looked a formality but, suddenly, things went horribly wrong.

Spider advanced along the line of the right post, but Peters' pass trundled two yards to his right and into the opposite corner of the net. However, this was a rare moment of jubilation for the visitors. The Irons might have won by six. In the end they got the victory but lost out a bit on the honour. Their goal came 11 minutes after the Belgian opener, but it was a good one. Sissons sped along the left wing and his long, diagonal centre was swept into the net, first time, by Budgie. This was one success, but it had to be set against an endless catalogue of near-things. Sissons hit the side-netting twice and was also denied by a post. Hurst forced Armand Seghers to make the save of the night and maybe his life.

So in the end West Ham's opponents deserved a fond farewell and the crowd of 24,000 (who paid record receipts) gave the plucky but outclassed Belgians a huge, spontaneous roar of sympathy as the game ended. Of course, this might have been ironic, as jeers and slow handclaps had been coming from spectators throughout the match in response to the defensive tactics deployed by the Belgians, who were seemingly intent on keeping the scoreline respectable. Nevertheless, West Ham were into the last 16. This had just been the preliminary round – a sobering thought as West Ham could expect subsequent challenges to be much more demanding.

For all this, news from other ties showed that the Irons not the only ones to struggle. The holders again slumped as Sporting bowed out to the English Second Division side Cardiff City, the Welsh Cup winners, who were already carrying on the Taff giantkilling tradition begun by Bangor City.

As West Ham were labouring against comparative minnows in European terms, over at Stamford Bridge, in a charity match, twice-European champions Benfica were giving Chelsea a lesson in the Continental game. The Blues were at the top of the First Division, and they were a good, thorough, enthusiastic young side and scored first, but all their sprinting got them nowhere in the end. In the second half the Eagles of Lisbon showed that subtlety and individual refinement of technique are superior to a method, however correct, which relies primarily on pace and determination. Chelsea were well beaten.

Chelsea had a team of quality with players like Peter Bonetti, Eddie McCreadie, John Hollins, Ron Harris, Bobby Tambling, Barry Bridges, Terry Venables and Peter Houseman. Indeed, this was the embryonic FA Cup and Cup-winners' Cup-winning side of the early 1970s, but this result showed how far they, West Ham and English football in general, had to go to achieve anything in Europe.

The next day, Slavia Sofia of Bulgaria put out Cork Celtic. The Turks, Galatasaray, were through on the toss of a coin, and the Fins of Haka had ousted Skeid of Oslo. Any one of this lot would have suited West Ham in the next round but they drew Spartak Sokolovo, later to be known as Sparta Prague. Greenwood and his team knew that they were a hard, disciplined side, who were leading the Czech League at the time. After going through the Spartak side, West Ham found them to be an awesome crew. Their trepidation would not have been allayed by the news that the first leg would be played at Upton Park.

The day before the match with Spartak the football headlines were dominated by the imminent transfer of Scottish international centre-forward Alan Gilzean from Dundee to Spurs. Gilzean had impressed at White Hart Lane, scoring twice in the John White Memorial Match. Bob Shankly, Dundee's manager at the time, was to meet with Bill Nicholson at Hampden Park for secret talks (so secret that the papers knew all about it). Scotland were also playing Northern Ireland in a World Cup qualifying match on the same night and names like Jim Baxter and Denis Law were plastered all over the place. Alan Ball and the encounter of England with Rumania at Under-23 level at Coventry was also exciting people working within the game. The 'innovative' 4-2-4 formation Rumania were using caused interest.

After a calf injury, John Bond was brought back into the side to play the Czechs. Joe Kirkup made way. Other than this, it was the same side that had beaten Leeds 3-1 the previous Saturday. Alan Sealey had played in this game, after being brought in for the match at Highbury where West Ham had beaten the Gunners 3-0. Sealey was thrilled about being involved in Europe again. Bond was prepared for a busy night dealing with Czech international Masek at outside-left, but the Hammers thought that defence would be their first consideration.

West Ham were not seen as a very attack-minded side at the time, and the cushion of a couple of goals, traditionally expected to take to the away leg of a tie, was not a foregone conclusion. It was thought that Peters and Ronnie Boyce would hold the key in midfield. Ron Greenwood's plan was to let Spartak do their defensive stuff, being the away team, and try to out manoeuvre them. The idea was that this would give West Ham control of the game, allowing Hurst, Byrne and Sissons to concentrate on goalgetting. Simple! But as is so often the case, it didn't work out like that.

For nearly an hour the Irons flung themselves at Spartak's solidly drilled defence, who never had less than seven men back and at times this went up to nine. It didn't make for exciting football, but it was effective, with the burly, uncompromising Gura closely marking Byrne, the equally daunting Steiningel holding on to Hurst and the towering Kos sweeping up behind the defence. The Hammers' main hope seemed to lie with young Sissons. The left-winger did well against Dyba early on, but the visitors' outside-right was a hard-running defender in this match. By half-time, he, alongside Voja and Mraz (who had focused on Boyce and Peters in midfield) had cut off Byrne's supply lines. With Moore out for this game, the side looked to Martin Peters for inspiration, but it was not happening.

The plans had gone awry. It began to look like one of those nights when everything you try just will not come off and a frustrating goalless draw was in prospect. The Hammers were left to fight it out, but that suited them, not least battling Sammy. Out on the right, Spartak conceded one of the string of free-kicks given against them. Sealey curled the ball into the goalmouth where it was beaten out by a defender and landed at the feet of John Bond. From about 25 yards out, Bond banged in a scorcher of a shot (with his 'wrong' foot, the left) which soared into the roof of the net.

Bond just loved to score and with just over half an hour of the leg remaining, the West Ham board and manager Ron Greenwood must have thanked their lucky stars that the veteran full-back had refused to sign for QPR some time earlier. He hadn't scored for three and a half years, but he could pick his moments. A Colchester lad, Bond came through the difficult way, playing first for North-East Essex Schools and Essex Army Cadets. An amateur with Colchester Casuals, he was signed by Ted Fenton in 1950, after catching Fenton's eye when he was manager of Colchester United, a non-League club at the time. Bond made his League debut in a 2-1 win at Coventry in February 1952 and he was in the Second Division championship side of 1957-58. Bond was something of a penalty and dead ball expert and although a defender, scored his share of goals (the first against Spartak was his 34th for the club), playing a number of games as centre-forward in the late 1950s.

One goal was not going to be enough to take to Prague, but the Czech defence now allowed Budgie to buzz and he began to spray passes round in the spaces which opened up. With under ten minutes left he sent a beauty to

Ronnie Boyce and then Sealey picked up Ron's volley on the left-hand edge of the Czech penalty-area. Alan struck it firmly and the ball hit the far post. As it came back out, one of the Spartak defenders inadvertently chipped the ball back to Sealey. This time he relaxed. He looked up at his target, chose his spot and fired. Kramerius, their 'keeper, had no chance. Sealey was ecstatic. He hadn't scored a goal since early April.

Now, throwing off their cloak of defence – just previously they had booted the ball out of the ground four times in succession in attempts to waste time – Spartak charged full-bloodedly at the West Ham defence. Even in the last minute they were still looking for a reply and Mraz swept a shot across the unprotected goal, but the Hammers held on. The game had attracted nearly 28,000 and the gate receipts were £10,600, a record for the Boleyn.

Even though England Under-23s thrashed Rumania 5-0, Scotland went to the top of their qualifying group with a thrilling 3-2 win over Northern Ireland, and Liverpool beat Anderlecht 3-0 in the European Cup at Anfield with goals from St John, Hunt and Yeats, it was West Ham who grabbed the imagination of the media. Everyone felt that something was happening down in the East End, the magic that comes of putting a Cockney battling spirit together with football intelligence and an effort to produce something akin to art. On that cold night, 25 November 1964, just east of the Tower, north of the river, the night was filled with a celebratory cacophony from the docks that could be heard by children in their beds from Tilbury to Chelsea, from Poplar to Houndsditch. Tug-boat toots and the mighty blast of the horns of disgorged cargo ships sang a 'knees up' of sound that signalled that the alliance of London pride and Essex grit, the stuff that made West Ham a place, not just a football team, had prevailed.

Bobby Moore, having missed the first leg, couldn't make the second leg either, so Boyce was switched and would play as sweeper in Czechoslovakia. Having been a member of the sides which won 3-0 at Stamford Bridge and drew at home to Leicester, Alan Sealey kept his place in the team. He got West Ham's first goal in the Chelsea game. They were flying high at the time and finished in third place in the First Division that season, so the Hammers did well.

In the next leg of the Hammers' European adventure, they had a lot to deal with: volatile opponents, a hostile crowd and a Bulgarian referee made their task a daunting one. Sparta, skilful, tough and encouraged by referee Hlavni Dinov to be rough, rolled wave after wave of attack at the line of defenders before them. The West Ham defence were magnificent and Spartak must have felt they were hammering a punch-bag. No matter how hard they hit, nor from what direction, the ball always came back at them.

In the 13th minute Byrne scuttled on to a long clearance from Bond, wrestled free from the desperate arms of Tichy and squared the ball for Sissons to score with supreme coolness from 20 yards. The goal was a perfect illustration of the counter-attack from a defensive position at which West Ham had become adept. The band of 120 Irons loyalists broke into exultant tone and, yet again in Europe, the sound of the *Bubbles* anthem floated across the ground, which was perched high on a hill above the friendly, sun-bathed city.

Unfortunately that was not the end of the story. Spartak were helped outrageously by the match officials and the referee's partiality reached its peak in the 36th minute. Bond was pushed, and as he fell his hand touched the ball. The outcome was a penalty. Standen watched Mraz carefully as the forward placed the ball deliberately on the spot. Then the West Ham goalkeeper went down into a crouch, still studying his would-be executioner. As the ball was hit, Standen flung himself far to his left, Mraz stared, fists clenched at the end of half-raised arms as the Hammers goalkeeper hurled himself towards the Czech missile. The crowd groaned as Standen intercepted. Justice!

Spartak scored in the 68th and 88th minutes and both goals followed mistakes that were unworthy of West Ham. Masek grabbed the first while Boyce stood motionless, Standen pushed a Taborsky long shot on to the bar, then lost his footing. The second came at a point when the penalty-area was populated by 18 players. Mraz was permitted to flick a header by Kraus into the net. However, these were the only moments in the game when Boyce was still. He pulled right back to sweep up loose ends in defence. He played the role as if to the manner born. It is adaptability and planning such as this that made West Ham the European power that they were becoming.

John Sissons and Johnny Byrne had a superb game. They were loners up front, but when the ball came up to them they held it until things developed around them. Although West Ham lost the game 2-1, they went through 3-2 on aggregate. But the desperate undertones of the game were spelt out in the cuts and bruises that the West Ham players sustained. Alan Sealey came off worse than most. He was taken to hospital immediately after the game and had seven stitches in an ugly gash on his left shin.

West Ham had been told that Spanish officials would be in charge of the second leg and this had been the case at Upton Park. Afterwards Greenwood said: "We certainly did not expect Iron Curtain officials. We shall have to take it up with UEFA."

This result, though, was a wonderful achievement for the East London side. They had played well, with control yet innovation. West Ham had out-played and out-thought class opposition with style and courage, as a team, each individual committed to the whole.

West Ham now had a three-month break before their next European game. Sealey's injury put him out for the best part of a month but he was back in the team for the club's biggest disappointment in this period when they lost their grip on the FA Cup in a bad way, 1-0 at Upton Park …to Chelsea. The Hammers had beaten relegation-bound Birmingham City in the third round, but the minute of silence before the fourth-round tie, for the death of Sir Winston Churchill, proved doubly fitting. Jim Standen parried Venables' shot for Tambling to score after ten minutes. It had to be said that West Ham had Chelsea on the back foot from then on, but it was not to be and the majority of the 37,000 spectators went home bitterly disappointed. Sealey got his first goal after the Spartak game in West Ham's 2-1 defeat at Bramall Lane. John Sissons set him up with a good pass, but overall the Irons were not playing well.

The highlight of the first part of 1965 came at Upton Park late in February when West Ham put an end to Liverpool's 21-match unbeaten run. This game also marked the end of West Ham's string of three straight defeats. Debutant Eddie Presland slammed in their first from 30 yards at the start of the second half, pulling the Hammers level after Roger Hunt's opener, scored halfway through the first half. Geoff Hurst got the winner with eight minutes left.

The third round of the Hammers' European adventure pitted them against Lausanne of Switzerland. The Swiss were managed by the legendary Karl Rappan who had massive experience of the game, having spent some 40 years at top level. He had been coach of the Swiss national side and had been named the 'Master of Swiss soccer'. His 'bolt' system was unique. It was based on a highly mobile game and required ten men to, theoretically, do the work of 13.

West Ham had met Lausanne before. In 1936 the Swiss won 1-0 and were the only team to beat the Hammers on an otherwise triumphant tour. In 1946 West Ham had thrashed them 7-1. But in the 1960s they were a different prospect. Lausanne were unlike the Czechs and a world away from the Belgians. They were much more flexible and their ranks were bursting with Swiss internationals. Their line-up was formidable:

**Rene Kunzi (goalkeeper):** A regular choice in the past few seasons, his consistency was reflected in Lausanne's fine defensive record. A Swiss 'B' international, he had just turned 26.

**Eugene Parlie (goalkeeper):** The experienced reserve was 36 and had 21 full caps.

**Andre Grobety (right-back):** A compact player with over 30 international appearances to his credit, he had played in the World Cup Finals in Chile.

**Ely Tacchella (centre-back):** Another regular international for his country in the early 1960s with a score of caps, he formed a fine twin centre-back partnership with Schneiter.

**Heinz Schneiter (centre-back):** He cost a five-figure fee when transferred from Young Boys in 1962. Tall and commanding, he played alongside Tacchella in the 1962 World Cup. He was 30.

**Eric Polencent (left-back):** An Under-23 international at the time, a promising 20-year-old defender, he had won himself a place in the team only a short time before, at the expense of the more experienced Hunziker.

**Richard Durr (wing-half):** He had also played in the Chile World Cup and had appeared regularly in the national team in the months before the tie. He was a lanky, long-striding, linkman who favoured attack. He was 26 years old.

**Kurt Armbruster (wing-half):** Among the 20 named for Chile, he did not eventually travel. A 30-year-old, capped twice, he took a midfield role but did not neglect his defensive duties.

**Norbert Eschmann (outside-right):** An outstanding forward, signed from Stade Français two season earlier, Eschmann had over a dozen Swiss caps. He suffered a broken leg in Chile during the World Cup. He was also

Lausanne's youth team coach, so, under Rappan, it was assured he knew his tactics.

**Pierre Kerkhoffs (centre-forward):** Top scorer for PSV Eindhoven in 1963-64, the Dutch international had succeeded in topping the Swiss scoring charts in this, his first season with 13 goals. He was 28.

**Robert Hosp (inside-left):** A 25-year-old attacking player with a keen eye for a goalscoring opportunity, he had made half a dozen international appearances.

**Charles Hertig (outside-left):** Another 25-year-old who made his debut for Switzerland in the last European Nations series, against Holland, he was also a former Swiss Under-23 international.

Lausanne was more or less the Swiss national side that itself was coming fresh from a World Cup qualifying victory in Belfast. This was part of their eventual group-winning performance which emulated their feat in the same competition in 1962 and would take them to England for the final stages in 1966.

At the time of the tie, Rappan's men were top of the Swiss League and would, by the end of the season, be champions. They had won the Swiss Cup against Chaux-de-Fonds, 2-0 in front of 51,000 in the Wankdorf Stadium. They were five times Swiss champions and their manager had predicted they would win their League and the Cup-winners' Cup. They were experienced European warriors, having campaigns in the Cup-winners' Cup and Fairs Cup behind them. So far in this tournament they had accounted for Honved, the crack Hungarian side, 2-1 on aggregate, and Slavia Sofia of Bucharest, 4-3 after a play-off in Rome.

The day before the Hammers flew out to Switzerland they had a League game at home to Sunderland. Eddie Bovington was carried off only three minutes into the match, so for the next 87 minutes the Hammers had to counter the relegation-threatened Rokermen a man short. Brian Dear was brought in for his first League game of the season – he'd had only seven games in three seasons – as Greenwood was resting Byrne for the Cup-winners' Cup game. Stag responded with a couple of good goals. The first came after ten minutes from a Geoff Hurst back-header. Sunderland equalised before half-time via

Harvey and after the break they went ahead through Heard. Then Dear ran on to a Hurst flick for his second to pull the Hammers level, but less than a minute later Herd scored the Sunderland winner. Peters had a goal disallowed and at the final whistle the Wearsiders had done a League double over the Irons and knocked them out of the League Cup in the first round.

Sunderland had given them another tough game. Now, following Sunday's flight, the Irons had to prepare for the quarter-final match on Tuesday. They came to the Olympic Stadium, in the shadow of the Alps, with the intention of playing defensively to set up the second leg on level terms.

Despite recent snow, the pitch was in good condition. Brian Dear was playing his first senior game outside Britain, being drafted into the side following his two goals and the injury to Eddie Bovington. It was Dear who put the Hammers in front, snapping up a chance in the 31st minute when Kunzi failed to hold a Boyce free-kick. Earlier, Armbruster had hit the bar. The Hammers' second came from Johnny Byrne, a brilliant solo effort eight minutes after the interval. Although a defensive error allowed the Swiss to halve that lead ten minutes from time, things looked good for the return in East London.

Yet the Swiss had their chances in the tense first 20 minutes as West Ham struggled to find the form that had eluded them since they were knocked out of the FA Cup. Armbruster thumped the ball against the bar from 18 yards and had another long-range effort headed away by Kirkup. Then Standen failed to hold a shot from Hertig, but Peters was there to clear things up.

The flying Dutchman, Kerkoffs, flashed a rising shot inches wide. He was potentially the most dangerous of the Lausanne forwards, but fluffed a couple of good chances. Had West Ham allowed the Swiss to score at that point, then they might well have gone on to take a commanding lead. As it was the Hammers settled down to some solid defensive stuff, and took a firm grip on the game.

Moore and Boyce, often playing behind our own full-backs, quietly and efficiently broke up many a Swiss move in its infancy. Brown, shadowing Kerkhoffs faithfully for much of the match, rarely put a foot wrong, and Kirkup and Peters made sure that the Lausanne wingers were given the minimum of opportunities to break through.

Early on, Dear cheekily flicked the ball into the net but was offside. Then, around the half-hour mark, West Ham made one of their few upfield sorties and Lausanne conceded an indirect free-kick. Ticker drove the ball over the wall at Kunzi, and the goalkeeper managed only to set up Dear, who stuck it home. If Kunzi had allowed the ball to pass untouched into the net, a goal couldn't have been given, the kick being indirect. To that extent West Ham had the fates on their side. To their credit, following that goal, Lausanne made even greater efforts to break through, but the Hammers stood firm until half-time.

On the restart, West Ham looked much more composed and in the 53rd minute their endeavour was rewarded. A clearance from a delayed free-kick by Moore bounced to Dear, who touched it to Byrne in midfield. Budgie smartly swept round one defender after another, over a 50-yard run, before racing into the penalty-area. He held off a final tackle to send in a well-placed shot. Kunzi touched the ball but could not prevent the second goal.

Ron Greenwood was to call this 'a brilliant goal' and it was. Every bit as good as anything seen in Brazil or Italy. Byrne's analysis gave nothing away: "I just kept going and then hit it." From then on West Ham sensibly concentrated on defence and Lausanne's attempts to close the margin became more and more frantic. Eventually West Ham let them through when Peters misplaced a clearance in his own packed 18-yard box and Hosp promptly slammed the ball into the net.

With the spectators now urging them on to even greater efforts, the home side forced three quick corners. However, when the final whistle sounded they had failed to close the gap, thanks to the headwork of Joe Kirkup, Moore's cool brain and the resilience of Ken Brown. West Ham had done well, but the game had turned into something of an intellectual battle for possession. The 500 travelling Hammers fans sent chants of "East Lon-don" echoing across the Alps as the 25,000 Lausanne supporters applauded both teams off the pitch.

Afterwards Greenwood commented: "I'm delighted. We did everything we came out here to do. We gave away a silly goal but the team played magnificently after the first 20 minutes …We were too defensive at this stage when we should have been going for more goals. We got a bit cocky and let Lausanne come back at us when we did not look in danger."

He had now seen the Swiss three times, once away from home. He said that they had played better than he would have thought. Of Brian Dear he said: "He took his goal well, showed no signs of nerves and did what we asked of him."

John Sissons got a nasty knock in Switzerland and finished the game limping, the injury keeping him out of the next game, at Blackburn. West Ham, meanwhile, were already looking forward to the next round. The Germans, Munich 1860 had a 4-0 first leg advantage over Legia Warsaw, whilst Torino had beaten the Fins, Haka Valkeakoski, 5-0.

The second-leg match against the Swiss was played with much more abandon, plenty of shots and near-misses making for an exciting night appreciated by the 32,000 who yet again broke the club record for gate receipts. It made for a good old-fashioned game of football as the Hammers' non-stop offensive was met by Lausanne fighting to get back into the tie. This gave rise to some fine entertainment. From the kick-off, both sides took risks, and West Ham had a fantastic opening burst which saw Hurst twice rattle the woodwork. Then Kunzi saved splendidly from a Dear effort but was lucky to deny Byrne. The Hammers were blitzing them and the big Lausanne defenders kicked and volleyed shots clear. At one point the Swiss gave away three corners in 30 seconds but, with under ten minutes to half-time, they threw a counter punch. For the first time in the leg the West Ham defence was caught napping when Durr took the ball to the right corner-flag and crossed it quickly into the goalmouth for Kerkoffs to head home.

The game didn't really need lifting but this goal elevated it to new heights. Within five minutes West Ham had scored twice. They were given the first by poor Tacchella, who swept Alan Sealey's centre past his own 'keeper. Sealey also played a part in the second goal when he got hold of the ball well and sent in a rocket at Kuenzi, who palmed it away. The ball seemed to go over the by-line, but Dear, from an extremely acute angle, planted it high in the net.

That should have settled the issue, but the Swiss were unwilling to give in. Four minutes after the interval they forced the industrious Kirkup to make a mistake, and there was Hertig, cutting in from the left. He hit the ball with his right foot into the far corner of the net. For the next ten minutes, West Ham were under intense pressure. An effort from Kerkoffs was saved by Standen with his legs before West Ham applied extra pace, trying to outrun the slow-it-down Swiss. This began to change the pattern of the game. On the hour the Hammers forced a corner. Sealey sent a curler into the goal-mouth and Peters, the outstanding player on a night of many heroes, calmly headed it home.

Although they now seemed to be fighting a lost cause, the Swiss soldiered on gallantly. Hosp smashed a shot against Standen's bar and ten minutes from time Eschmann scored the game's most spectacular goal with an overhead kick that left Standen rooted to the ground in disbelief and earned rapturous applause even from the Hammers fans.

But West Ham were in no mood to give way now and with barely and minute to go, Dear thumped the ball into the net to clinch victory.

Winning this tie had been no mean achievement. West Ham were the only side to beat the Swiss at home that season. Boyce, playing at right-half, had been immaculate, prising open the Lausanne defence. Just a few days later he became a father for the first time, a double celebration if ever there was one. Hurst was a tower of strength and Byrne linked defence and attack with style. Moore was his usual impeccable self and Peters appeared to be the perfect full-back. They all looked England class, with the World Cup just over a year away…

In the semi-final draw West Ham were first out of the hat to face the team they most wanted to avoid, the Spanish side, Real Zaragoza. Their ground was 200 miles from the nearest airport, in Barcelona, and they were, by far, the best team the Hammers had come up against in the competition. Their team was practically the Spanish national side and it was going to be a difficult tie. The other worry was that West Ham's League form was not boding well for the encounter – ten defeats in 13 games from a run which started in December and was not to finish until the end of March.

The first leg of the tie was at the Boleyn Ground. Geoff Hurst and Ron Boyce had been to see the Spanish play in the last round against Cardiff, in Wales, a month earlier. They sang the praises of 'Las Cinquos Magnificos'. Ronnie Boyce recalled:

"Zaragoza's 'Magnificent Five' forward line, was made up of five internationals."

This included Marcelino, Villa and Lapetra who had replaced the great Ghento as Spain's outside-left. They had helped Zaragoza find European glory the previous season, winning the Fairs Cup. And they had beaten Barcelona and Atletico Madrid in the process of claiming the Franco National Cup that had qualified them to take part in the Cup-winners' Cup. And as if all that was not enough, Zaragoza could score goals. Their victory over Valetta of Malta in the preliminary round of the tournament had proved this. The Spanish had won 8-1 over the two legs. Ron Greenwood was destined to be vindicated when he predicted that they would be tough and uncompromising in defence, quicksilver, lethal destroyers in attack.

The big Wednesday night came and in the first couple of minutes Marcelino went close, but with only nine minutes gone a packed crowd saw local boy Brian Dear get his eighth goal in as many games. The move began with Hurst, who sent a pass bouncing out to Sissons on the left. Sissons cleverly drew Cortizo out of position, then crossed towards the far post where Dear was waiting to head it home. Less than a quarter-of-an-hour later, Budgie got a cracker. Moore chipped a free-kick upfield, and this was collected by the alert Brown, who had left the magnificent Marcelino to work on the right wing. Brown crossed to Sissons. For a moment or two Sissons looked like losing control, but he flicked the ball into the middle for Byrne, who took the pass on his chest, let it drop and volleyed home. The ball smashed into the roof of the net past the prancing Yarza. Budgie had made contact from almost 20 yards out.

Throughout the first half Dear and Sissons flashed wicked-looking shots inches over. Marcelino shot wide and Canario almost scored. West Ham had the potential to kill the tie in the second period, but were never going to score a hat-full as Greenwood went for a play-it-safe policy. West Ham came out after the break with a nine-man defence. The crowd hated it. The Hammers had just two men up and relied on the 'big boot' to find them. They lost momentum, gave the Spaniards' defence a rest and allowed their fast, highly-skilled attack of Canario, Marcelino, Santos and Lapetra to take advantage. They now looked quite capable of out-smarting Moore and the rest of the Hammers' defence.

After hitting the post from the right in the 53rd minute, Canario halved West Ham's lead after ten minutes of the second half. The experienced Brazilian wandered out to the left, tapped the ball through Moore's legs, dribbled into the six-yard box and then shot. It hit Standen on the arm and he effectively scooped the ball into the net. Boyce had a great chance to make it 3-1, but slashed wide. Then Canario had a better opportunity to lay on the equaliser but his shot went high into the silent crowd. After that Zaragoza were happy to play out time, confident that they could win the tie in front of their own supporters. The Spanish defence, that had booted with all the thunder of a Fourth Division side in the first half, grew more confident as West Ham, desperately needing goals, faltered and slid back on the defensive. The giant Santamaria inspired some excellent defensive play which West Ham's two lonely strikers and the occasional three-pronged attacks, could not break in the second half.

This said, as Ronnie Boyce remembered: "Ken Brown had never played better for the Irons. He always matched Marcelino in the air."

The 35,000 fans, who paid £13,000 gate receipts to cheer the Hammers, rose as one person to applaud the Spaniards at the close. For the West Ham players there were only boos and hope. But the result gave them some kind of chance for the second leg, although, by the next morning, most of the national newspapers had already written off their chances of reaching the Final. Haven't the press always loved West Ham?

Ron Greenwood was disappointed after getting two early goals. He noted that the Spanish had played better as the game went on and were as good as he thought they would be. He saw it as the toughest game his side had played since he became manager. The Zaragoza manager was very pleased with the result, but he did not expect an easy game on his team's home turf.

West Ham's League fixtures concluded just five days before the second leg of the semi-final. The Saturday after the first leg they beat Chelsea at Upton Park. On Good Friday, the Hammers were out at the Boleyn Ground again, and this time the opposition was West Bromwich Albion as another Canning Town lad took centre stage. The Cockney confidence of Brian Dear, who came in for injured Johnny Byrne, punctured, plundered and pulverised sad Albion to a decisive defeat with five goals of his own. However, it was the sleek, cultured elegance of Martin Peters which engineered the slaughter. From his first talented touch, Peters, the supreme artist, took the game by the scruff of the neck and controlled it. West Ham had such contrasting brilliance at wing-half: Moore, the superb defender, Peters the versatile attacker.

It was Peters the great who sparked the goal spree with a memorable half-volley from the 18-yard line after 31 commanding but frustrating minutes. How apt that Peters should send Stag off on the road to goal glory. It was a typical piece of intelligent running off the ball from Martin and a slide rule pass that left Dear the simple task of touching the ball home. Jeff Astle made it 2-1 just on half-time but it was only the lull before the storm, Brian Dear's own one-man goal storm, four second-half goals. He demonstrated his power after 55 minutes when he crashed home after a dazzling crossfield run by Brabrook, a centre by Burkett and a header on by the impressive-as-ever, Geoff Hurst. Dear, always the opportunist, showed this talent in the 58th minute when his snap-shot from a Sissons-Peters move zipped through the stunned Potter's legs.

Stag, when concentrating, could position himself as good as any forward in the First Division. Just a couple of minutes after his second goal he was on the spot to shoot home after Potter had parried Hurst's drive against the post, and again in the 65th minute when he tapped in after a fine Kirkup run and low Brabrook cross. It was nearly a record-equalling six goals in one game when his best effort, a flashing header, grazed the bar and went over. All the same, Dear had gained a post-war record which had the 27,000 fans cheering the man who had scored 23 goals for the Reserves that season. He wiped out John Dick's four-goal League best against Rotherham and Johnny Byrne's four-goal League Cup spree against Workington two seasons previously. And he just failed to equal Vic Watson's 36-year-old record of six (against Leeds) at Upton Park but joined Syd Puddefoot as a five-goal Hammer (Puddefoot had achieved this in an FA Cup game against Chesterfield in 1913). Brian's fistful of goals brought his tally to 13 goals in ten League and European Cup-winners' Cup games. Five goals in 20 minutes is still a First Division record in terms of speed. It was revenge for the four goals that West Brom's Billy Richardson banged past West Ham back in the early 1930s, although West Brom themselves had some revenge, winning 4-2 at The Hawthorns in the penultimate match of the season.

In their final match of our Division one campaign, West Ham met Blackpool at the Boleyn. The game started badly, Moir robbed Boyce and made the most of the ball only six minutes into the game. Shortly after the break Ken Brown headed home the second goal of his West Ham first-team career. Dear got the Hammers' second and the match-winner in the 79th minute, putting away a cross from Sissons. The two points pushed West Ham up to finish ninth in the League. Johnny Byrne was top scorer, netting 29, and Martin Peters won the Hammer of the year. West Ham had only four draws all season, equalling the fewest ever of the 1934-35 season.

Just as the Irons left London for Spain on Monday, Jim Standen heard that his wife, Elize, had given birth to their third daughter. The players took this as a good omen.

Brian Dear recalls the welcome the team got in Spain: "At the reception on the Tuesday before the game we each got a bottle of sherry and a silver ashtray. Nice, but maybe they wanted us to have a good smoke and drink before the game."

Greenwood wasn't taking any chances. Before the match his team trained behind closed doors. Ernie Gregory, the 43-year-old reserve-team manager, went in goal and played brilliantly. "I wonder if they'll give me a month's trial?" he asked.

International forward Villa, a 26-year-old local boy, was coming back into the Zaragoza team that night. He hadn't played in London, but had scored three goals in a recent domestic cup game. Not having Byrne available, Greenwood had decided against playing with a centre-forward, but to strike down the wings: Sissons was on the left, Sealey on the right. Hurst and Dear went deep. These tactics would leave the centre-half as the spare man, rather than a full-back, who would be free to boost the attack. West Ham did not want the tie to end in a draw – that would mean a play-off in Marseilles three days later.

Despite the task ahead, the Hammers felt confident. As Bobby Moore pointed out, the Spaniards had to get two goals to win and West Ham had scored first in all their European games. This was a night of fine team work, an evening on which West Ham, a side often said to lack that little extra 'devil', fought with courage, determination and superbly-disciplined defensive skill.

From kick-off to final whistle, Zaragoza's launched attack after attack but West Ham's defence held and, consequently, much of their shooting was from long range. However, this artillery was not the most accurate barrage and it didn't look like beating the alert Standen. It was probably Bobby Moore's best game to date. He put on a true captain's display, and it received support from the rest of the team. Standen, Kirkup, Burkett, Peters and Brown gave everything they had. The same could be said of Boyce, who, although nominally chosen as a right-winger, played an important role as an extra defender. The burden of attack rested on the shoulders of Hurst, Sissons, Dear and Sealey. There were times in the first half when Dear and John Sissons looked like boys lost in a grown-up world. But it was this pair who, between them, in the end clinched a place in the Final for West Ham.

When the first 20 minutes had gone by without a goal, optimistic Hammers fans began to think the danger period had passed, and that West Ham might be able to relax. However, three minutes later, the Spaniards levelled the aggregate score. A corner-kick curled into the penalty box, Marcelino headed the ball forward and Standen could only push it away. The ball bounced to Lapetra, who eagerly slammed it home. Lapetra should have scored again before half-time but at a crucial moment in the second half, following a long period when the Spanish had dominated the game, Peters cleared the ball to Dear. He chested it down and passed to Sissons. The teenager took the ball into the Spanish penalty-area and calmly steered it into the corner of the net with his right foot as Yarza, the Zaragoza 'keeper, moved towards him. Just a week or so before, West Ham fans had been jeering young Johnny.

After the goal, Standen and Moore continued to fight an heroic rearguard, snuffing out one attack after another. Marcelino curled in a shot inches wide and Ken Brown headed a Canario drive off the line. It was a hard game, but West Ham managed to hold on.

The Hammers conceded 19 fouls in the first half alone, and Zaragoza were convinced that the Dutch referee, Leo Horn, had 'beaten' them, claiming three penalties should have been given.

Hammers' chairman, Reg Pratt, was right afterwards when he said that the supporters were 'wonderful', giving the team 'unequalled support'. They had each paid £15 for their flight (plus £1 for an in-flight lunch). Some of them had left East London at 7am to make the 10am flight out and would not get back until the early hours of the next morning. No British club had ever taken so many supporters into Europe before. More than 1,500 had travelled to Belgium, Czechoslovakia, Switzerland and Spain to cheer their team on. They were marvellous, West Ham's 12th man.

Roque Olsen, the Zaragoza manager, was predictable in his post-match analysis, saying that he thought West Ham were lucky and that the Spaniards had enough chances in the first half to have won the game in comfort. Greenwood gave his team all the credit after the match, but it was his ideas that did the trick. Moore said that once West Ham got their goal, he knew that they would hold on. John Sissons reckoned he felt ten feet tall when he saw his shot go in. It had been only the second goal that he had scored with his right foot all season. Reg Pratt summed it all up when he remarked what a wonderful achievement and magnificent effort it was to reach two Wembley Finals in just over a year.

Zaragoza had been heralded as the 'new Real Madrid'. They had taken two British scalps before meeting West Ham, having beaten Dundee in the first round and accounted for Cardiff in the quarter-finals. The 11 Cockney crusaders had avenged all that. This had been Bobby Moore's match. He had even been brilliant in the air (not always his strong point). He inspired the defence, who with the aid of Boyce and Hurst, had destroyed Europe's best club forward line in the process. They were allowed only three clear chances.

West Ham were only the second British team to reach the Final of a major European tournament. They would meet either Torino or Munich at Wembley on 19 May 1965. Spurs had won the European Cup-winners' Cup three years earlier, but the Hammers had the chance to become the first British team to win European glory on their own soil. And, unlike the Tottenham side, these Irons were all English.

The newspapers were full of West Ham the next day. The Hammers had put the likes of Yashin, Puskas and di Stefano, who had played in a tribute match for Stanley Matthews the same night, in the shadows. The resignation of Malcolm Allison from Plymouth also made the news. This was something of an irony on the day West Ham had made the biggest Final in their history. Allison, one of the architects of the club's culture, was out of work and seeking fresh employment for his bold ideas. A colourful individualist, he had also been with Cambridge University, Bath City and Toronto City since leaving

Upton Park. You can't help thinking what would have happened if he had stayed on.

So, following a warm up against Shamrock Rovers in Dublin on 12 May it was back to Wembley, the venue had been decided well in advance of the tournament and West Ham's Final opponents, were the West German club, Munich 1860. They had defeated Union Luxembourg 10-0, Porto 4-0, and Torino 5-3 after a play-off in Switzerland.

Bobby Moore knew what had given his team the edge in all their matches – the presence of Martin Peters, who had just established himself in the side. "In Europe you need more skill," said Moore, "and Martin added an extra quality to our game."

Before the Final, Ron Greenwood sent some of the players to Germany: Said Moore: "They went to see 1860 play in a Cup game in Germany. I wasn't able to go, but they got a good idea what to expect in the Final."

Alan Sealey recalled: "Eight players, Joe, Jack, Martin, Ronnie, Geoff, Brian, John Sissons and myself along with club officials Albert Walker and Eddie Chapman had gone see the play-off between Torino and Munich six days after our draw in Spain. Bobby was on England duty and Ron couldn't make it, but Greenwood had seen them beat Chelsea 2-0 in August.

"It was obvious that Munich were an impressive, well-organised side. They did well against the skilful Italians, who were emerging as one of the best sides in their country and would have proved difficult opponents for any side in the world. Ron told us to watch our immediate opponent in one of the teams, I chose Munich. They had some good players. Hans Rebele, their outside-left was one of their youngest players at 22. A nippy winger who had played well in Europe, he'd once been an inside-forward. I watched their backs carefully. Manfred Wagner, on the right of the defence, was their longest-serving player. He'd earned a reputation for his versatility. He could play in either full-back position and revert to wing-half if he had a mind. On the left was Rudolf Steiner. He was another one who could move over if he had to. Their centre-half, Hans Reich, was not yet 23 and had been with the club as a youngster. He'd played at right-half and right-back. Their style was almost typically English with two fast wingers, a hard-hitting centre-forward and a solid defence."

West Ham returned to the twin towers for the second year running. They had to reshuffle because Peter Brabrook and Johnny Byrne were both injured. The Hammers were England's last hope in Europe. Liverpool had been beaten in the European Cup in Milan. The Lions of Munich (the Teutonic Millwall?) roared into Wembley knowing, like West Ham, that they had to win to stay on the money-spinning European soccer circuit. They were out of their League race and out of the cup they had won the year before by beating Eintracht Frankfurt 2-0 in the Final. They had been eliminated by giant-killers Mainz 05 in an early-round replay.

Munich are the oldest club in Germany. The 1860 in their title refers to the founding of the sports club. The football section didn't come into being until 1899. It was only a few years before the Final that they had emerged from the shadow of Bayern and Wacker, Munich's other big clubs. Honours were few under the regional system, which involved top clubs meeting in end-of-season play-offs. TSV had reached this stage only once, in 1931, when they lost to Hertha of Berlin 3-2. It was 11 years before they won their first Cup Final, beating Schalke '04 by 2-0. Under former Dutch national coach Max Merkel, the 45-year-old ex-Austrian international of SC Rapid, they won their first League championship and entered the Bundesliga when it was formed in 1963. They had not been out of the top six in the 1964-65 season, bettering their seventh place of the previous term.

The 1965 Cup-winners' Cup Final had one of the biggest audiences ever for a football match. Eddie Bovington, the teak tough, iron-man of the FA Cup winning side, was fit, but he would not get a place in the team, as Bobby Moore came back okay from England games against West Germany and Sweden. The whole Munich team had turned out to watch Moore in the former game.

Tickets for the Final had been sold out in a few days. At Upton Park the allocation went at a rate of 4,000 an hour on the Sunday they went on sale. About 30 million people watched the match on the television all over Europe. It was a warm evening with the kind of atmosphere that can only be experienced under the floodlights of Wembley at the start of an English spring.

Byrne had been injured in the England-Scotland game and so Brian Dear had been brought in. This was a worry, even though Dear had done well in Spain. Again, Hurst was going to play behind the main attack which was made up of Alan Sealey and Sissons. The team looked very different from the FA Cup winning side of the previous year. The right flank had been transformed. John Bond had made way for Joe Kirkup at right-back, Martin Peters had come into Eddie Bovington's right-half position and the right-wing place had been transferred from Peter Brabrook to Sealey.

West Ham went into the game with the best record of any British club in Europe, and two good teams, neither keen to go to a replay at the Feyenoord Stadium in Rotterdam a couple of days later, promised a memorable encounter. No one was to be disappointed and from the first kick West Ham went full throttle at the Germans, who were playing in all white, a change from their usual blue and white.

It was a cracking first half, there was some immaculate football displayed, and although no one managed to score, it could have been 3-3. Before 15 minutes had been played, Sissons had put a shot wide from some 12 feet out.

Peter Radenkovic, the 30-year-old, black-garbed Yugoslav in the Munich goal – the Press called him Peter the Great – pulled off a string of magnificent saves, foiling Dear more than once. In Germany, where he had played for five years, Radenkovic was seen as something of a clown, but he was one of the best 'keepers in the Bundesliga, good in the air and going to ground. He came from a club called Wormatia Worms!

Both Dear and Sealey failed to connect with a Sissons cross which, if diverted, would almost certainly have put the Hammers ahead. Hennes Kuppers, the fair-haired inside-right, was maybe Munich's best forward and he also had his chance to open the scoring. At 26 he was one of those perpetual motion performers. Two months before the Final he had partnered outside-right Alfred Heiss at international level against the Italy. The pair won their first caps together in December 1962. Heiss was a speedy winger and his outstanding club form that season had given him West Germany's number-7 shirt.

The second 45 minutes started where the last period left off. Dear again went close, and Sissons hammered a shot against a post. Sealey put the ball in the net a couple of minutes later, but he had instinctively used his hands and it didn't count.

Rudi Brunnenmeier, Munich's all-action skipper and West German international centre-forward, had nearly been transferred to Torino, but the Italian

FA had barred new foreign imports until the end of July 1966. Brunnenmeier had a bullet-like shot and blinding pace, his 24 Bundesliga goals in 1964-65 were the product of that combination. He had been the first Munich player to be capped that season and had recently scored for his country in a 1-1 draw against Sweden. Inside-left Peter Grosser was tall, lean and clever with the ball. At 25 he had missed only one League match all season. These two and Kuppers were denied only by the skill and courage of Standen. At one point, the Hammers 'keeper hurled himself across goal to deflect a shot from Grosser and just seconds later saved from the blond Kuppers.

With only about 20 minutes of the match remaining, Ronnie Boyce intercepted just over the halfway line, immediately drawing two men. 'Ticker' carried the ball up the right, past the full-back. Sealey went in close and then Boyce placed a perfect pass between two Munich defenders, leaving Alan with just the left-back to worry about. Boyce gave it to Sammy just right, and at the right time. He went forward and fired a bullet of a drive from the edge of the box. It went beyond Radenkovic from what looked like an impossible angle and whistled in, from about 12 yards, into the high right-hand angle. Nobody was going to get near that. Sealey somersaulted out of pure delight and followed this with a bit of a dance. He said afterwards: "It could have gone over the bar as easy as flying in the top corner of the net, but without going over the top, I can say that I could hit a ball. I can't say I had any feelings. It's all over...a sudden rush of blood, that's all."

This is how the BBC radio described it: "Hurst, looking for a man, decides to sling one over left-footed but he finds Bena. He didn't mean to do that, but the ball bounces off Bena fortunately to Grosser, his inside-left, who is tricking West Ham players left, right and centre now, and then slings a good pass there for ...oh, but the left-half missed it and its Boyce coming through for West Ham. A chance here for Sealey inside the box. Can he get in a shot? It's a goal! A goal for West Ham. So, West Ham are a goal ahead from Sealey, 24 minutes of the second half. A mistake by the German left-half Luttrop gave Sealey his chance and from a narrow angle he fairly belted the ball into the Munich net."

That goal was regularly screened on television for a while, as part of an advertisement for Oxo. It was typical of the type of goals West Ham been scoring in and out of Europe. Sealey went on: "I remember the ball hitting the roof of the net. It was my style of goal, the kind I would score."

It was a great moment, and a terrific way to celebrate his marriage, just four days earlier, to Janice Gilbert, a former Dagenham Town Show beauty queen. The honeymoon had been rearranged twice, because of West Ham's European commitments. Sealey was last of the senior Boleyn bachelor boys. Alan again:

"When I came to West Ham from Orient I never dreamed all this could happen to me. I've been to Ghana, Rhodesia, America, Austria and Germany and, of course, the European Cup-winners' Cup travels. When I went on that first trip to Africa, I played with people like Jackie Dick, Malcolm Musgrove, Ian Crawford, Lawrie Leslie and Brian Rhodes. It seems strange that they had all gone by the Final. A year before I had sat on the sidelines at Wembley and watched us win the FA Cup. Now it was great to be back, this time playing and scoring. I know the other lads who missed Wembley last time – Martin Peters, Brian Dear and Joe Kirkup – all felt the same. Martin had, of course, played there for England Schoolboys but that was not quite the same. It had been a great four years for me."

In the fraction of a second after a crucial goal has been scored, there is a space in time. Herein the roar that is to emerge in recognition is squeezed into a quietness, not a total silence, but sound retreats. In this tiny period, between an occurrence and the realisation of the same, there is a gap made for what is to become and regard for that which is passing away. This was palpable as the fans watched the ball enter the goal. The Munich supporters gazed incredulously at the ball as it bounced, happily, inside of the net. The bellow of the Irons supporters gouged out a dome in the dusky skies. The Munich fans turned their eyes up from the ball to stare, shocked and questioning, at the voice of all the Hammers, the fount of the massive noise. The roar smashed hard into every niche of the famous, old stadium. The German supporters intuitively dipped down as one, trying to avoid what seemed like a wall of sound coming their way.

West Ham had caught the Germans on the ropes and just two minutes later the knockout blow was delivered. Dear, having got by Munich's defence with a late run, was poleaxed by a desperate German defender and a free-kick was awarded. The Hammers had the kind of thing they were going to do, sorted out well in advance. Alan Sealey describes the tactics: "We used to make a nice big hole that Bobby could just knock the ball into and we would pull people wide. We would just nominate somebody to make for the hole. I was the last one that should have gone because I was the worst header of the ball in the world, but I saw the hole and went early. Hurst ran over the ball leaving Boyce to send it to Moore, a commanding figure on the night, to lift it. Bob floated the ball in from an attacking left-half position, 15 or 20 yards outside the penalty-area. He drove it in towards the far post, in my direction. I was supposed to run in and head the ball. That was the intention, but, as I say, heading wasn't the strongest part of my game. Sure enough, I missed it, the ball whizzed by me and then, luckily, it hit Martin Peters, who had moved into the middle from a characteristically late run. He didn't quite control it, the ball must have gone out of his vision or something, and it hit him on the leg. That got everyone on the wrong foot and, as the ball bobbled, it ran for me. That lack of control turned out to be a perfect pass. It came beautifully, if unintentionally, into my path about five yards out. I'm lethal from that range. It only needed turning in. I applied the finishing touch."

Again, the radio commentary: "And a free-kick to West Ham. Some of the most cunning free-kick takers these West Ham boys. I wonder what they've got up their sleeves now. West Ham, that brilliant goal ahead by Alan Sealey, and now looking for another one. Here comes Hurst, runs over the ball, it goes to Boyce, to Moore, Moore clipping it forward ...and ...oh ...and ...oh, it's a goal! Another goal for West Ham! Sealey the scorer again! West Ham two-nil up now and surely that must be the killer goal."

Ron Greenwood remembers the work and faith that went into that goal: "We had repeatedly rehearsed the moves that led to the second goal in the European Cup-winners' Cup Final. There was a young lad called Trevor Dawkins at the club at the time and we went through it with him. I remember Alan saying that 'it would never work'. I was delighted that Alan was the match-winner that night at Wembley."

West Ham could have had three more goals in that final period of the game. Sissons hit the post again with a right-foot shot and Dear, twice, had Radenkovic deflecting shots wide. But that was it. 2-0.

As the final whistle was sounded, delirious fans, tossing claret and blue bowlers and scarves high into the night air, had to be dragged away from Sealey and the rest of the team. Bobby Moore led the way up to get the trophy from Gustav Wiederkehr, the president of the UEFA. Brian Dear carried a captured Munich flag in triumph in the lap of honour, and Ken Brown cuddled a huge claret and blue hammer. Ron Greenwood, Budgie Byrne, Eddie Bovington, Peter Brabrook, Alan Dickie, Tony Scott and John Bond stood on the touchline and applauded.

It was a classic match, the end of 810 minutes of football in four different countries. Even the referee Mr Zolt, a Hungarian, said what 'a good and wonderfully clean game it had been,' and that 'West Ham and Munich are two fine teams'. It was one of the great Wembley Finals, and the high-point in the history of West Ham United. But the game would give rise to many more stories over the years. Alan Dickie shared just one. Like so many players of his generation 'Spider' is a romantic and generous man: "All the players who played in the Cup-winners' Cup winning team got a gold Omega watch from the directors, inscribed with their name and 'WHUFC CWCW 1965'. I gave it to my son for his 21st birthday. He asked me what he should do with it. I told him to give it to his son on his 21st."

The Wembley Final had been a satisfying affair. Both teams had played the fast, open football that the 100,000 spectators had wanted to see. Munich tried to match West Ham by playing attacking football, and this had made for an entertaining game that swung back and forth. Both sides had played with flair and determination. One Fleet Street sports journalist wrote: 'There could have been no greater match to put before the greatest night audience in England's football history.'

After the match, the team received a telegram of congratulation from the Prime Minister, Harold Wilson. The First Secretary of State, George Brown, a West Ham supporter, was guest of honour at the banquet that evening.

This game, alongside the FA Cup Final, would be a cross-roads for the English game. Nothing would be the same again. West Ham had carried in the future with their dreams. The past was now a memory.

Bobby Moore, meanwhile, was looking forward to the European Cup. That was typical of him, always up for the next hurdle. He said that the Cup-winners' Cup Final had been West Ham's best-ever team effort: "There was a lot of good football and we played really well against a good side."

He was right. The game had been an example of what working together can achieve. Jack Burkett had been as solid as a rock at left-back, playing just behind Moore. Burkett had sustained a back injury on Boxing Day and had fought his way back into the team to face Zaragoza. Greenwood said : "When Jack returned, we started looking like a team again." Jim Standen had yet another good day. An instinctive save, with his legs, from the Munich skipper Brunnen, may well have been critical to the final result. Boyce had made the first goal. It was a great pass. Sealey recalled: "I saw the 'keeper was slightly out of position and so decided to shoot."

John Sissons thought he had scored when he hit the post. He was desperate to make up for that miss and he worked like a Trojan. Ken Brown, who thought the whole experience was better than winning the FA Cup, had been a giant in the centre of defence. Ron Greenwood was full of praise for the whole team, but he was correct when he said: "This was Bobby Moore's greatest game. Technical perfection."

Of course, the match had over 100,000 individual stories. One of the more unusual involved a little Bavarian factory worker, Anton Gailinger. He pedalled 700 miles to be at the game. The 43-year-old set off, with no ticket, a week before the match. He knew just one word of English: 'Wembley'. An East Ham lorry driver, Jim Seal, saw him slogging along the Dover road towards London on Wednesday. Mr Seal picked him up and offered him the hospitality of his own home. An East End newspaper, the *Stratford Express*, got Anton a ticket to the game and set up a tour of London after the match. Following his team's demise the poor bloke rode around the City near to tears.

Alan Sealey, looking back at the day, was to comment: "That Wembley day passed me by so quickly. It came and went. You have your little bit of success and you go home. You don't really take it all in, but it was a marvellous night. It had to be the best night of my career. My dad, God rest his soul, was there, and that's all you want in life really, to give your parents just something back for what they gave you. If you do that you have achieved what you want."

An odd chemistry had made the night. Sealey and Greenwood were two very different football people, but they both enjoyed the night of their lives:

Sealey, a bustling striker who grew up next door to West Ham's ground; Greenwood, a northerner and very much a coach. It's peculiar how people's lives come together.

About threequarters of the 100,000 fans who attended Wembley – the biggest crowd ever to watch a Cup-winners' Cup Final – were Hammers supporters. They paid an average ticket price of around 15 shillings (75p).

One supporter, Danny, remembers the post-match events: "The queue at Wembley Park station was over a mile long at one point. It didn't matter to us, though. Many of us were still outside the stadium in the early hours of the next day. It was the night that dockland didn't sleep. Ships and tankers paid a foghorn tribute up and down the Thames, accompanying millions of joyful renditions of *Bubbles*."

They must have wore themselves out as Ronnie Boyce recalls: "When we came back to East London, not a soul was about. This felt odd after the huge reception we'd got bringing the FA Cup home."

Danny continues: "That Sunday only about 5,000 people turned up, about 20,000 fewer than our average home gate. It was a real surprise because the team's return from the FA Cup Final was greeted by hundreds of thousands lining the streets. But the arrangements had been made at the last minute and many street parties took place in the afternoon. When Bobby Moore spoke to the supporters he said that without them it would not have been possible and Ron Greenwood told them that the side were proud to represent them in the world."

Among the telegrams which poured into Greenwood's office was one from Bill Shankly, whose Liverpool side had lost to Inter-Milan in the European Cup semi-final. It read: "Well done. I feel that British club teams are more than ready for these European clubs."

Chelsea sent two telegrams, one from Stamford Bridge and one from Tommy Docherty, leading the Chelsea party in Australia. Bill Nicholson, manager of Spurs wrote: "Those were the days. Hope they are yours too."

From Fulham manager Vic Buckingham: "Well done you East End lot – a real West End show."

As an East Ender, Alan Sealey was a typical example of what West Ham were built of: "The ideas that Ron came up with, working with us, were too unbelievable for words. We used to come in every day and there was something different. Being a bunch of young lads we were just so keen to listen, learn and develop. Things started to happen from the moment that Ron arrived. This was invaluable, but I think if you look at the team, nine or ten came through the system. They weren't bought, they were local lads."

Of course, Sealey was right. John Sissons came from West London, but the majority of the team were local, Cockney or Essex boys. Sealey again: "Bobby Moore was a little bit older than us, but of those who played in the Final, there were Geoff, Martin, John Sissons, Ronnie Boyce, Jack Burkett, and Brian Dear who had all come through at a similar age."

This meant that the side had the resources of camaraderie and togetherness. People like Ken Brown and Jim Standen, who were a little bit older, stabilised the whole thing, but as Alan said: "We all came through together and we all did things together."

West Ham later found out that they had beaten two teams who would be playing in the European Cup the following season. Not only did Lausanne win the Swiss title, but Spartak Prague also topped the Czech League, by seven points form Dukla.

Ron Greenwood was in his element against the foreign sides, starting from the point when he was put in charge of the England Under-23s while at Arsenal. Although he relished these encounters with continental clubs, he would describe the experience as 'interesting' because it was 'testing'. He saw it as his teams' proving ground and a kind of football laboratory. He loved to travel abroad and watch people. He built up a footballing encyclopaedia within his own mind. When he came to West Ham and got into Europe, he had the opportunity to put into practice all the things that he'd got in his head. Alan Sealey said of Greenwood's idea of play: "It was brilliant because it agreed with us, it suited our players, it was to do with movement. If you're playing from the back, then there's got to be a lot of movement up front to let the ball get there. It's got to be built up. We had the players to do this. We revelled in it. We loved it."

Greenwood later remarked that winning the Cup-winners' Cup was not ultimate success and that West Ham still had to win the European Cup. For him, only then would West Ham be a great team. After Wembley he declared this as the aim of the club. When the Hammers had come back from the USA, a couple of years earlier, Greenwood had called it a new era for the club and he had been right. He saw West Ham's success being founded on a belief by everyone in the club and that this had to be built upon. This had caused a team of great style to be developed in London's East End. A team who passed the ball. A team with players like Martin Peters, Johnny Byrne, Bobby Moore and Geoff Hurst.

Sealey asked himself: "Why was I part of this creative evening? The great referee in the sky might have just looked down, stretched out his finger and touched Alan Sealey on the shoulder, but I was an aggressive, very quick forward. Ron took on many of my ideas about what I wanted to do. I tried to be innovative and he cottoned on to this. Sometimes my mind raced ahead of myself, but a lot of the time it paid off, as at Wembley in 1965 in the Cup-winners' Cup Final. They were two great goals. Since those goals, a lot of people have said how good it was to see an East Ender do the business. I have always said that it was my pleasure."

But most people, like Johnny Byrne, who were at Wembley for those 90 minutes in 1965, simply thought that it was 'Sammy's finest hour and his night'.

# 1965-66

RON Greenwood continued to be something of an enigma for West Ham supporters. For some reason he was not as 'loveable' as the likes Shankly or Busby. Paul, who was 15 at the time of the Cup-winners' Cup triumph, reflects on the man at the helm at Upton Park: "Bill Shankly, Joe Mercer, Jock Stein and Matt Busby seemed to have a different attitude to the game than Greenwood, who didn't seem to have any sense of humour or fun. Maybe his very serious attitude to football had something to do with the fact that, unlike Shankly, Stein and Busby for example, he had never really done anything else. I mean, when you've had to work on a coal face, down a pit, you probably have some idea of proportion. You might get upset about results, but maybe not fall into a deep depression or, as it sometimes seemed from a distance in Greenwood's case, a sulk. But he did get better as he got older."

According to Ronnie Boyce: "Everyone understood that Ron had a huge knowledge of the game and great perception. He was a champion of the way the game should be played. He liked it to be open, he liked it to be attractive. He wanted the game to be honest. Football was, for him, at its best, a battle of wits. He viewed any match on a slightly higher plane than most other managers. He was a real student of the game, always looking to expand his knowledge, but he was also a realistic man."

One former player commented: "He was often accused of being a blackboard theorist, and that, to some extent, was true, but there was never a more practical manager than Ron Greenwood. These things did not go together. I mean, you can't be a no nonsense philosopher can you."

In the same way Greenwood's rather detached attitude, that didn't always make for good 'people management', was contradicted by his obvious understanding of how people could get the best out of themselves and learn to contribute this to the work of the whole. He seemed to understand humanity well, but this was not matched by his awareness of individual human sensibilities. These contradictions perhaps demonstrate a paradoxical nature.

Another ex-player said: "Greenwood, quite rightly, got a lot of credit for what happened at West Ham in the mid-1960s. However, you've got to remember that when he arrived at Upton Park, the place had a way of doing things that did not really change when Ron came along, but he built and strengthened the structure. What happened in 1965 wasn't the result of just one mind or person, with a number of others just following instructions. Dozens of people were involved, all pulling together, handing on and working on ideas and moves over years, from the late 1950s in fact.

"This was the 'Academy'. Straightforward stuff done with quality, but with an ethical code and a sense of morality. True, our big ideas and principals could be literally kicked off the park, but West Ham's football was a gospel and Ron was its prophet. For him, the way you played was much more important than getting results; if you could not get results righteously, then the game wasn't worth playing.

Greenwood's belief was that a commitment to skill, fairness and generosity of spirit (team work) were the only means to attain the highest levels in football, or anything else. Ron spelt out what he thought about the game, what he expected of the players, and even if they didn't catch on to everything he said, like putting players in vacuums, they appreciated that he had intelligent ideas.

"Greenwood was great on different styles of play that were new to the English game. His was a continental approach to football; a fluid, passing game. When West Ham got into European games they tended to do pretty well. For some reason, the Hammers could not sustain this kind of poetry over a 42-game programme. That was West Ham's big problem.

"We were always different from other clubs in London. The Hammers belonged to their own patch. Players and fans identified with each other. You felt when you went to Upton Park that you were actually part of something quite special. Expression of ideas was important. Ron had players who believed in what he believed in. It's no good if a manager says what he wants and the players don't believe in it. We gelled together. Ron developed his ideas with the players – that is, he didn't just come and transplant a way of doing things. I think that he came to the club with the notion of creating a kind of 'Arsenal light'. What was produced was something quite unique, and I think even he was surprised.

"West Ham were seen as a side that will never threaten to win the League, that's for more consistent sides. But in the Cups it was a different story altogether. Ron, in the end, almost came to accept this belief, that we were better suited for Cup football than the nine month rigours of a League Championship. The suspicion grew in his own mind, almost into a certainty, over the period in which we were winning the FA Cup. We had won the Cup with quite a bit of style. In fact the semi-final was taken beautifully, with panache. As such, I feel that this level of Ron's thinking limited us; it smacked of a kind of excuse (more than a reason) and he never gave it a clear rationale. It became part of a negative myth that he paid into, the other part of which was that we were an easy team to play against. People used to say that they loved playing against West Ham, because we allowed them to play. This rumour or legend started with Greenwood. In the 1950s, West Ham were always thought of as a hard team, that gave little away."

For all this, Europe was really what Ron had been waiting for:

"He was so pleased that the Cup-winners' Cup Final was seen all over the continent and he congratulated Munich for making it such a good game. We were admirably suited to the European game. West Ham players who were injured were sent out to spy on the opposition. They came back and were able to talk to players on players' terms with a player's view of things. We went into games thoroughly prepared. Ron adapted tactics to suit the occasion and the score, whether West Ham played at home or away."

The Cup-winners' Cup was a great achievement for Ron Greenwood, though. It was a game in which his principles and beliefs fell in line with the way West Ham played:

"It was the perfect example of how he wanted the game thought about and performed. I don't know if it ever happened for him again. Maybe that would have been the best time for him to leave the club. It's difficult to build on something that has already reached your ideal. It's got to be all down hill when you've come to the top of the mountain, hasn't it? A Malcolm Allison or a Noel Cantwell coming in at that time would have driven West Ham on to bigger and better things and a move to somewhere like Arsenal or Chelsea would have given Ron a more comfortable situation in terms of his personality."

As it was his problems with the post-match celebrations were to be indicative of the next few years:

"It was a real mess up. The team complained about it because all Ron had been concerned about was getting to the stadium and doing well. No arrangements had been made for anything afterwards. At Wembley they had the two teams sat down but there had been no arrangements made for the wives. So all the families of the players were left standing outside somewhere. Ron was occupied for some time after the match taking drinks and bits of food out to the wives. He did his best, but that was a bit of a lash-up."

Three weeks after Wembley, West Ham were again taking part in the New York International Tournament. Johnny Byrne's return to fitness meant that goalkeeper Alan Dickie could not make the trip to America with the rest of the team (only 16 could go). West Ham were also waiting for the go-ahead for a two-leg challenge with European Cup holders Inter-Milan at Wembley. This never happened, but the idea was taken on by UEFA and in 1972 the European Super Cup was born.

Bobby Moore, led West Ham to two great triumphs, played more games for the club than any other man in the club's history and led England to her greatest football triumph in the summer of 1966.

Geoff Hurst, moved up front from wing-half by Ron Greenwood and for the next ten seasons was West Ham's best hope of a goal. He scored 248 in 499 games for the Hammers and, of course, hit a hat-trick in the 1966 World Cup Final.

Alan Sealey – unlucky to miss out on the 1964 FA Cup Final, 12 months later he was the toast of East London after his two goals won the Cup-winners' Cup for the Hammers. Then a freak accident effectively ended his League career.

Martin Peters was another player unlucky to miss the Cup Final against Preston when he was left out after making 36 League and Cup appearances that season. But like Alan Sealey he won a Cup-winners' Cup medal the following year, and with Moore and Hurst shared in England's World Cup triumph in 1966.

Ronnie Boyce's phenomenal work-rate was legendary and with the prospect of extra-time in the 1964 FA Cup Final looming, he kept running to head Peter Brabrook's cross into the net to give the Hammers the trophy for the first time.

Peter Brabrook was born close to Upton Park but the Hammers had to pay Chelsea £35,000 for his signature. He repaid them with 43 goals in 214 appearances and it was his centre that led to Boyce's last-gasp Wembley winner in 1964.

Johnny Byrne was capped for England as a Fourth Division player with Crystal Palace, cost a record £65,000 when the Hammers signed him, and hit an average of a goal every two games with 107 in 205 appearances for the club. He missed the Cup-winners' Final after being injured while playing for England.

Ken Brown made 455 senior appearances for West Ham as a commanding centre-half. Born at Forest Gate, he spent 15 years as a player at Upton Park and his career spanned the days of Ernie Gregory and Malcolm Allison in the early 1950s, to the European triumph of 1965.

Jim Standen played for Arsenal and Luton before coming to Upton but his best days were with the Hammers, for whom he made 235 appearances and was the goalkeeper in both the 1964 FA Cup Final and the 1965 Cup-winners' Cup Final. A fine cricketer, he also played for Worcestershire when they won the County Championship.

On the brink of glory. It's August 1963 and Ron Greenwood chats to his first-team squad on West Ham's training ground at Chadwell Heath.

John Sissons draws West Ham level in the 1964 FA Cup Final against Preston North End at Wembley after Doug Holden had given the Lancashire side a tenth-minute lead. At 17, Sissons was the youngest-ever Cup Final goalscorer.

Five minutes before half-time Alex Dawson restores Preston's lead with a powerful header after 17-year-old Howard Kendall had won a corner.

Geoff Hurst's 52nd-minute header spins off the crossbar and over the line to put the Hammers back on level terms once more.

Ronnie Boyce watches his last-minute header flash past Preston's George Ross and Alan Kelly – and West Ham United have won the FA Cup for the first time in their history.

Bobby Moore takes a drink from the FA Cup after West Ham's thrilling victory.

Eddie Bovington and Jim Standen take the Cup on a victory run.

Johnny Byrne has the lid of the FA Cup in one hand and the famous giant hammer in the other.

From left to right: John Sissons, Ronnie Boyce and Geoff Hurst pose with the Cup in the Wembley dressing-room.

Brian Dear looks up to see his effort beat Real Zaragoza goalkeeper Enrique Yarza in the European Cup-winners' Cup semi-final first leg at Upton Park in April 1965.

Alan Sealey scores his – and West Ham's – second goal inside two minutes to put beyond doubt the result of the 1965 Cup-winners' Cup Final.

West Ham United, with yet another giant hammer, pictured after their Wembley victory over TSV Munich 1860.

West Ham players show off the European Cup-winners' Cup to thousands of fans lining the streets after a civic reception at East Ham Town Hall in May 1965.

Bobby Moore and Olympiakos captain Polychroniou are embraced by Russian referee Bachramov before the Cup-winners' Cup match in Athens in December 1965. Moore and Bachramov would meet again seven months later when Bachramov was the linesmen who allowed Geoff Hurst's controversial "over the line" goal in the World Cup Final.

West Ham's youth side successfully defended their International Trophy in Hamburg. They got to keep the cup which they had now won three years running. Bill Kitchener captained a side which included Paul Heffer, Frank Lampard, Harry Redknapp, Roger Cross and Trevor Hartley, who was voted best player in the West Ham team.

The Hammers' opening game of the 1965 American tournament ended in defeat when they lost to New Yorkers 2-1 at Randall's Island. Then they met Munich 1860 in a repeat of the Cup-winners' Cup Final and won 2-1, although Munich didn't put out a full-strength team. Peters and Sealey got the West Ham goals.

The Hammers then met Portuguesa, a Brazilian club, in the Shea Stadium which had never before been used for soccer. West Ham lost 6-3. They had their chances, and the scoreline was somewhat generous to the Brazilians, but it really was a case of South American football beating the British brand.

In the next game, West Ham lost again to New Yorkers, conceding three goals. The Hammers also had games against an Italian club and another match against Portuguesa. They could not qualify, whatever they did, so those games became no more than a work-out. All in all it was very disappointing and the Hammers looked a shadow of the team that had gone to the US in 1963. The energy, urgency and enthusiasm of that first triumph was absent. Maybe all the thrills of the past two years had taken their toll.

The 1965-66 season opened with bad news. West Ham's double-scoring Cup-winners' Cup hero had broken a leg in pre-season training. It was initially thought that he would be out for the season, but it was to be the start of the end of his short career.

Ken Brown, former England international and veteran of West Ham's cup campaigns of the 1960s recalls: "We had a good cricketing side at West Ham, good enough for us to consider touring at one point. Alan was one of our better players, good with the bat and in the field. One day, during pre-season training, he was after taking the last catch in a lunchtime knock about. It was a press day and he backed into a bench used for team photographs. He broke his leg and his footballing days were as good as over."

Trevor Hartley, a member of the West Ham side that won the FA Youth Cup in 1963, also remembers the tragic event: "After playing in the European

Cup-winners' Cup Final side at Wembley, Sammy was unfortunate enough to break his leg in the next pre-season training at Chadwell Heath. The silly thing is that it occurred during our lunch break, that's not a pun. He was playing cricket and, while chasing the ball, he ran smack into a wooden bench."

Brain Dear recalled: "Sammy broke both his tibia and his fibula that day at the training ground. Just before we had a photo session. It was strange, because I had my leg in plaster at the time and the press got us to pose as if we were fencing with my crutches. We always used to say, 'never touch someone else's crutches.'"

Bill Lansdowne senior, at that time in charge of the West Ham 'A' team: "If anybody ever asks me about Alan Sealey, my mind always goes back to that fateful day at Chadwell Heath training ground. We had finished the morning's team photo shoot and had lunch. I was sitting on the pavilion steps watching some of the players indulging in an impromptu game of cricket – Alan loved cricket almost as much as football. A ball was skied and Alan set off to take the catch. Unfortunately he ran into a gym bench and shattered his leg."

Jack Burkett, the Hammers Cup-winners' Cup defender elaborates: "When Alan broke his leg playing cricket, the injury that ended his career, he was more worried about taking the catch than the pain and consequences of what had happened to him. This was an example of what a dedicated sportsman Alan was."

And Eddie Presland lamented: "It was so tragic that playing the game he loved ended Alan's footballing career. It was such a bad break, the bottom half of his leg was wobbling about."

Paul Heffer adds: "Unfortunately, the memory of Alan that will live with me forever is of the disastrous game of cricket we were both playing in …this really ended his career as a top player."

The incident seemed to affect the morale of the West Ham team. They lost their opening game of the season, 3-0 away to West Bromwich Albion, and could only scrape a draw against Sunderland in their first home match.

However, history was made at the Boleyn Ground on 28 August when Peter Bennett became the first-ever Division One substitute after 53 minutes, the Football League having ruled that injured players could be replaced during the course of play. Leeds dropped their first points of the season that day and West Ham notched up their first win. Peters and Hurst got one apiece after

Peacock (the man with the name echoing his club's nickname) got the opener for Leeds after 13 minutes. Harry Redknapp hit the post when his cross was missed by Gary Sprake. Peter Lorimer returned the complement by nearly demolishing Standen's goal when he hit the up-right with one of his specials.

The League, however, was of secondary importance in terms of the Hammers' European ambitions. West Ham faced the Greek side, Olympiakos, in their first game in the new Cup-winners' Cup campaign. The first leg was at the Boleyn Ground.

Derek, who took up attending Upton Park late in life, most of his foot-balling experience being in the back streets of Kingston, Jamaica, recalled: "This Greek lot were quite a handful. They were like barbarians at Upton Park in the first leg, spitting, kicking and elbowing all over the place."

Geoff Hurst got to a pass from Bobby Moore to blast the first past Fronimidis. Hurst got a second with his head. Just over ten minutes after half-time Byrne jumped on the 'keeper's mistake to make it 3-0. Brabrook finished them off when he nodded in the fourth with 72 minutes gone.

Derek continued: "John Charles was the only new boy to European foot-ball in West Ham's line up. He was just 21 and looked a little incredulous at times, aghast at the behaviour of the Greeks, but he did well enough to keep his place for the second leg."

John Charles was a Canning Town boy, and one of the first black players to break through in London football, 'Charlo' was a good full-back and always strove to live up to one of the most famous names in football. He captained West Ham's Youth Cup winning side, won England youth honours and made his League bow in a 1-0 home defeat against Blackburn, all in 1963.

Before the second leg, West Ham achieved good Upton Park wins against Chelsea and Everton and were unlucky to come out worse in a five-goal game at Highbury. The quarter-final of the League Cup was not at all heartening, though. West Ham had already had a bit of a bumpy ride in this competition, having been taken to a replay by Bristol Rovers in the second round, and although they had got past Mansfield relatively comfortably, 4-0 at Upton Park, Second Division Rotherham made them work hard in round four. They hit the post and caused Brown to clear off the line in the Hammers' 2-1 win at the Millmoor Ground.

In the last eight, West Ham faced a trip to Blundell Park. This would be the third Third Division side they had met in the competition. Grimsby had already put paid to the hopes of Palace, Bolton and Preston. Matt Tees, the leading scorer in the Football League, gave the Londoners a fright after 11 minutes, John Charles pulled them level just after the half-hour, but Grimsby went ahead again in the final 15 minutes. Then Geoff Hurst scrambled the equaliser. This was a relief, of course, but also a curse because the replay would have to be squeezed into an already overcrowded fixture list.

In Greece, West Ham got a firecracker of a welcome, literally. The 45,000 crowd were hurling bangers around the huge Olympiakos soccer bowl well before the match. Indeed, about an hour before kick-off they were lobbing them at the West Ham team as they inspected the pitch. The bombardment continued throughout the game and a thunderflash was burning away in Jim Standen's goal as he took up his place.

It was indeed a European baptism of fire for young John Charles, on his first trip abroad with the team. Injuries meant that Martin Peters was moved to centre-forward. Both Standen and Hurst had been suffering with stomach bugs and this was part of the reason why Hurst played something of a defensive role that night. From the off it was clear that the Greeks were a rough and uncompromising side and after 20 minutes, the Greek World Cup skipper, Polychoniou, left Martin Peters. with a nasty gash on his shin. The same player got the first goal, converting a penalty. Ken Brown was picked out as the offender by the referee, Mr Bahramov, a Russian who was later to find fame in a World Cup Final with heavy West Ham involvement. The decision was a complete mystery. Even Ron Greenwood questioned him.

West Ham were not doing too well. Too many passes out of defence were going astray, but the Hammers had a couple of first-half shots and one, from Martin Peters, was particularly unlucky, being just inches wide. Then again, West Ham's first goal was somewhat fortunate. Stefanakos missed a chip forward by Sissons and Peters scored with an angled shot that was deflected past the 'keeper, Fronimidis, by a defender. Peters said later that he had meant it to go to Johnny Byrne.

The second goal was an Irons special. Byrne sent John Sissons away and he jinked around a couple of defenders before flighting a perfect cross to the head of Peters. Not surprisingly, both Peters' goals were greeted by the home crowd with almost perfect silence. West Ham's 120 or so fans, of course, went mad.

A couple of minutes or so after Peters' second, Eddie Bovington scored a strange own goal, sending a high ball past Jim Standen. At this, the Greek crowd became animated, but were stilled and silent as the teams left the field following the final whistle. A 2-2 scoreline on the night sent the Hammers through 6-2 on aggregate.

After the match, Greenwood identified Jim Standen as man-of-the-match, pointing out the magnificence of two saves in the first part of the game. Standen was born in Edmonton in 1935 and had been kept out of the Arsenal side by brilliant Welsh international Jack Kelsey. He played 35 League games for the Gunners. Even when he moved on to Luton, he had to play second fiddle, to England's Ron Baynham, but made 36 League appearances in a couple of seasons with the Hatters. Standen was one of a breed of footballing cricketers and won a County Championship medal with Worcestershire. In one season he had topped the first-class bowling averages with 64 wickets at an average of 13 runs, and altogether took 313 wickets between 1960 and 1970.

Many West Ham fans will remember Jim for one performance in September 1963 when he held out almost single-handedly against Liverpool at Anfield, including efforts from Hunt, St John and a Moran penalty, to help The Hammers go away with a rare victory.

Shortly before Christmas, West Ham found ourselves back in the League Cup semi-finals. They had squeezed past Grimsby, Hurst maintaining his record of scoring in every round after future England manager Graham Taylor had attempted to tackle Peter Brabrook as he made his way down the line. The skilful winger was too much for Taylor and got in the cross which allowed Hurst to get the only goal of the replay. The semi-final finished in a 10-3 aggregate win over Cardiff City, their 5-1 win in the second leg of this tie being a record away victory for West Ham in the League Cup. So on went the Hammers into the last two-leg Final of this competition (from 1967 the League Cup would be decided by a Wembley Final – just West Ham's luck!).

In January 1966, John Bond had left West Ham for Torquay United after 16 years and 428 appearances for the Hammers. The following month, West Ham were held 3-3 by Blackburn at Upton Park in the fourth round of the FA

Cup before going out in the replay at Ewood Park. It was a bit of a mess, the Hammers going down 4-1 to the side that would end the season at the foot of the First Division, 13 points behind the next club. Even this score flattered West Ham's performance. Rovers hit the woodwork four times. Ken Brown was out with tonsillitis so, in what seemed to many fans a monumental moment of madness, Greenwood decided to play the cultured Boyce at centre-half. Boyce had been out for five months and, partly as a consequence of the change, the entire defence, including Moore, was at sixes and sevens all afternoon.

West Ham now had a rather crowded fixture list in March: two Cup-winners' Cup quarter-final games and the two-leg League Cup Final, on top of four matches in Division One. Eight games in three weeks!

The Hammers' grip on the Cup-winners' Cup seemed to loosen at Upton Park when they failed to create the big lead they had hoped to take to East Germany for the second leg. They left themselves an uphill task in Magdeburg. Unless there was to be a marked improvement in their performance, West Ham would disappear from the competition.

For a team now so experienced at this level of football, West Ham were surprisingly easily thrown out of their stride at Upton Park by Ernst Kuemmel's FC Magdeburg, a sound but far from great German team. They allowed themselves to be hassled into mistakes and their work seemed always to be hurried. The long-ball game they played resulted in them giving too much possession to their opponents. The Hammers snatched at shots and the ball flew high or wide again and again, even from close range. At the same time, errors were forced by the close-covering, intelligent marking and swift interception of the Germans. With Busch sweeping up behind a four-man line of defenders, and Segger and Seguin harassing in midfield, when Magdeburg were not launching counter-attacks, they were tying down the off-colour Boyce and hard-working Peters for long periods. Byrne was almost always closely guarded, and Hurst could never find the time he needed for a well-directed shot. Brabrook rarely got through on the right, and Sissons too often was left to strike on his own.

Not surprisingly, West Ham did not get their noses in front until a minute after the interval, when Byrne hammered a cross from Peters into the net, after

Hurst had just failed to meet the ball with his head. Thereafter, the Irons launched raid after raid, but few were carefully built and none was accurately finished.

They squandered their chances of building a tie-winning lead by trying to batter their way through the wall the Germans had erected. They were not, however, without hope of squeezing into the semi-finals, provided they could revert to their counter-attacking style in East Germany. This would surely prove far more effective against a fit, fast and earnest side like Magdeburg, than the old fashioned 'hit hard and run' stuff seen at Upton Park.

Following a 4-2 win against Villa in the League at Upton Park, the Hammers faced West Brom at the Boleyn Ground in the first leg of the 1966 League Cup Final. Two strange goals gave the Hammers the game. Bobby Moore's goal was a cross rather than a shot, and the West Brom players were sure that the out-of-form Byrne (whose name was booed by the home fans when it was announced) had fouled their 'keeper before he won West Ham the game in the 90th minute. Jeff Astle had replied for the Baggies on the hour. Four days before the return game against Magdeburg, the Hammers beat Blackburn in the League, 4-1 at Upton Park.

Then, in East Germany, West Ham achieved a noble end by harshly efficient means. They were uncompromising in defence, hard and well-ordered overall. Magdeburg, meanwhile, proved to be a team with greater ability, vision and bite than they suggested in the first leg, but they too were a side well-versed in a few of the game's naughtier bits.

It was all pressure on the Hammers in the first half. Hirshmann hit the base of West Ham's post with a 20-yard free-kick in the opening minute, Sparwasser blasted over from two yards, and after 55 minutes Standen had to catapult across his goal to turn away Seguin's 25-yard drive.

The goals came in the space of 45 seconds midway through the second half and it was Magdeburg who scored first to silence the happy little band of 200 roving West Ham supporters. In the 77th minute, Sparwasser, soon to win his first full cap, handled the ball but Mr Laurax, the otherwise admirable Belgian referee, did not see it. Sparwasser centred and with West Ham's defence dithering for the only time in the match, Walter was able to score easily.

It took just 45 seconds for the Irons to equalise. Hurst swung the ball across from left to the far right, Brabrook pushed it inside and Sissons beat the agile Blochwitz from five yards.

It was a rare Hammers attack and it was the Londoners' defence who took the honours. Burnett showed why Greenwood felt able to let Joe Kirkup go to Chelsea; Brown and Bovington relished every moment of the battle, and Standen could not to be faulted. Ronnie Boyce, still not the 'Ticker' the crowd knew and loved from the previous season, and Martin Peters were the link between defence and the three-man attack, Brabrook, Sissons and the gallant Geoff Hurst, but both had played better. For all this, West Ham had achieved a 2-1 win over the two legs.

On the same evening the Football League, despite a Jimmy Greaves goal, lost 3-1 to the Scottish League. Dunfermline gained a one-goal lead over West Ham's Cup-winners' Cup semi-final opponents of the previous season, Real Zaragoza, in the first leg of their Fairs Cup quarter-final in Scotland. Dunfermline had the better of the first half, playing crisp, penetrating football, but the Zaragoza defence stood up to terrific pressure. Santamaria, the Spanish centre-half, was injured in a clash with Dunfermline's outside-right and resumed with his head bandaged. Zaragoza should have taken a lead on the resumption when Villa broke through, but shot wide. The Scots got their goal near the end through Paton. The Spanish went on to the Final of the Fairs Cup, but lost to their 'neighbours' Barcelona over the two legs.

West Ham were through to their second European semi-final, but the potential opponents were big boys. The draw the next day in Cannes included Liverpool, Celtic and Borussia Dortmund of West Germany. Most of the public and the press wanted to draw Dortmund. Success would mean that West Ham would defend the trophy in an all-British final in Britain.

At this time the British transfer market was hotting up. Allan Clarke moved from Walsall to Fulham for £40,000 and West Ham's very own Martin Britt went to relegation-threatened Blackburn for £17,000. Manchester City, pushing their promotion bid, paid out £45,000 to bring the Bury winger Colin Bell to Maine Road, and Rodney Marsh made the short trip from Fulham to Queen's Park Rangers at a cost to the Third Division club of £15,000. Looking at all this as a boy, I was mystified as to why Ron Greenwood wasn't involved. I could see Bell and Marsh as the perfect type of West Ham players and Allan

Clarke, even though still very young, could have offered great cover for any of the Hammers' first-choice forwards. Why wasn't Greenwood building on what he had?

West Ham now had to fit in two legs of a European semi-final, six First Division matches and the League Cup Final second leg over the next 21 days. This, following the last schedule, seemed incredibly demanding. Given their selection options, how would they hold it all together? They needed cover badly. Tired cup legs were being sapped by League games which were themselves still important enough.

The pace soon began to tell and West Ham lost 2-1 to Blackpool before goals from Kaye, Brown, Clark and Williams, all in the first half at The Hawthorns, ended their hopes of the League Cup with a 4-1 defeat. Then Fulham beat them 3-1 before the Hammers managed a draw against Burnley on 2 April. On 5 April, they ran out at Upton Park in the first leg of the European Cup-winners' Cup semi-final.

The tiredness showed against Dortmund, who were one of the best clubs in Europe at the time. They had hammered Floriana (Malta) 5-1 and 8-0, but had been given a fright by CSKA, the Bulgarian Cup holders. In the second leg, a 3-0 lead was almost swallowed up by a 4-2 defeat in Sofia. In the quarter-finals they drew 1-1 in Madrid with Atletico and won 1-0 at home. Lothar Emmerich had scored 14 goals up to the semi-finals.

One supporter, Joe, recalls: "It was early springtime when we met the Germans at Upton Park. Nobody seemed to have told Borussia that teams playing away in Europe are suppose to defend. They took the game to West Ham at every opportunity. The night did not begin too promisingly. Byrne was captain in place of Moore. Bobby looked to be on his way from Upton Park. He was the last but one man to take the field and was booed as he came out. Moore, however, was soon to win the supporters over to his side in the best way he knew, by stamping his authority on the game. He was magnificent."

This was the Moore who England would need during the coming summer. Others were also turning it on. Bloomfield was at his most cunning, Byrne darted about incisively, Brown stuck relentlessly to his job, and Peters was at his ubiquitous best.

It was Martin Peters who put the Hammers in front just before half-time. Greenwood had brought in the 32-year-old Jimmy Bloomfield, an old pal from his days at Brentford, and it was Bloomfield who gave Peters the ball midway in Borussia's half. With Byrne running free on the left, it looked as if the movement would continue that way. But Peters suddenly cut inside, drifted past two defenders and scored with a crisp, low drive.

West Ham pushed remorselessly forward in search of the second goal they needed, but it did not come. In the final stages Borussia went on the offensive and provided a thunderclap finish to a brilliant and combative game, hitting the Hammers twice in the last four minutes through Lothar Emmerich, West Germany's leading scorer. First Libuda, a wraith-like figure, gave Emmerich the chance to score from 12 yards. With only two minutes left, Held crossed from the left and it was Emmerich, waiting by the far post, who slid the ball smoothly past Standen. He had knocked in both his goals with his right foot, his left had done all the damage in the competition thus far.

Emmerich's priceless opportunism gave West Ham much to do in the second leg. Dortmund were a side of crushing efficiency, wide skill and indomitable spirit. The match had throbbed with all the best in football.

Alf Ramsey, England's team manager, was there to see it all. At the start of the match Martin Peters may not have been included in Ramsey's first list of 40 World Cup potentials. However, his performance must have put him there. Peters proved beyond all doubt that he had the perception and range of skill to tax the best. But West Ham had run out of steam in the final stages.

After the game Ron Greenwood said: "The way it ended was cruel but a game lasts 90 minutes. We have not yet given up hope. Dortmund are a good side, but they were not in it. I told my players how good this West German side was, to buck them up. But we did not let them be good. I thought Bloomfield was the best player on the field and Byrne has been appointed captain for the rest of the season."

Bobby Moore told the German players: "You will have a hard game over there."

Brave words, but anyone who was at the match could see that West Ham had a mountain to climb in Germany.

Things looked as if they were turning round when the Hammers beat

Spurs. If they could win 4-1 at White Hart Lane, surely they could do the same in Germany. But then a 6-2 hiding at Stamford Bridge reversed this philosophy.

A player in the West Ham squad of the time recalls: "The team spent the 48 hours before the match with Borussia talking with Ron Greenwood about the value of an early West Ham goal and the importance of holding the German's early assaults. The away goals meant that we would need to win 2-0 or 3-1. At the Rote Erde Stadium, Dortmund, who were sitting on top of their League, scored with the first movement of the game. So much for theory."

The Germans cut the West Ham defence in two when Sturm gave Sigi Held a chance to cross the ball to Lothar Emmerich. The tall, dark, round-shouldered winger headed against the bar, but banged home the rebound after only 27 seconds.

Emmerich had an awkward gait and moderate ability, but he had a feel for scoring goals. He was not satisfied with the one either. He scored again in the 29th minute with a bullet of a shot from a free-kick following a foul by Bobby Moore. West Ham built their defensive wall with meticulous care, but the lethal left foot, fired from a brisk seven-pace run-up, found the gap that did not seem to exist. This brought his goal tally to 43 that winter.

West Ham did their best and kept going with dogged persistence long after the tie had been won and lost, and Byrne managed to get on the score sheet two minutes before half-time. Brabrook broke free on the right and Budgie headed his centre past Tilkowski in the Borussia goal. But with only three minutes left, Cyliax, their right-back, was allowed to move up and his 25-yard shot hit Brown before spinning over Standen's head. West Ham ended up well beaten, 3-1.

Barney, an intrepid traveller recalls: "The night had begun with the band of the Royal Artillery thumping out some English marches. By the end, the 32,500 crowd, several hundred perched on a humped-backed bridge, of all things, at one end of the ground, were well happy that their team had mastered the side which had beaten Munich 1860 in last year's Final. At least we had the consolation that it took one of the best sides in Europe to take the Cup from us."

On the same evening, George Best was never able to get into the first leg of the European Cup semi-final and Manchester United, also including Charlton and Law, were as good as put out, losing 2-0 to Partizan Belgrade in Yugoslavia. West Ham, meanwhile, won their next three games, against Arsenal, Spurs and Manchester United.

In the Cup-winners' Cup Final, staged once again at Hampden, Borussia met Liverpool, a side conditioned to European football the previous season. The Merseysiders had done well against strong opposition, beating Juventus, Standard Liege and Honved to set up a semi-final meeting with Celtic. In the first leg at Parkhead, Liverpool, without leading scorer Roger Hunt, struggled to withstand Celtic's attacking momentum and were fortunate to escape with a single-goal defeat. At Anfield the roles were reversed, but by half-time Liverpool were still trailing to that single goal. A venomous free-kick from Tommy Smith levelled the scores and then Geoff Strong, who had spent much of the half limping because of an injury, managed to find some extra spring in his legs and rose above the Celtic defence to score. With a minute left it appeared the Scots had pulled level, but the referee blew for offside.

In the Final, the Germans were stronger all round, with a particularly formidable defence. Indeed, they were tactically more sound overall. Siggi Held put them ahead after the interval, only for Roger Hunt to equalise from a controversial centre, that might have upset less resilient teams than the Germans. Then, with just seconds left, Hunt failed with a simple chance and the match went into extra-time. In the 107th minute the Liverpool goalkeeper, Tommy Lawrence, under pressure from Held, was forced to punch the ball from the edge of his area, a sin for a British 'keeper in those days when failure to 'hold the ball' was seen as a nasty foreign weakness. Libuda pounced on the clearance and blasted at the ball from 40 yards out. It took a deflection off the Liverpool centre-half Ron Yeats and whipped past the stranded Lawrence. West Ham had gone out to the winners.

A hectic season left West Ham in 12th place in the First Division and nothing else. Hovering around the foot of the table for most of the season, they picked up near the end. Only five teams won at Upton Park: Leicester City, Liverpool, Fulham, Nottingham Forest and Borussia Dortmund. In the League, five goals were conceded at Forest, Leeds and Sheffield United. Chelsea managed six at Stamford Bridge, prior to which Bobby Moore had been stripped of the captaincy.

## World Cup winners

Wembley again. On a bright, English summer's day. Martin Peters, Geoff Hurst and Bobby Moore were all playing. In the season just ended, both Moore and Peters had turned out 63 times for West Ham, and Hurst had played just one game less. The West Germans had Borussia Dortmund's Lothar Emmerich, the man who destroyed West Ham in the Cup-winners' Cup, and his team-mates Sigi Held and Tilkowski in goal.

Millions of words have been written and spoken about England's performance that day. Not a lot more needs to be said. Indeed, all the chatter covers up the fact that England hadn't looked good before the semi-final and have never really looked like getting to a World Cup Final since. It has also diverted us from seeing that English football has never built on that success in the way Brazil did and Germany have. However, what seems to have been forgotten, to some extent, is the part the culture of West Ham United played that day at Wembley. What follows looks to address this, just a little.

In the early part of July 1966, the Queen and the Duke of Edinburgh had visited Northern Ireland. The Troubles that have brought so much tragedy to the province for the last 30 years were still some way away, but nevertheless Ulster was becoming uneasy and bottles and bricks were hurled at the royal car. The 'battle of Red Lion Square' took place around this time, outside the US Embassy. It was a protest mounted, in the main, by students agitating against American bombing of North Vietnam. Thirty demonstrators were arrested during violent scenes which included a charge by mounted police. Myra Hindley and Ian Brady, the 'Moors Murderers', were convicted of the torture and murder of three children. Hindley had, on the eve of the England-Uruguay game which opened the tournament, lodged an appeal against her conviction.

Also at this time the Beatles, who were at the zenith of their fame, flew to Manilla to be met by the marines and tens of thousands of screaming teenage girls. Not long afterwards they were more or less chucked out of the Philippines, having missed an appointment to meet the wife of President Marcos. Still, life has its compensations, *Paperback Writer* was number one.

Whilst it was pretty certain that Bobby Moore would play for England in the World Cup, Peters and Hurst had not been so sure of a place even in the squad and neither were chosen for the opening match. Sir Geoff remembers:

"Even though I was probably the most in-form striker in the country, at the time you just don't realise you're good enough to be in the squad."

Even when Hurst was chosen for the final 22, becoming a first-choice striker was not his only consideration: "I'd finally broken into the card school and we were playing morning, noon and night for a shilling a game. We didn't know what pound notes were then."

But life under Ramsey wasn't all beer and skittles, it seemed to be mostly skittles in fact: "There was no real drinking as such, which was down to Alf picking the right people and keeping things strict."

Wembley, on Monday, 11 July 1966, was a cauldron of nerves. Ladislao Mazurkiewicz, the Uruguayan 'keeper, gave a faultless display of clean handling, intelligent anticipation, and cool courage, to became the first foreign goalkeeper to prevent England from scoring at Wembley. It was the 30th time England had played non-British opposition there. This game is rarely noted by those who have written about England in 1966, but it was probably their best performance in tournament, given the crucial nature of the match – it was England, the hosts, and the tournament's first game – and the quality of the opposition, who were probably the strongest of the South American challengers.

Just before the World Cup, Mazurkiewicz had won honours with Penarol, the club who that year became South American champions for the third time and went on to contest the World Club Championship. 'Mazurko' twice prevented the Real Madrid attack from scoring, ensuring that it was Penarol who would reign supreme on the face of the earth. Throughout the 1960s, Penarol seized Real Madrid's crown, the eminent team of the previous decade.

As Mazurkiewicz stood in the goalmouth he could see his counterpart, Gordon Banks, away in the distance. In front of him stood some legendary names and others destined to become legends. They included Jimmy Greaves and Bobby Charlton. These men, led by Bobby Moore, in the past year had swept aside the likes of European Nations Cup winners, Spain, in Madrid. The semi-finalists in the same competition, Hungary, and Denmark (in Copenhagen) had been vanquished. West Germany had been beaten on their own soil and at Wembley. After a 1-0 defeat by Argentina more than two years previously in Rio, England had lost only one game. They had won 14 and drawn just six. Twelve of these matches had been played beyond England's shores. The attack had scored a total of 42 goals and the defence conceded only 20. Since losing 4-2 to Uruguay in the 1954 World Cup quarter-finals, England had enjoyed a 2-1 win over them at Wembley in 1964. This England side was no mean team.

But Uruguay were also a team in the process of becoming such. The following year they would be the champions of South America, leaving the likes of Brazil and Argentina in their wake. However, historically they had been no slouches. Their record of success in South America was bettered only by Argentina, who had a much bigger population and by far the superiority in terms of facilities. Make no mistake, Uruguay were serious contenders for the title.

Alf Ramsey was himself from 'West Ham' country, born into a poor family in Dagenham in the 1920s. He was always going to make Bobby Moore skipper, even though there was a rumour that Norman Hunter might get the nod, but the choice of Moore as captain was crucial. No one knew what was needed in the same way that he did. Not enough credit has been given to him for his leadership and insight during the whole of the 1966 finals. However, his most critical effort was in this first game. England dared not lose; the way the defence worked would be so important. This match would dictate the course of the rest of England's tournament.

Every spectator in the stadium seemed to be English. Uruguay fielded a team based around Penarol. Before five minutes had passed England had won three corners, Connelly and Wilson crashed a path through the heavily-built, sky-blue barricade erected by the Latin Americans. This signalled the transition of the game into an aggressive confrontation premised on desperation and desire. Knowing that Banks was discomfited by the setting sun, Rocha and Cortes sent in drives from nearly 30 yards to severely test the English 'keeper. Connelly, the Manchester United winger, was in fantastic form. He cut in from the right. The moment was pregnant. Mazurkiewicz moved backwards and Connelly shot over. Stiles appeared to punch Rocha. Bobby Charlton and Moore were crudely brought down. Connelly and Ball retaliated following terrible tackles.

Mazurkiewicz was doing his job well. Although the shots rained in, his goal survived. A point of tenuous balance and chronic equilibrium had been reached. From now on spirit and not tactics would decide the fates.

After the break, the English came out blazing with tremendous effort and West Ham's Bobby Moore was in constant action. Now Mazurkiewicz played with terrific concentration. If he protected the net then maybe the two lone front runners could find an opportunity. The players that besieged his goal-keeper domain were to become the best combined footballing force on the planet, but still he kept them out.

Uruguay drew breath and strained every sinew in an effort to hold on. In the final 20 minutes Bobby Charlton gathered the ball. Mazurkiewicz and Charlton; one on one. Their eyes met for a fleeting moment. Angels faced each other. An unstoppable force met the immovable object. Such moments are rare and real. Anything could happen. Connelly deflected the searing shot, Mazurkiewicz somehow got in the way and sent it to safety. This was all too soon followed by a Greaves cross,. Mazurkiewicz's fist beat Connelly to the ball.

Mazurkiewicz continued to play brilliantly, absorbing the English attack that had been reinforced by the intimidation of the towering centre-half, Jack Charlton. Indeed, Uruguay, a nation of less than three million, nearly snatched it from the country of football's birth, who chose their side from tens of millions, when near the end, Rocha pivoted in front of Moore to strike a dipping volley. But Moore had done enough to put the great man off his shot and it fell just wide of Banks' right-hand post.

The final whistle sounded and the Uruguayans were ecstatic. Their opponents had earned 16 corner-kicks, only one had been awarded to them. England had fired 15 shots at Mazurkiewicz and he had thwarted every effort.

Martin Peters was included in England's next game, which ended in a 1-0 defeat of Mexico, despite the Mexican 'keeper praying under the crossbar before the game. Peters kept his place against the French, and England qualified for the quarter-finals, but the 2-0 result did not reflect a poor game.

As host nation, England were doing no better than all right. It was plain that if they were to live up to Ramsey's pre-tournament boast, that his side would win the World Cup, something significant was needed. Moore could not be faulted in his role, but it was clear that the potential triangle between him, Peters and, 'A.N.Other', was not being completed. So Ramsey decided to couple the chain so often used at West Ham. It was a well-disguised act of desperation, albeit low level, something just short of panic. It was hard to recall when Ramsey, or any England manager, had called 30 per cent of their side from one club. Geoff Hurst was brought in for the quarter-final against Argentina. Many were surprised that he would replace Jimmy Greaves. Looking back even Hurst was impressed: "It was one hell of a decision to leave Jimmy out, when you think about it. After all, he was the world's greatest goalscorer. Jim's never held it against me personally, but without question it was one hell of a blow for him. We all have disappointments in our careers and it was a huge setback for Jimmy."

For all this, Hurst's 40 goals in 57 domestic games for West Ham, which got him into the final squad of 22, were pretty good credentials in themselves. He was not yet 24. This game would give him his tenth international cap. He had four Under-23 caps. He recalls: "Alf announced the team after training and I was in. I remember I just kept thinking to myself: My time's arrived."

Although born in Ashton-under-Lyne, Lancashire, Hurst was brought up in the East End. The England youth international blossomed from a competent wing-half, who by determination and hard work became one of the most feared strikers in the First Division. Charlie, his dad, was a professional with Oldham, Bristol Rovers and Rochdale before finally coming south to play for Chelmsford City.

Hurst junior made his first senior appearance for West Ham against Fulham in a Floodlight Cup game in December 1958. He signed professional forms four months later. His baptism in the First Division came against Nottingham Forest in February 1960. His first goal at senior level was in a 4-2 win against Wolves at Upton Park in December 1961.

Hurst started as a wing-half in 1962-63, but his first-team appearances increased after Ron Greenwood called him to his office to tell him he was looking for someone big and strong, and not afraid to graft, to play inside-left for him at home to Liverpool. Hurst did the job and the Hammers won 1-0. His first season as a regular first-teamer was 1963-64, when he scored 23 goals, and he and Byrne built up a terrific partnership. Hurst rated Byrne as the best player he had worked with, and in the season before the World Cup, Hurst was the First Division's top scorer.

Geoff Hurst was an unselfish runner off the ball, and perfected the near-post run that produced so many goals. He had massive strength in the penalty-area. He took a lot of pounding from close marking, but was always brave and strong. He was capable of shielding the ball, waiting to move or lay off devastating passes. Ron Greenwood turned him from a run-of-the-mill wing-half into a powerful and explosive forward. No one thought he would make the switch. It seemed to take him an age of hard work and patience. He ran himself into the ground, yet he appeared always to be just short. He put up with his share of abuse from the supporters and press and made it. He could also have been a decent cricketer, playing for Essex schools in the same team as Bobby Moore, and he turned out for Essex seconds for three summers, playing one Championship match against Lancashire at Liverpool in 1962.

The game against the Argentineans was, again, not a great performance by England. But as Sir Geoff Hurst recalls: "I was spat at, punched in the throat and elbowed, so it was rewarding to score the winner with a typical West Ham near-post goal."

England played against ten men for much of the match, Antonio Rattin having got his marching orders ten minutes before the break. Hurst's first chance was reward for his endurance and strength. Just into the second half, Ray Wilson got a ball from Bobby Moore and centred. Hurst hit it hard but Roma, the Boca Juniors goalkeeper, pulled off a fine save.

The goal, when it came, was patent 'West Ham'. It had 'Made in Chadwell Heath' written all over it. Peters curled in a high cross from the left. Hurst leapt high at the near post. The header went into the right-hand corner. Bobby Charlton said of it: "It was the best goal I ever saw in my time with England – an unstoppable header."

In a television interview afterwards, Alf Ramsey called the Argentineans 'animals' – and that is what the game is largely remembered for – but this match also opened up Geoff Hurst's perception of himself: "By now, I knew I was making a significant contribution. I still wasn't aware of the tension and the pressure, but then I was only a kid and I took it all in my stride."

The three Hammers kept their place for the semi-final game against Portugal, when England played well as a team. Moore marshalled his defence brilliantly to defend England's one-goal lead, and Peters was a constant threat, creating plenty of space for Bobby Charlton to exploit. Eleven minutes from the end Hurst shook off Carlos and made his way to the right-hand goal-line. He sent the ball back to Bobby Charlton for the Manchester United striker, who would be named European Footballer of the Year in 1966, to bury his second goal. Eusebio, the European Footballer of the Year in 1965, scored from the spot, but England went through to the World Cup Final.

*Doctor Zhivago* won five Academy Awards and was nominated for 12. Vietnam was fast becoming a mass graveyard for Americans, who were still ruthlessly bombing the north of that country. And the first Englishmen to line up in a World Cup Final, stood where the first English team to win any international trophy had stood in 1965. Three of those original conquerors were back on the Wembley turf. Sir Geoff again: "As soon as Alf told me I was in the Final, I was on the phone to my wife Judith. Then I found out that my room mate Martin Peters was in too, and we congratulated each other. It would have been horrible for one of us to have been left out."

On the morning of the Final it was business as usual as the team prepared to leave the Hendon Hall Hotel for one last time: "We just weren't aware of the momentous day that was ahead of us. Without question, it was THE biggest day in this country's sporting history.

Nobby Stiles spent the morning trying to find a Catholic Church in Golders Green, even though George Cohen was trying to explain he might find it difficult in one of London's biggest Jewish communities.

Bobby Charlton and Roger Hunt had distracted themselves by going shopping for shoes! One finds it hard to imagine such a laid back attitude considering the effort given to security in recent Finals. Sir Geoff recalled: "There was none of the tremendous hype you see today, only about 20 or 30 people saw us off from the hotel. But on the coach we were all very upbeat."

Once the game started Hurst was a marked man: "Horst Hottges, a full-back, came across to mark me straight away. He obviously wasn't familiar with marking tall central strikers like myself and I knew then that I was going to have a good game."

With the game not a quarter-of-an-hour old, Haller put West Germany in front. In retrospect Sir Geoff didn't see this as a catastrophe: "Sure, it was a set-back – but we certainly weren't going to drop our heads. It was still early days."

Just six minutes later Moore was tripped by Wolfgang Overath. Sir Geoff takes up the story: "Bobby went down and immediately got up to take the free-kick. Being club mates we were on the same wavelength and he knew I was looking for the early one."

Moore's speed in taking the free-kick surprised the German defence. It was long and accurate, Hurst timed his run perfectly on the right – and headed home. Sir Geoff continues: "By going that split second earlier I had the edge and headed past Tilkowski. I was absolutely elated. I kept jumping up and down thinking, 'I've done it!' I never celebrated goals like that and it looks so ridiculous now, but it was sheer joy."

With just over 12 minutes of ordinary time left, Hurst shot, following a cross by Alan Ball. The West German defence could only send the ball out to Martin Peters who fired in the second goal – another Hammers goal – to put England ahead. Again, in Sir Geoff's words: "I was amazed to see little Bally hit the cross so far. My shot took a deflection and it looped up. Martin managed to keep it down and hit the target."

With less than a minute remaining Weber pulled West Germany level to take the game into extra-time:

"Alf said a very simple thing as we watched the tired Germans prepare for extra-time: 'You've won the World Cup once, now go and do it again'."

Like the rest of the men on the field, Hurst was practically exhausted:

"I'd made a run and realised I was physically and mentally shattered. But then Hottges signalled to me to take it easy. Seeing him in a worse state than myself gave me an extra boost."

Ten minutes into extra-time, Hurst made it into the middle as Ball mustered up the energy for one final burst down the flank.

"Bally didn't even look up, he just knew he had to whip it into the near post. I'd made my run marginally too early and the ball was going behind me so I had to control it, take a second touch and... BANG!"

Geoff Hurst had scored his second with a devastating near-post drive– but did the ball cross the line?

"I had the worst view in the stadium because I was on my backside and thinking, 'Is it in or isn't it?' I was knackered and just had my hands on my knees. It was agony while the referee, Dienst, went over to the Russian linesman, Bakhramov. Although it was only seconds, it seemed ages until he eventually gave a huge nod. I've said it for over 30 years now, Roger Hunt – a preda-tor – had the best view and instinctively he'd have tried to put it in to claim the World Cup winner. Instead he shouted, 'It's there!' and wheeled away. That's good enough for me. I still believe today that it was a goal, even though the film is inconclusive. I'll never change my mind about that."

The last goal of the 1966 World Cup Final was taken straight out of the West Ham/Ron Greenwood coaching files; another all-Irons effort. Moore's long pass, finishing his masterful performance, sent Hurst through. The shot was massive and unstoppable. Sir Geoff elaborates: "Mooro showed so much composure in chesting the ball down in his own area with just seconds to go in the World Cup Final. It says so much about his greatness. Jack was screaming for him to get it out of the ground. He would! Bobby hit a great pass upfield. I was so tired I just decided to hit the ball with everything left in me. If it had gone over it would have wasted a few precious seconds, but the ball just popped up off the turf and I hit it on the sheer bone of my instep and it just flew in!

"Even an hour after the game I wasn't sure whether it had counted. No one seemed to know. I had my winners' medal but it wasn't until I got changed and went back out on to the pitch and looked up at the scoreboard, that I realised I'd got three. At the time the hat-trick wasn't important, it was winning that counted then."

England had won the World Cup, but the victory owed a lot to West Ham United, not just in the persona of the three players who took such crucial roles in the Final. The culture of the East London club had fostered the football that had given England something original and unique – the merging of the tradi-tional qualities of the English game with the best of continental technique and, in the shape of Martin Peters, sheer genius.

The squad received £1,000 each for winning, plus £300 from Adidas and the choice of a sponsored navy or white raincoat. But the victory changed the life of those in the team, particularly Geoff Hurst:

"A few days later I had to go and collect the trophy for ending up as England's top scorer with four goals …they sent a big limousine to my semi-detached chalet in Hornchurch which I'd bought two years earlier for £5,050. That made a big change from my second-hand Ford Anglia which cost me £460. In those days they only used limos for Royal occasions.

"Looking back, that was the first sign that things were starting to change. Before the World Cup, I'd phone restaurants and say I was a friend of Bobby Moore. Now, suddenly, I could book a table in my own name. At the time I was only on about £45 per week and I spent my £1,000 bonus for winning the World Cup on the house. West Ham then offered to double that and I was about to sign, but then I found out that Bobby Moore was on a six-year contract worth £140 per week. That was the benchmark for me and after some discussion the club agreed.

"I traded in the Anglia for a second-hand Morris 1100 which cost about £1,200 and we moved into a house in Chigwell for £12,750."

Matt Busby made a £200,000 bid for Hurst before the end of 1966. This would have broke the British transfer record, but Ron Greenwood sent a concise telegram back to the Manchester United manager. It read: 'No.'

Geoff Hurst did not regret missing the chance to move on to a bigger club, although it may have given him opportunities he was never to have with the Hammers:

"I was very happy with West Ham, my career was going well and I've never been one to think that the grass is greener on the other side. It's all about the time and the place and even now I have no regrets, I don't feel I missed out. I had a good career and when you've scored three goals in a World Cup Final you tend to be reasonably happy. Now, 30 years on, it's significant because it's a hard record to beat. I'm very proud."

The years from 1963 to 1966 had been the greatest time in the history of West Ham United and English football in general. As far as West Ham is concerned, the seeds of this development went right back to the beginnings of the club, but the most recent root-line had been the work of Ted Fenton, Ernie Gregory, Wally St Pier, Malcolm Allison, Noel Cantwell, Bobby Moore and Ron Greenwood. None of these men have had the recognition they deserved. In particular, it is nothing less than appalling that Bobby Moore had no role in the organisation and development of English football at a senior or national level. He spent some of his best intellectual years in the backwaters of the lower divisions. With the greatest of respect to the men who have led England over the last few decades, Graham Taylor, Bobby Robson, Terry Venables and Glenn Hoddle, they would be the first to say that as a player they never developed the insight or talent that Moore had. None of them could boast his pedigree in domestic, Cup, European or World football, or be seen as such a natural successor to Alf Ramsey and Ron Greenwood. The question that history will ask of the tsars of English soccer in the late 1970s and 80s era will be: 'Why not the captain in the red shirt? Why not Bobby Moore?' There can be no satisfactory answer.

# We Live in Hope

## 1966-67

**B**EFORE the cheers following England's World Cup success in 1966 had melted away, a small Welsh coal mining village suffered the appalling loss of 116 children and 28 adults when a slag heap engulfed their school in Aberfan. The following Easter, the tanker *Torrey Canyon* spewed 120,000 tons of crude oil, much of it on the beaches of Devon and Cornwall, with inestimable damage to wildlife.

Football, meanwhile, still held centre stage in many people's minds and West Ham's first game of the season, against Chelsea, saw the World Cup winning trio take to the park first. They got a thunderous welcome from the 36,000 crowd who had turned up. Peter Bonetti, the Chelsea 'keeper, was as acrobatic as his nickname implied and the Hammers lost 2-1. The talk on the terraces was that Greenwood was going after 'the Cat'.

Although Moore, Hurst and Peters won the World Cup for England in the summer of 1966, they could not prevent West Ham's poor start to the new season when the club went five games without a win. And as the season developed, the Hammers' form became increasingly eccentric. Whereas points were readily picked up away from Upton Park, the team did not record a home League win until the end of October, when both Byrne and Sissons were dropped for the game against Nottingham Forest. Hurst got two early on and Bovington made it three with seven minutes left. Storey-Moore got one back for Forest in the dying minutes.

The ability to score goals was still there, but seemingly in the wrong place, at the wrong time, as far as the Hammers were concerned. In September, in the Football League's game against the Irish League, Johnny Byrne got four and Geoff Hurst two in the Football League's 12-0 win.

Spurs and Arsenal were beaten in the League Cup, though, and this lined up a formidable confrontation with Leeds United at the Boleyn Ground in November. Before the match Don Revie said that he would be playing for a draw. His tactics went wrong somewhere. Having walloped Fulham 6-1 in the League a couple of days earlier, West Ham achieved their biggest-ever win in the League Cup against the foundation of the great Leeds team of the 1970s, a team which included Billy Bremner, Jack Charlton, Norman Hunter and Johnny Giles. Both Sissons and Hurst got hat-tricks in the 7-0 win, and Peters chipped in with the other.

A few days later, West Ham were at White Hart Lane in the League, lining up against the likes of Pat Jennings, Cyril Knowles, Allan Mullery, Mike England, Dave Mackay, Jimmy Greaves, Alan Gilzean and Terry Venables. It was breathtaking and a brilliant display of attacking football ended in a magnificent 4-3 victory for the Irons. Sissons and Hurst were again on the scoresheet along with Brabrook and Byrne.

A 3-0 home win against Newcastle made it four wins in a row by the Irons – perhaps things were turning around. But the good run was ended with Leeds getting their revenge at Elland Road, where the Hammers lost 2-1. West Ham beat West Brom 3-0 at the Boleyn and then it was the League Cup quarter-final at Bloomfield Road. Blackpool were destined for Division Two that season and although they were no easy pushovers, West Ham beat them 3-1. Hurst got a couple in the first half, one from nearly 20 yards out, and Byrne got the third early in the second period.

Before the Hammers met Chelsea in the League they suffered a 4-2 defeat at Turf Moor. Burnley were then the most successful home side in the First Division and West Ham were the best away team, so one could have bet this would have been a pretty entertaining match. Jim Standen had to take a deal of the blame for the second goal when he missed a centre, but he made up for this by saving a penalty from Irvine following a foul by John Charles on the superb Willie Morgan.

Thus, the match at Stamford Bridge on 17 December was approached with some trepidation. It was a remarkable game as the Hammers shared ten goals with the Blues, letting them get back on even terms twice in the process.

Chelsea had only won three games at Stamford Bridge that season, and West Ham looked to be ahead early on, but John Byrne was called offside. However, in the 24th minute, the Hammers took the lead. The ex-Chelsea man Brabrook knocked in a corner from Sissons. Then Byrne and Hurst created the chance that Peters took well to make the score 2-0 up and West Ham looked to be coasting. However, in last moments of the first-half, Baldwin scored for the Blues after goalmouth ruck.

Five minutes into the second half, Hateley scored from 25 yards out, and on the hour Chelsea took the lead when Charlie Cooke got the goal of the game, a terrific volley via Baldwin and Hateley. Then the Hammers drew level when Sissons beat Bonetti with a curving drive.

With just over half an hour to go, Sissons got his second, a belter from 40 yards. Two minutes later 'Chopper' Harris handled in the area. Byrne took the penalty to see Bonetti make a marvellous save, but then Budgie picked up the rebound, swerved past McCreadie, then ex-Hammer Kirkup – 5-3 to the Irons.

With ten minutes left Moore was judged to have fouled Hateley and Bobby Tambling scored from the spot before Chelsea equalised in last minute of injury time by way of Tambling, from a cross by Charlie Cooke. It was the last kick of the game.

West Ham were up at Blackpool again on Boxing Day and both teams went down to Upton Park the very next day. It made for three December victories over the club at the foot of Division One. West Ham beat them 4-1 at Bloomfield Road and 4-0 at the Boleyn Ground, where one of three goals in the last ten minutes was scored from a classic Bobby Moore strike from over 30 yards out.

West Ham had scored 32 goals in just nine League games in November and December, but the League Cup seemed to became their focus for the season at this point. The Hammers won only one of their next eight games in Division One. They were taken to a replay by Third Division Swindon in the FA Cup, and then bundled out by them at the County Ground. Ron Greenwood commented: "This was the blackest month we have known."

The League Cup semi-final gave West Ham the opportunity to avenge the Final defeat of the previous season at the hands of West Bromwich Albion. However, history was to repeat itself at The Hawthorns.

Albion took the field in the second half with a four-goal lead and that was how the score remained, so the second leg was something of a non-event. The 2-2 draw at Upton Park meant that the first Wembley League Cup Final would not include West Ham and as such, neither would it provide a fourth successive Cup Final appearance to Moore and Hurst. Peters, of course, would have had a hat-trick of Wembley Finals.

The let-down of the League Cup semi-final was followed by a home draw against Sunderland and a visit to Goodison Park, where FA Cup holders Everton completed the double over the Hammers, winning 4-0, having beaten them 3-2 at Upton Park in early October.

Everton had been eliminated from the Cup-winners' Cup by West Ham's old foes, Real Zaragoza, in the early rounds. But Rangers improved on rivals Celtic, the Scottish representatives of the year before. In the first round they beat Glentoran of Northern Ireland 1-1 and 4-0, and after removing, the holders and the Hammers' tormentors of the previous season, Borussia Dortmund, 2-1 on aggregate, they beat Real Zaragoza. It was ironic that with the new away goals rule (from this tournament onwards, in the event of two teams being level on aggregate, the away goals counted double – a rule not without its critics at the time) a deadlock resulted when both teams won 2-0 at home. The tie had to be settled by the toss of a coin.

In the semi-finals the Scots defeated Slavia Sofia 2-0, winning narrowly in each leg with goals from Wilson and Henderson.

Bayern Munich reached the Final with three odd-goal victories, over Tatan Presov (Czechoslovakia) 4-3, Shamrock Rovers (Eire) 4-3, and the Austrians, Rapid Vienna, 2-1. Then they defeated Standard Liege 2-0 and 3-1 in the last four. The West Germans were fortunate that the Final was held in Nuremberg, a near neighbour of Munich. But although they always had the edge on their Scottish opponents, they still needed extra-time to win a boring game 1-0, with a goal by Roth.

Not long after West Ham's defeat at Goodison, Johnny Byrne returned to his former club, Crystal Palace. Byrne was originally from West Horsley in

Surrey and although his parents were Irish, he was as Cockney as any of his team-mates. An England youth international, Byrne joined Palace in July 1956. In 1961 he scored 30 goals in the Glaziers' climb out of the Fourth Division. He came to Upton Park from Crystal Palace with Ron Brett, Budgie had one cap when he joined West Ham. He was the first-ever Fourth Division player to win an England cap for the Under-23s and one of the very few Third Division players to be picked for full England honours.

He was nicknamed Budgie because of his constant chattering, on and off the field. An inside-forward blessed with great skills and good shot, he was tagged the 'English Di Stefano' at West Ham. He was sold back to Palace for £45,000. He moved to Fulham little more than a year later, for £18,000. After spending 12 months at Craven Cottage, he went on to manage Durban City in South Africa.

In all Budgie won ten full caps. If he had avoided injury, he would have undoubtedly played many more games for his country. This would probably have included appearances in the 1966 World Cup. He scored a hat-trick, including the 87th-minute winner, for England against Portugal in 1964. For West Ham he scored an average of a goal every two games and netted 28 times in 34 Cup ties for the Hammers.

The win over Aston Villa at Upton Park at the close of March put an end to a terrible run which provided only a single victory in three months. Between beating Villa again at Villa Park, helping them on their way to the Second Division, West Ham won against Burnley at the Boleyn Ground. Something of a mini-revival seemed in the offering.

But West Ham finished the season on a low note. Seven defeats, and a draw against Manchester City in the final game. They finished in 16th place, although they were scoring goals all season. In fact only the champions, Manchester United, scored more than West Ham in the League: the Hammers got 80, whilst United netted 84. However, the significant figure was that United had conceded only 45, whereas West Ham let in 84. The Irons scored 100 goals in all competitions and Geoff Hurst, who was voted 'Hammer of the Year', got 41 of these.

In the last weeks of the season, a number of youngsters were given first-team chances. From the performances of these players, who had graduated from the junior ranks, it was evident that the signing of some experienced defenders was to be a priority if First Division football was going to be maintained at Upton Park. During the summer of 1967, Billy Bonds, a rugged fullback, was purchased from Charlton Athletic, John Cushley came from Glasgow Celtic, and Bobby Ferguson, a Scottish international goalkeeper, was recruited from Kilmarnock. Ron Greenwood had the opportunity to sign World Cup 'keeper Gordon Banks, but instead he went for Ferguson, not wanting to let down his old Brentford pal, Malcolm McDonald, the Kilmarnock manager, to whom he had apparently promised a world record fee to take the erratic Ferguson off his hands.

Jim Standen had to make way for Ferguson. In six seasons between the sticks for West Ham he played 235 games. Now he went off to Detroit Cougars, although he re-appeared in three matches in 1967-68. Cushley filled the place vacated by Ken Brown, who had joined Torquay United.

After the Cups – FA, Cup-winners and World – this was the first season for some time that Hammers fans had nothing to congratulate themselves about. Something had gone. The magic had died. Perhaps the 'Allison effect' had finally worn off. Maybe Budgie's injury, sustained in the service of his country against the Scots, had robbed West Ham of too much.

One former player reflected: "Probably we just didn't have enough players of the very top quality to last the whole season. We had lost Byrne, Alan Sealey, Ken Brown, John Bond and, at the end of the season, Jim Standen, who had been past his best for most of the season. The great side was breaking up. We relied far too much on the World Cup men, in the belief that they could do it on their own."

Added to this, Bobby Moore had been unsettled for some time. There had been problems registering him for the World Cup as he had refused to sign a contract at West Ham following the 1965-66 season. None of these excuses were good enough, though. West Ham had literally been at the top of the world and somehow the administration and management of the club could not handle this. The achievement and ambition of the players and the supporters had outgrown the managerial structures that surrounded them.

In European football it had been a good year for Britain and, in particular, Scotland. Leeds had got to the Final of the Fairs Cup, to be beaten by Dynamo

Zagreb. Rangers had got to the Cup-winners' Cup Final. But Jock Stein's Celtic, an all-Scottish side, beat an international select in the shape of Inter-Milan in Lisbon, to become the first British side to win the premier European trophy, the European Champions Cup.

Mazzola put Inter ahead with a penalty after only seven minutes. Then Bertie Auld and Tommy Gemmill hit the bar before Gemmill scored with a 20-yard drive in the 63rd minute. With five minutes to go before extra-time would have to be played, Bobby Murdoch drove in a shot that cannoned in off of Steve Chalmers. Thus the 'Lions of Lisbon' were born.

Under Stein, Celtic built on this, something Greenwood and West Ham did not do. The following decades would punish the East London club harshly for this tardiness.

# 1967-68

THE late 1960s would see an epidemic of world conflicts, including the Six-Day War in the Middle East, civil war in Nigeria over secessionist Biafra, the invasion of Czechoslovakia by the Soviet Union and of Cambodia by the forces of the United States and South Vietnam. Northern Ireland would experience its first civil rights demonstrations, while a wave of student protests would engulf many of the universities and cities of western Europe. Individuals became bywords of violence, whether as victims of perpetrators: Martin Luther King and Senator Robert Kennedy were assassinated; Lt. William Calley would be prosecuted for his part in the massacre of Vietnamese peasants in the village of My Lai.

The news from the Boleyn Ground was not quite so dramatic at the start of the 1967-68 season. John Cushley, Bobby Ferguson and Billy Bonds, the three newcomers, played in the first game at Upton Park, which Sheffield Wednesday won. A meagre three points were gained from the first six games, which included a 5-1 defeat at White Hart Lane. West Ham held out until nine minutes from half-time when Jimmy Greaves got away from John Charles. Three minutes later Jones put Spurs two up with his head, a goal which was followed by a minor pitch invasion. Greenwood played Peters at full-back in this game but after Alan Mullery scored about halfway through the second half and a 76th-minute Greaves penalty, following a Bonds tackle, it was obvious that Greenwood 's plan had fallen in on itself. A goal by Saul a minute later confirmed this fact. Sissons got a consolation goal for the Hammers ten minutes before time.

Spurs were out of Europe in the second round of the Cup-winners' Cup. They had done well to see off Hadjuk Split in the first round, but they were eliminated on the away goals rule against Olympic Lyon. Holders Bayern lasted until the semi-finals, but there they were beaten 2-0 on aggregate by AC Milan. The Italians, who had gained earlier success in the Champions Cup, had a happy first entry to the Cup-winners' Cup. In round one they had accounted for Levski (Bulgaria) 6-1, then went through on the away goals rule against the Hungarians of Vasas Gyor after a 3-3 tie. In the quarter-finals, Standard Liege forced them into a play-off before Milan emerged 4-2 winners overall.

For the fourth successive year a German side reached the Final. This time it was SV Hamburg. They had beaten the Danish Cup winners, Randers Freja, Wislaw of Poland, Olympic Lyon (conquerors of Spurs) after a play-off, and the gallant Welshmen of Cardiff City in the semi-finals. Cardiff's finest hour had been in the quarter-finals where, with five reserves in their side, they defeated Moscow Torpedo 1-0 in a play-off in Augsburg. Hamburg, however, beat them 3-2 in Cardiff after a 1-1 draw in Germany.

The Final at Rotterdam proved considerably easier for Milan than many of their earlier matches, and their two-goal win from a Kurre Hamrin first-half double did not sufficiently reflect their superiority over Hamburg.

Trevor Brooking made his debut for the Hammers in the 3-3 draw at Turf Moor. Bobby Moore cleared off the line twice, after scoring just ten minutes into the game.

At Roker Park in September, the Hammers got a 5-1 win and Bobby Moore scored for each side. When he turned in a cross past Ferguson, it looked like the home side's Roker Park unbeaten record was safe. Then Peters scored the first of three goals in three minutes and Redknapp and Moore each fired in from 30 yards. This was followed by another 5-1 victory in the League Cup at Walsall, a result which equalled West Ham's record for an away win in this competition and seemed to spark a temporary revival for the club.

Having looked good in winning 5-0 against Third Division Walsall, and Geoff Hurst getting all four goals in a 4-1 victory over Bolton (which brought Hurst's tally in this competition to 25 in five years), West Ham went out of the League Cup in the fourth round, losing 2-0 to Huddersfield from the depths of the Second Division. Ferguson had a poor game as the Yorkshiremen eased past the Hammers.

At Upton Park in mid-November, 19-year-old Frank Lampard was drafted into the first team to face Manchester City, the eventual League champions, but Francis Lee and Tony Coleman ran him ragged as Lee scored twice in City's 3-2 win, which left West Ham with the worst home record in the entire Football League.

By the day before Christmas Eve, the Hammers were still in the lower reaches of the table. Then maximum points were taken from three games, as Spurs were beaten and Brian Dear netted five times in two games against Leicester City. At one point, Geoff Hurst was the division's joint top-scorer with Peter Lorimer of Leeds United.

In February, against the team which would finish bottom of the table that season, West Ham knocked in five goals in 22 minutes to win 7-2 after Bobby Robson's Fulham had scored first. In the same month, two goals in the last ten minutes helped the Irons to a 3-0 FA Cup win at Stoke.

Like the League Cup, the FA Cup also gave West Ham just three games. Good away wins against First Division opponents Burnley (3-1) and Stoke (3-0) gave them a deal of hope. As such, watching them being booted out in the fifth round by Sheffield United at home was particularly horrible. In the end Bobby Moore found himself playing centre-forward. The Blades manager, John Harris, said afterwards: "We love playing West Ham." Of course, that helped tremendously, but not as much as them getting relegated along with Fulham at the end of the season.

This unexpected Cup embarrassment at Upton Park saw West Ham lose confidence and sink to within a point of 21st place in the table before wins over Newcastle United – Brooking got a hat-trick in the 5-0 home victory against the Magpies – Forest and Liverpool recovered the situation.

West Ham finished an indifferent season with a lack-lustre draw with FA Cup Finalists Everton at Upton Park. The Toffees had rested Alan Ball, Joe

Royle, Brian Labone, Ray Wilson and goalkeeper Gordon West. If the Hammers had won the match they would have at least finished in the top half of the First Division. As it was they ended in 12th place, five points clear of relegation. It was clear that the dreams and hopes which the fans had carried for West Ham a couple of years earlier, had collapsed.

Geoff Hurst was top scorer with the decent tally of 25 goals, which made him the club's top marksman for the third year on the trot. Bobby Moore won the Hammer of the Year award for the third time.

West Ham supporters again had to look to the England team for some consolation as Moore captained his country to the top of their all-British group in the European Nations Cup and Hurst and Peters lined up with him in all the group games when the Home International Championship doubled as European qualifying games. Hurst had been top marksman in the group with four goals, Peters had bagged a couple. Peters scored in the 2-1 quarter-final second-leg win in Madrid. Peters and Moore had also been in the team that had defeated the Spanish 1-0 at Wembley in the first leg.

Many West Ham fans wondered aloud whether their three England players were saving their very best for their country. This attitude was understandable; after all, West Ham seemed to be going nowhere. Indicative of this situation was that one of the best games the Hammers played all season was when Alf Ramsey was at Upton Park. Against Liverpool in April, Moore and Peters were on top form, and even though Hurst was unfit, he played in midfield and still managed to force Tommy Lawrence into the save of the match before Peters ran in on the blind side to head home Harry Redknapp's centre. The 1-0 defeat at the hands of the Irons put an end to Liverpool's title hopes; they finished in third place, just three points behind the champions, 17 points clear of West Ham.

But as far as the hard core of supporters are concerned, the club is more than its results, and more even than those who play the games. It is as much about what they have inside them. Supporter Joe illustrates this with the memory of an away match: "I was one of the few West Ham supporters at Stoke in the League. I knew most of the others by name. It was the arse end of February 1968. I was standing with the lowest number of people to watch the Irons that season, just over 16,000. Terry Conroy reached up and grabbed the ball inside the box, the referee gave a free-kick to the Irons …outside the box. Two quick goals sunk us. Cushley's miscued pass went to Eastham, who always did well against West Ham. He turned the ball to Dobing who buried it. Mahoney got the second with a tasty volley just a minute later. We gave our support. Bobby gave us an apologetic thumbs-up as he left the field. This kind of stuff isn't easy. It takes loyalty, patience, endurance, yes, even love."

Leeds went one better than their performance in Europe the previous season. They won the Fairs Cup, beating the experienced Hungarians, Ferencvaros, by a single goal over two legs. Celtic were unable to win the World Club Championship, though, losing out to the Argentineans of Racing Club.

Manchester United became the second British and first English club to win the European Cup, beating Benfica 4-1. Like Tottenham's team which won the Cup-winners' Cup in 1963, they were very much a British team. George Best, the young Northern Ireland international, was United's star turn. He was to become the European Footballer of the Year in 1968. His team-mate Bobby Charlton was runner-up.

# 1968-69

BEFORE the start of the season, Moore and Peters had faced Yugoslavia in the European Nations Cup semi-final in Florence. They were unlucky to have lost 1-0 in a game which saw Alan Mullery the first player ever to be sent-off playing for England in a full international. On the domestic front, Alan Stephenson, who was signed from Crystal Palace for a big fee in March 1968, was at the centre of the defence for the first game of the season, at St James's Park. Hammer-to-be Pop Robson put the Geordies ahead but Brian Dear saved a point in the last minute of injury time. Peters miscued Harry Redknapp's low cross against the post and Dear snapped up the rebound. This result was not unexpected since West Ham had won only once in 36 tries up there – something about 'the law of averages'. A win in the Potteries and a home victory against Forest meant the season had started well enough, and the next two games saw the Hammers lose 4-1 to Everton at Upton Park but beat Coventry 2-1 at Highfield Road.

At the end of August, the FA Cup holders, West Bromwich Albion, visited the Boleyn Ground. West Ham had beaten Burnley 5-0 at Upton Park the previous week. The referee had been knocked out in that game and had to be replaced by an off-duty League official plucked from the crowd. He must have been an Irons fan as he ignored Brooking being an age offside and gave the fourth goal at the end of the first half. With this victory still fresh in the memory, the fans felt a decent match was in prospect against West Brom. And so it was. Martin Peters got a hat-trick, giving him a personal total of seven goals in seven games. Hurst outshone Jeff Astle, the man eyeing up his place in the England team. The other goal came from Harry Redknapp. West Ham had won three games in a row, scoring 11 and conceding only one. They sat proudly on top of Division One.

West Brom, meanwhile, held their own in the Cup-winners' Cup. Two good games against Club Brugge saw the Baggies get through on away goals. This was followed by a 5-1 aggregate win against Dinamo Bucuresti. In the last eight they were drawn against the Scottish Cup winners, Dunfermline.

The League Cup provided a nine-goal extravaganza at Upton Park when the Hammers defeated Second Division Bolton, 7-2. Hurst, who had scored all four in the previous season's League Cup defeat of Bolton, added three more. Nat Lofthouse, Bolton's caretaker manager, said that the Irons were 'magnificent'.

The Irons' run in the League continued with five draws which included one at Old Trafford and another at Stamford Bridge. So that was only one defeat in a dozen outings.

In the next round of the League Cup, Coventry City earned themselves a replay at Upton Park. Bill Glazier, the Sky Blues' 'keeper, made a terrific effort to deny Redknapp's volley and brought off three fantastic saves from Moore, who had been pushed forward. At Highfield Road there was a riotous end to the first half. Ernie Hunt shoved John Charles in the back and scored in the confusion. Seconds later, John Tudor was given a goal that was yards offside. And on the stroke of half-time, just a minute after Coventry's second goal, Geoff Hurst volleyed powerfully home. The Midlanders grabbed a third, eight minutes after the restart, and although Peters snatched a second for West Ham in the dying minutes, it was Coventry who went through to meet Swindon Town.

West Ham's collective head went down a little after this and their unbeaten away sequence and general good League run ended with a visit to Turf Moor on 8 October 1968. Burnley, being weighed down by injuries, put out their youngest side ever to face West Ham and the result was the Hammers' first away defeat of the season. John Murray got his first-ever first-team goal and the first of the thirsty Clarets' three that day. Steve Kindon made his debut for them and the speedy, former rugby wing-threequarter scored and tormented West Ham all afternoon. Brooking made the Hammers' inadequate reply on the hour, but by then Dobson had put the game beyond the reach of the shell-shocked Irons.

Elland Road then beckoned and Harry Redknapp became only the second Hammer to be sent-off since the arrival of Ron Greenwood. Bremner had hurt Harry, so 'Aitch' went after him. The little Scot's swallow dive resulted in Giles getting the second for the eventual champions. The Irons had no reply.

In the next League outing, Geoff Hurst hit the jackpot with six splendid goals against Sunderland. Hurst broke the club record for goals in one game during a match that had looked like being a bit of an average affair. But Geoff claimed a hat-trick in each half.

Not 20 minutes of the match had ticked by before Hurst got his first, banging in a Martin Peters centre. Later he confessed to punching the ball over the line. Under five minutes later, Bobby Moore scored the first of his two goals for the season. Charlie Hurley conceded the free-kick and Moore made it pay. That was 20 goals in a decade. But they were nearly all worth waiting for.

Around a half-hour had gone by when Hurst doubled his account. A nice back-post header. A bit before the break he put away a Redknapp corner.

A neat interchange involving Sissons, Trevor Brooking and Peters led to the fourth Hurst goal. Under 15 minutes later it was 6-0 to West Ham and five to Geoff. Brooking sliced through the Rokermen's defence for the seventh. Less than a minute later, Trevor latched on to a feeble effort from Herd. He sent it to Redknapp who made the cross for Hurst to claim his half-dozen

This result sparked a deal of optimism at Upton Park. By October, the Hammers had won only five of their first 14 games. They were without a victory in seven games. It's funny how a pretty impressive record can so quickly turn around.

Ironically, Montgomery, the Sunderland goalkeeper, had a good game. Without him West Ham would have notched up a cricket score. A couple of months after their mauling at the Boleyn Ground, Sunderland beat the Hammers by the odd goal of three at Roker Park.

November saw the opening of the new East Terrace at Upton Park, and two months later, the seating area was in use for the third-round FA Cup tie against Bristol City. The whole complex replaced the wooden terracing, affectionately known as the 'Chicken Run', which had stood since the club's very early days at the Boleyn Ground. Its passing caused many a nostalgic tear.

West Ham won only three of the ten games between the slaughter of Sunderland and the New Year. Doris remembers one bright spot: "I saw the 4-3 home win over Queen's Park Rangers on the telly. All the other Division One games put together produced only two more goals than this one. Rangers were 3-1 down at one stage, but got back to 3-3. Old Les Allen was a real pain to our defence, but in the end the best goal of the game, a volley by Harry, did for them."

The best performance of that period was a 4-0 home win against Leicester. Woollett knocked in a Hurst centre to open the scoring with an own-goal. Brian Dear, recalled on his eighth anniversary as a West Ham professional, marked the occasion with a couple of goals, one either side of an effort by Martin Peters. 'Stag' had now put seven past Peter Shilton, their goalkeeper, in three games.

Thirty-two thousand saw West Ham's Cup match against Bristol City. It was the first-ever Cup meeting between the sides, although West Ham had played an FA Cup first-round second replay against Swansea at Aston Gate in 1922. Moore smashed the ball into the face of a trombonist before the game, accidentally of course. In the tenth minute, Galley put City, who were 20th in Division Two at the time, in front. Martin Peters equalised with a devastating downward header that went through a defender's legs. Then Martin got number two in the second half and Hurst made it three for the Hammers, who went through 3-2 after a last-minute goal by Skirton. Following a two-goal victory in the fourth-round, at Leeds Road against Second Division

Huddersfield Town, West Ham were drawn against Third Division Mansfield Town, the game was to be played at Field Mill on 8 February.

The day was a disaster for football as severe weather conditions curtailed the entire Cup programme of eight games, plus all but four League fixtures. After a series of postponements, the tie finally got under way on 26 February, when the Stags won 3-0.

The first League win of the New Year came at the beginning of March, at the Boleyn Ground, when the visitors were Newcastle. West Ham managed to pull themselves together after the debacle in the Cup. Brooking scored after just two minutes. Peters got number two, stabbing home a Redknapp cross, and Hurst netted the third just after Newcastle had got back into the game when a 45-yard cross from Welsh international Ron Davies floated in over Ferguson's head; another joke goal to add to the growing portfolio of the Scotsman signed by Greenwood in preference to arguably the greatest goal-keeper ever.

Wins against Forest, away, and Coventry, at Upton Park, gave the Hammers another three-game run of victories. A bad 3-1 defeat at the hands of Ipswich in front of nearly 33,000 Hammers fans, was followed by the last win of the season. Wolves arrived at the Boleyn with a reputation for hard play. They lived up to it, conceding 24 free-kicks, two of which produced goals for the Hammers. Peters headed the first from Moore's chip. A blunder by goal-keeper Parkes gave West Ham their second when he dropped Brooking's shot over the line before Peters got his second and West Ham's third in the 63rd minute. The final results of the term gave the Hammers five draws and saw them beaten four times.

In the Cup-winners' Cup, like the European Cup of that year, there had to be a re-draw of the first round to keep the Eastern European and Western countries apart. This resulted in the withdrawal of some of the communist countries. Justice was perhaps done. The dispute had arisen because of the invasion of Czechoslovakia by the Soviet Union, and in the event it was a Czech side, Slovan Bratislava, who emerged as winners.

Bratislava started slowly by beating the unknown Yugoslavian side, Bor, 3-2, but looked a better team when they accounted for Porto 4-1. Torino were their quarter-final victims, 1-0 and 2-1. In the semi-finals they drew 1-1 in

Scotland against Dunfermline and won 1-0 at home. Dunfermline had beaten West Brom in the quarter-finals, holding them to goalless draw at home and winning 1-0 away.

Barcelona, experienced campaigners in Europe, ploughed through Lugano (Switzerland) 4-0, the Norwegians of Lyn Oslo, luckily, 5-4 (playing both legs at home because of the conditions in Norway) and 1FC Cologne were beaten 6-3. This lined up the Final in Berne with Slovan.

The Czechs were off to a fine start with a goal from Cvetler in the second minute. Further goals from full-back Hrivnak and winger Jan Capkovic, answered only by a single from Zaldua for Barcelona, put Slovan well on the road to success. Although Rexach added a second for the Spaniards, direct from a corner, their destiny was to lose another European Final – on the same soil where their hopes had faded eight years earlier against Benfica in the Champions Cup.

Newcastle kept up the English domination of the Fairs Cup, like Leeds beating a Hungarian team, this time Ujpest Dozsa, over the two-legged Final.

West Ham finished eighth in the First Division. Their 50 goals against was the club's best defensive record since 1923-24. They had earned ten draws away from home, and 18 all together, both totals being records for the club. Hurst finished the season as leading scorer yet again, with 31 goals, and was voted Hammer of the Year again. Martin Peters was the next highest marksman with 21. Neither of these two missed a game all season.

# 1969-70

THE final game of the 1960s saw Bobby Moore's 387th appearance – a post-war record for a West Ham player. The Hammers should have made sure of two points in the first half, but too many chances went begging and in the end they were lucky to get a 1-1 draw with Forest, the team that had put them out of the League Cup in the third round the previous September. In 27 League games before the New Year, West Ham won only seven and suffered 13 defeats, four of them at home.

The end of a decade of support. Hundreds of times I had waited on the score, mostly in a mixture of dread and anticipation. Why? West Ham have filled all the crevices in my life. I have been all round the world. Nothing has been constant. Yet, at the heart of it all has been the Hammers. The fickle, strange, mad entity that haunts my winter days and for whom I long throughout the summer.

So often my devotion has been unrequited. Many times I have hated my care for those who make a habit of disappointing and frustrating the likes of me, who spend so much in the way of money, emotion and sentiment on them. West Ham have always been in me, my mind and my soul have corners that are forever theirs. If I am anything, I am West Ham. All I have been cannot be more than this.

The first four months of 1970 saw one-quarter of the world's states engaged in armed force in one way or another. Just before the World Cup opened, four students were shot dead by National Guardsmen during campus riots at Ohio State University in the USA.

But man had walked on the moon, Concorde had made its maiden flight, colour television had arrived in Britain, Dr Christian Barnard had performed the world's first heart-transplant operation, and early in 1970, the discovery of oil and gas reserves off the coast of Scotland looked like saving Britain's flagging economy. Other 'good' news included the availability of male vasectomy on the National Health, and Richard Nixon had been elected as the new president of the United States.

An American oil company paid £2.4 million for London Bridge, took it apart and rebuilt it over the Colorado River, only to find out that they had bought the wrong bridge. They thought they were getting Tower Bridge. The old halfpenny was taken out of circulation and the seven-sided 50p piece was born as the first decimal coin. The consternation and hiatus this caused could only have happened in Britain. The death sentence was abolished as the breathalyser was brought in. The future of international cricket was threatened when South Africa declined to accept a visiting England team because, Basil D'Oliveira, a 'coloured' player, was included.

The West Ham record in the past decade as follows:

**League**

| Played | Won | Drawn | Lost | For | Against |
|---|---|---|---|---|---|
| 425 | 153 | 103 | 167 | 725 | 760 |

**Cups**

| 89 | 32 | 14 | 33 | 132 | 96 |
|---|---|---|---|---|---|

**Overall**

| 514 | 185 | 117 | 200 | 857 | 856 |
|---|---|---|---|---|---|

It's surprising how right this looks. Not one thing or the other really.

We were all English at one time, mostly London, mainly East London. By the end of the 1969-70 season, West Ham had a Welsh lad, a few Scots and the mighty Clyde Best from Bermuda. Stephenson and Bennett, were country boys and Eustace was a Tyke. Still, the bulk of the side were locals: Billy Bonds (Woolwich), John Charles (Canning Town), Martin Peters (Plaistow), Jimmy Greaves and Bobby Moore (Dagenham), Pat Holland and Harry Redknapp (Poplar), Paul Heffer (Upton Park), Peter Grotier (Stratford), Roger Cross, Frank Lampard and Ronnie Boyce (East Ham), Trevor Brooking (Barking). Sissons and Miller were both Londoners while Geoff Hurst was brought up in Barking.

Today, the picture is just a little different, but West Ham is still an East London club. If you go to Chadwell Heath, the West Ham training ground, Dave, the car park attendant, will tell you of the Hammers manager, Harry Redknapp: "'E's got time for everyone has 'Arry, no matter who or what."

Harry, the grandson of a bookie's runner, says: "I talk to all of them punters out there, everyday. It's their club. It's not my club. It's not the chairman's club. This club belongs to the punters. It belongs to the people. Big Dave looks after the car park …You've got to have people talking from the same level. I'm from the East End. So the punters feel they can say: 'What the 'ell's 'appening 'Arry?' to me. There's a very selfish attitude in football. Chairmen are not concerned about the whole of football. They've no real understanding of people who support their game. They're not in touch with the real punter. They see it as only making money for their club, pushing their shares up. They're on a different planet."

While Harry was still not having too much concern about signing foreign players at the start of the 1998-99 season, bringing in Chilean defender Javier Margas and Marc Keller from France, he saw this as being related to the financial rewards now dictating the situation: "Wages have gone crazy. People like Bobby Moore went out of the game with nothing. In his day, players stayed at one club for years. Now they've all got agents who get them more money, so the agent cops more. The punters don't care where they come from – Outer Mongolia for all they care. But it don't matter as long as these imports bring them success. Still I'd love it if every player was homegrown, but that's not the reality is it?"

However, Harry is not so phlegmatic about foreign coaches: "I talk to everybody who wants to talk to me about the club. You're not going to get that with foreign coaches are you? Apart from Wenger, the Premiership has only been won by British managers. It's all about having decent players. I don't care where you come from, you can't turn bad players into good."

For Harry, English players will come through, but they will not be 'pampered'. According to Harry, players who 'get above their station' at Upton Park get 'pulled down to earth'. At West Ham, it's 'punters before profit'. A few years ago, when West Ham were near the foot of the League, Harry was angry when he discovered his players were having a Christmas booze up: "I couldn't believe where their front was. They're going to get on an open-deck bus and go through the streets passing the blokes who work all day for a living. If I was them, I'd wanna hide."

As such, there is still some respect and loyalty towards the roots of West Ham as a club.

The best day in the claret and blue chronicles stays with me; another corner of my obsession. Every year I study the goings on in the European Cup-winners' Cup. For me, it is West Ham's cup. The winners, each year, hold on to it until the Hammers can again campaign for it. Like Arthur, we wait in slumber until the day comes when we are needed to dignify and colour the football landscape of Europe. As when Alan Sealey painted the sky above Wembley in hope and glory.

But Alan didn't consider his display against Munich as a career best. Indeed, he commented: "I played quite ordinarily that night." Instead, he cited his best performance as the contribution to a 1-1 draw with Burnley at Upton Park on 7 October 1963: "I was great that night. Never a bad ball all the game …I scored the equaliser …it went right for me. It was an all-round performance and I will never forget the satisfaction I felt. You remember a few good games in your career above the rest. This match against Burnley was exceptional to me. That night it was a dream – all my mates tell me that was my best game."

That Monday night, Alan did rip the Lancastrian defence apart with a display of wing-craft rarely seen now. He scored West Ham's equalising goal with a shot from 20 yards out. It was after this game that he overheard Ron Greenwood discussing his contribution on the telephone. Ron had told Walter Winterbottom, the former England manager, that Alan had put on the best display of running off the ball that he had ever seen.

In 1969, England's Cup-winners' Cup representatives, Manchester City, came to the East End early in December. Alf Ramsey watched his World Cup trio have a collective nightmare at Upton Park, while Francis Lee and Colin Bell tore the Hammers apart. Bobby Ferguson, fast becoming an East London legend, helped City along with each of their four goals. Although West Ham did put a number of attacks together, they got nothing from City who played so well as a defensive unit whenever the Irons came forward.

How, in the latter half of the 1960s, we could have done with the Alan Sealey of that Burnley game in 1963. Following the euphoria of the 1965 Cup-winners' Cup win, which meant that West Ham, as holders, would play in the tournament in the 1965-66 season, with a bye in the first round, fate was not kind to Alan. Injury kept him out for most of the new campaign, and he played just four more League games for West Ham in the 1966-67 season. As Bill Lansdowne senior lamented: "The injury was to end such a bright career. I was in charge of the 'A' team when Alan was trying to make his comeback. It was heartbreaking to watch him have to battle to get fit."

But in the couple of the tour games he played in, one of them was, ironically, against Munich. The Irons won the match and the Hammers took the United Nations Trophy for Fair Play at the same time. As Alan pointed out: "West Ham players don't kick the opposition."

Sealey eventually left the Hammers for Plymouth for a fee of £8,000. He played just four games for Argyle. He said that the set-up at Plymouth was not what he was used to. He felt let down over a house, but it was not a good time for him overall; his father had died around that time and this didn't help things. Plymouth were in Devon and in relegation trouble, Alan was in London trying to take over his father's business interests. It simply couldn't work.

At the age of 28, Alan was playing part-time with Southern League Romford FC and running the family business, supplying information to betting shops. However, he seemed happy and was getting a decent living.

How did Alan rate as a player? Ron Greenwood said: "Alan was a good footballer, a team player."

Eddie Presland knew Alan as a player as well as anybody: "I think the first game of football I played against Alan was for West Ham colts. He was playing for Fairbairn House Boys' Club …He was a cute player. He knew when a tackle was coming in and would be able to skip over it, a bit like Harry Redknapp. This gave him a bit of a reputation among the supporters for being frightened, but there's a difference between being frightened and being clever. Who wants to get clogged? Alan was a good player. He was very fast and probably underrated."

Martin Britt, former England youth International and centre-forward, who was with West Ham between 1963 and 1965, confirms Presland's analysis: "Alan had a strong right foot and a fine turn of speed. At one point the fans seemed to think that Alan was none too brave, but this was not the case."

Midfield maestro of the 1960s Cup-winning sides, Ronnie Boyce: "My very first recollection of playing in the same side as Alan was when we were both in the reserves. He scored from the by-line. We never got to see the best of Alan. He was a good crosser of the ball and could pass well."

Defender Ken Brown concluded: "Alan was a player with pace and a powerful shot."

Ron Penn, Alan's good friend of many years standing, backs this up: "Alan certainly had a powerful shot."

For full-back Joe Kirkup: "Alan Sealey will always remain for me one of the core of good club professionals who served West Ham well, alongside the stars like Bobby, Martin, Geoff and Budgie. I thought Jimmy Greaves summed him up pretty well after the funeral when he said: 'Alan was never the best footballer in the world, but it is a measure of the man that ALL of his team-mates were at his funeral to say their farewells to a good friend.'"

Eddie Baily: "Alan, as a player, could have done with that bit extra, but he scored his goals at Wembley and I think he achieved his best. Alan was a very talented young man, quick-witted, cocky and artful. He worked hard."

Brian Dear: "Sammy was quick and was a good, natural sportsman; he was gifted, but needed to be pushed."

But, former player, assistant manager and finally manager of the club, John Lyall saw Alan as: "…a good player, able to play the ball early, like Pop Robson later on. He could finish and volley the ball well. This skill, to use the ball early, the ability to picture in his mind where he wanted the ball to go, meant that he was comfortable working alongside players of the class of Hurst, Byrne, Peters and Moore. They could anticipate where Alan was going to send the ball."

Ernie Gregory told: "Reg Pratt sent me to look at Alan down at Orient. Straight away I was impressed by his speed and the way he could stand on the ball and hit it, he didn't need any back lift. He just hit it from standing."

He went on to describe Alan's first goal at Wembley as "an example of this skill" and continued: "He was an intelligent player, with pace and could dribble a ball tight to him. He knew the game and could shoot from any angle."

Bobby Howe, who was with the Hammers as a player throughout most of the 1960s up to the early 1970s and is now Director of Coaching Education for US Soccer in Chicago, saw Alan "epitomising the flair and style of West Ham on and off the field; his outstanding shooting ability excited the fans during games".

Alan Dickie, who was constant cover for Jim Stanton in the victorious Cup-winners' Cup campaign concluded: "As a player Alan was not a schemer. He came to Upton Park as a centre-forward, but played a lot on the sides. He gave John Dick, who had a great left foot, some decent service and got in plenty of good crosses for Geoff Hurst."

He testified to Alan's courage: "We were playing in Europe, in a bleak, freezing cold stadium. Alan got injured and had to be brought off. We were all sitting on the touch-line, so I could see that part of his shin bone had come through the skin. Alan was shaking. I couldn't believe what I was hearing when Bill Jenkins, our physiotherapist, told Alan not to worry and that he was going to send him back on."

There is no doubt in the mind of Johnny Byrne: "Sammy's footballing prowess was proven beyond all doubt when in the European Cup-winners' Cup Final against Munich he bagged both of our goals. With much bigger names on the field that night at Wembley, he proved that he could write his name in the record books."

But perhaps Jack Burkett, who played in both the FA Cup and Cup-winners' Cup winning sides, and who is currently working with the PFA Youth Training Scheme, gave the most telling analysis of Alan as a player: "One of the things we used to do in training was have the defenders playing the forwards. Alan would mark me and I would have to try to beat him. All I can say is that I was glad that I didn't have to play against him every week. When Peter Brabrook defended, he would try to get the better of you with a clever move or trick, but Alan would come at you with his pace.

"I don't think Alan reached his full potential as a player. We all had to fight for our place and he had to compete with Peter Brabrook a lot of the time, and then there was the injury, after which he was never the same player.

"As a player, Alan was unpredictable and this, together with his speed, meant that he could score and make goals off the line. Maybe he should have been an out-and-out front man.

"If you had to pick someone to be on your side in the trenches, Alan would be your man. As I say, he was a fast runner. I was lucky enough to be fairly speedy myself, but Alan would always be looking to help and motivate those who were not blessed with the same gifts. He'd encourage others along, even running backwards alongside them to assist them."

In the 14 games up to West Ham's next meeting with Manchester City in mid-March 1970, they notched up only two wins. One of their eight defeats was at the hands of Second Division Middlesbrough in the third round of the FA Cup. Three marginal offside decisions were given against the Hammers. The 'Boro were happy to make use of a spoiling strategy. In the second half, both Moore and Billy Bonds were booked.

Almost spring at Maine Road, and West Ham went looking for revenge. Martin Peters was no longer with the club, and City had both Bell and Summerbee missing. Jimmy Greaves, who came to West Ham with £200,000 when Peters moved to Spurs, scored two typically nonchalant goals in the first half. Ronnie Boyce sent a brilliant shot from the centre of the park, beating Joe Corrigan for a goal which was sandwiched between two Hurst efforts.

Backwards and forwards we swing. From the ridiculous to the sublime. This is our culture, be it 1960 or 1970. West Ham are the chameleons of the game.

In Europe, Manchester City saved their best for Maine Road. They had to play the first leg of every round away from home, and managed only one win in four matches abroad. But once they had got their opponents back to Manchester, it was a different story with four victories and 14 goals. City twice hit five, the most notable time being their 5-1 victory over Schalke in the semi-finals after a 1-0 setback in West Germany. With their indifferent away form, the omens might not have appeared too good for their trip to Vienna to play the Polish side, Gornik, in the Final. However, Lee, as so often, was irrepressible. In tandem with Neil Young he was responsible for both goals. The first came early in the match when Lee's shot hit a post and Young scored from the rebound. Then just before half-time, Young was brought down by the Polish goalkeeper and Lee converted the penalty.

Gornik scored a consolation goal in the second half but that was not going to stop City collecting their fourth trophy in three years. They were the first British side since West Ham to win this tournament and only the third in its history.

West Ham ended the 1969-70 season in 17th place with a total of 36 points making for their lowest tally since returning to the top flight ten years earlier. Bobby Moore was top Hammer again. Geoff Hurst got just 18 goals, but this made him top scorer for the fifth time running, albeit it with his lowest haul in that time.

It was the end of ten years of football. Again, West Ham had won no silver, but they had won a few games and the gold of our hearts. That is the glory of the Irons; we can never actually be defeated, even when we lose we win. Even if we were relegated, we would rejoice in being 'us'. We'll be back. First Division,

Southern League. We are still here. Come to Upton Park. Blow Bubbles, be a Hammer, celebrate with the Irons. At the Boleyn you will hear fans roar. You will see people involved in creating identity.

We, at Upton Park will continue to support. It may take another ten years, it may take 100 years, but when we next win that cup, when we finally take the title, it will be all the sweeter. We will take part in a *relationship*; a growthful, developmental, challenging, *two way thing*. At the home of the Hammers, more than a century of passionate and loving support has been given by hundreds of thousands of people, generation after generation of mainly working class folk, many of whom have used the game as a source of hope and happiness within lives often dominated by poverty. There is something humane in this support. It is likely that it is a manifestation of some deep human needs, based on the collectiveness and connectiveness that we have come to call 'community'. Certainly, if support had no basis in our humanity, it would probably not exist.

The existence of West Ham United, and football in general, is based on a partnership between players and supporters. The product is 'the club'. It is really as simple as that. What the supporter hopes for from his or her affiliation is an essentially benign warm, inter-supportive conjoining. This association takes place within a boundary that is the area from which the team borrows its name. The conjunction between supporter and team is an exercise in mutuality, and involves confirmation of identity. At its root it is kindness and care, and Alan Sealey was well endowed with such qualities, as Alan Dickie testified: "Alan played in my first-team debut. We were up at Bolton [West Ham had played three different 'keepers in three games]. The match was being played on a Saturday evening, due to an illness scare up there. I was really overawed by the journey up, in a first-class carriage, eating on a Pullman. Bolton won the game 1-0. I was denied a clean sheet in the last minute when Wyn Davies forced Martin Peters into an error and Holden's 25-yard drive flew in off the post. Mind you, that was at about 9.20pm, the game should have been finished at around 9.10pm. After the match, the great Nat Lofthouse was asking players to sign a ball. I was shocked when Alan called out, 'What about our goalkeeper?' I was speechless when Lofthouse approached me. 'The Lion of Vienna' was asking for my autograph!"

And Trevor Hartley recalls: "My earliest and most pleasing memory of Alan was when I took my first steps into the Chadwell Heath training ground as a young professional footballer, in preparation for the 1964-65 season. Obviously, senior players were split from us youngsters and enjoyed the 'senior' dressing-room. However, on that first morning Alan and Bobby Moore were the first senior players to seek me out and wish me every success at the club. That greeting certainly settled me down and gave me a good indication of how friendly the club was."

Jack Burkett relates that: "I was good friends with Harry Cripps, who, like Bobby and Alan, passed on before his time. Harry and Alan were similar in that they would do anything for you, even if it meant they had to sacrifice their time. I saw Alan shortly before he died. He didn't show his problem, he carried it well. I think that's an example of how much he considered the feelings of others. If you had a daughter you would be happy with Alan as a son-in law."

Ron Penn remembered how consistent Alan was in terms of his concern for others: "There were no flowers at the funeral. The money that would have gone on flowers was given to charity."

Alan Sealey has no gravestone, no obituary. His ashes were scattered in a garden of remembrance in an East London cemetery. His obituary must be our memory of him. Forever, one of *The First and Last Englishmen.*

In June 1970, the England World Cup squad's single, *Back Home,* was knocked off the top of the music charts by *Yellow River,* by Christie. Unemployment stood at 600,000, thought to be an appalling figure at the time. Industrial strife was turning violent following a two month strike at the Pilkington glass factory. Skinheads and 'greasers' were battling it out in the seaside resorts of the South East, as massive earthquakes were ravaging Peru. South Africa's cricketers had their invitation to tour Britain withdrawn because of their racist selection procedures.

Following England's exit from the 1970 World Cup in Mexico, knocked out by West Germany in the quarter-finals, Bobby Moore, captain of Ramsey's team, the strongest-ever England squad to leave Britain's shores, was runner-up to Gerd Muller, the leading scorer in the World Cup of that year, in the pole for the European Footballer of the Year. It had been two years since an English player had got in the top two and it wouldn't happen again until Kevin Keegan finished runner-up in 1977. There have been only three British and two English players in this position since Bobby.

Brazil won the World Cup, beating Italy (conquerors of West Germany in the last four) 4-1 in the Final. Brazil had been the only team to beat England in their group matches, by a single Jairzinho goal. Moore had played brilliantly, but that's another story (Geoff Hurst and Martin Peters were also in the side, Peters scoring England's second goal in their 3-2 defeat by West Germany, after extra-time).

The final game West Ham played in the 1969-70 season ended in a 2-1 defeat at the hands of Arsenal, the European Fairs Cup winners of that year, at Highbury.

> U N I ...T E D, United are the team for me...
> West Ham United,
> There's only one West Ham United,
> West Ham U-nite-ed,
> There's only one West Ham United.
> Viva Bobby Moore,
> Viva Bobby Moore,
> Viva,
> Viva,
> Viva Bobby Moore,
> Viva.
> Al-lan See-lee, Al-lan See-lee...
> UP THE HAMMERS!
> Guu-on-you-I-ons!

# Tributes

URING Alan Sealey's career at West Ham, 46 other players appeared in the first team. Of these, Brian, Bobby Moore, Jimmy Bloomfield and Ron Brett are no longer with us. Together with Alan they gave 34 seasons to the club. These five players turned out 863 times for the Hammers. Bobby Moore played alongside Alan 97 times. Bobby was a youth International, played eight games for the England Under-23s and, of course, was awarded 108 international caps.

This noble handful of players scored 58 times for West Ham. They are all sadly missed, but they may be making a pretty good five-a-side team somewhere.

Below are some of the tributes paid to Alan by his other colleagues, his friends and ones he loved. They have contributed to this and other parts of *The First and Last Englishmen* from all over Britain, South Africa and the USA. They include many of those who turned out for West Ham in the 1964-65 European Cup-winners' Cup and the FA Cup winning teams. The players who have remembered Alan here, as a group served the Hammers for a total of 181 seasons as players and many more years in management, scouting and coaching capacities. Between them they made 3,653 appearances and the outfield players scored 733 goals. They have played many schoolboy and youth internationals between them. There are four full and five Under-23 England players. As a group they gained 100 senior caps while they were with West Ham. These men represent both those who knew Alan throughout his time with the Irons and those who were with him at the club for just a short while, but all agree that Alan was a good player, a sociable, affable man and a fine human being.

First, their manager, the man who also led England to the final stages of the European Nations Cup and the 1982 World Cup.

## Ron Greenwood

Ron Greenwood was the only manager Alan was to know whilst he was with the Hammers.

At nearly 77 years of age he remains a thoughtful and intelligent assessor of the game and must rate as one of the most successful England managers and one the great footballing minds of the century.

> "Alan was a really bubbly character, a popular young man and a good chap. He was a nice lad."

## Ronnie Boyce

Ron Boyce, who is currently coaching at Millwall, turned out for West Ham 339 times, scoring some incredibly important goals in his tally of 29, including two in the semi-final of the 1964 FA Cup against Manchester United and the winner in the Final. He scored the crucial away goal against La Gantoise in West Ham's first-ever competitive European game and took over from Bobby Moore as skipper when the captain fell ill before the vital away leg of the second round against Spartak Sokolovo.

Ronnie was one of the best West Ham players never to get a full cap for England, although he played schoolboy soccer for East Ham, London, Essex and England and also won youth honours for his country. However, he was called into the Under-23 squad at one point and was on the fringes of Alf Ramsey's plans in the mid-1960s. Perhaps he was unlucky that he was playing at a time when Alan Ball was doing such a great job linking the England midfield and attack.

Geoff Hurst once said of Ron that he was "a players' player – a tremendous worker but people do not appreciate his value to the team". For Ron Greenwood, Boyce was: "In other people's eyes …a most underrated player, but to us he was invaluable. The thing that impressed me most about his play was his ability to do the simple things quickly and effectively." But 'Boycie' could also read the game. In a World Cup match Pele, noticing that the opposing 'keeper was out of his area, nearly scored a goal from near the halfway line. The whole football watching population of the earth eulogised and wondered at the feat. But Ron went one better, scoring from inside his own half in a Division One game in at Maine Road in 1970.

Boyce is a true West Ham man. Although he first saw light in East Ham, his father was born, one of 13 children, in Canning Town. As a boy of about ten I used to sell firewood to his dad, who owned a local shop. Mr Boyce was, like his son, a quiet, reserved man, but he would always give me a 'two bob' tip.

Ron Boyce has been a distinguished servant of West Ham and the game of football. No one better represents the lineage of players at Upton Park that have graced the game with flair and skill. However, Ronnie, with a few others, has also made the world a better place with his loyalty, friendliness, compassion, kindness and most noticeably, his integrity as a human being. His good-mannered, honest, modest and gentlemanly attitude is a credit to his East End roots. He was and remains a prince of the game.

> "Alan was a good bloke. Not a bad bone in his body. No one could have anything but good to say about Alan. It's so sad that he is not with us any more."

## Johnny Byrne

Budgie Byrne, game for game, was comparable to Geoff Hurst as a goalscorer for England and West Ham and better than Vic Watson, West Ham's highest ever goalscorer.

Johnny was *the* star of the West Ham team in the early 1960s. He played ten full internationals for his country, and if not for the injury picked up in a match against Scotland, he would no doubt have made the 1966 World Cup squad. Eight goals came with those ten caps. He got a couple on his international debut against Switzerland, both in a 2-1 victory over Uruguay at Wembley in 1964 and a hat-trick against Portugal in Lisbon the same season, including the 87th-minute winner. Having played for and managed the very successful Durban City for many years, he is now the owner-manager of Santos FC in South Africa.

"I would like to pay my respects to both Alan's first wife, Janice, and second wife, Barbara, who are both fine ladies. Unfortunately, the saddest part about life is that in time we all move on and invariably lose touch with one another. This was the case with Sammy. It was probably due to the fact that I have lived here in South Africa for the last 28 years. I could write no end of stories about him. I do believe that I could tell a million tales about the both of us. Sammy was a great character. Yes, Sammy, you came, you conquered and you went, but you will be remembered in the football records at West Ham forever.

Budgie, Margaret and family"

## Martin Peters MBE

Alan was in the team for Martin's debut game. The last time they appeared together in the same team in competitive game was the final match of the 1966-67 season at Upton Park when the visitors were Manchester City. Peters scored 14 goals in the games in which he played in the same attack as Alan.

Martin is traditionally the last name mentioned when the 'holy trinity' of West Ham is listed: "Moore, Hurst and Peters." But he was the most complete player of the three, probably the best all-round player of his era and maybe any era. Geoff Hurst was a phenomenal goal machine, but he, like Bobby, was a 'made' player. Hard graft and, in Moore's case, active study of the game, made them what they were. Hurst had tremendous physical gifts. Bobby was a footballing genius, blessed with mental agility, foresight, a calm, almost religious insight, and amazing balance. There is little doubt that Bobby became, as Pele had it, 'the best defender in the world.' Few would argue that he could easily wear this crown. Geoff and Bobby became world-class players because of their concentration, focus, dedication and discipline. However, Peters is probably the finest player ever to pull on a West Ham shirt. A footballing aristocrat; a professional of infinite grace, immaculate natural skill and elegant poise. If ever a man made the game a beautiful thing to watch, it was Martin Peters.

"Alan was a good team-mate and a fine person."

## John Sissons

John Sissons played in 265 games for West Ham, netting 53 times. John was in the same first team as Alan on 35 occasions. A schoolboy and Under-23 international, John's contribution to both the FA and European Cup-winners' Cup victories was invaluable in terms of both creating and scoring goals. Sissons was the young artist of these sides, the most pulchritudinous of players to watch; fast, balanced and skilful. He now lives in Cape Town, South Africa.

"I am so pleased you are doing something in memory of Alan Sealey and am proud to be asked to contribute to this tribute to him. He enjoyed life tremendously. We all miss him terribly."

## Ken Brown

Ken Brown, an England International, during his time at the club played 455 games for the first team (he made his debut in February 1953). Ken was present in all but ten of the 128 matches that Alan Sealey played for the Irons. He became a successful manager with Norwich City, winning the League Cup and twice taking the club into the top grade. Now, nearing 70, he is involved in the leisure industry. Ken carries many of the positive traits of his former team-mates; he is a kind, thoughtful and affable man.

"It was tragic how Alan's career ended. Like Bobby, it was terrible that he passed away at such a young age."

## Brian Dear

Brian Dear and Alan Sealey played together in the West Ham first team just 14 times. In those matches Brian scored 11 goals, an average of 0.78 goals per game. In the 85 occasions that Brian turned out for the Irons he netted 39 goals; this amounts to 0.45 goals each match. Alan played in Brian's debut game, a goalless draw at Molineux in 1962.

> "Sam liked a good time. We had some laughs. He was a great bloke."

## John Lyall

John Lyall won England youth honours and would have undoubtedly gone on to a distinguished playing career at West Ham had he not been dogged by injuries. As it was he played just nine games alongside Alan Sealey, but was with the Irons for the whole time Alan was associated with the club

John took over from Ron Greenwood in 1974 and guided the Hammers to FA Cup victory the following year, and the Final of the European Cup-winners' Cup in 1976. In 1980 his team won the FA Cup again and in 1981 he steered West Ham to the Second Division championship. In the same year West Ham reached the quarter-final of the Cup-winners' Cup and were unlucky to be taken to a replay by Liverpool in the League Cup Final. They lost at Villa Park by the odd goal of three.

Under John, West Ham became one of the most feared cup-fighting teams in England. Apart from the above triumphs he twice reached the sixth round of the FA Cup and the semi-finals of the League Cup in 1989.

In 1985-86, John piloted the Hammers to their highest position ever in the First Division. They finished third, four points behind champions Liverpool and two short of runners-up Everton. The Irons were eight points clear of fourth-placed Manchester United.

John Lyall is a man with integrity. An honest person, he always gave enormous credit to his mentor Ron Greenwood. John did a great deal to establish the Hammers' reputation for open, entertaining football, even in the most adverse conditions and in the face of criticism from less talented observers:

"Alan would always greet you with a grin or a smile. He was a typical Cockney, lovable and bright."

## Ernie Gregory

Joining the ground staff in 1936, Ernie Gregory was a member of the 1958 Second Division championship side and an England 'B' international. Ernie would have certainly have gained many full England caps if he had taken the opportunity of moving to Arsenal in the mid-1950s, but he chose to stay loyal to the Hammers. After his playing career ended in 1959 he took on a range of coaching and team administration jobs at the club, up to the late 1980s. It is likely that Ernie was the best all round 'keeper West Ham has ever had, in terms of his general understanding of the role and the game in general. Now, nearing 80 years of age, he is still a sharp observer of the game.

"Alan was a nice kid. I loved him."

## Bobby Howe

Bobby Howe is a former Essex Schools star. He signed as a professional in the same year as he played in the West Ham Youth Cup-winning side. Bobby, a chivalrous and considerate person, is now the Director of Coaching Education for US Soccer in Chicago.

"Alan is sadly missed."

## Jack Burkett

Jack Burkett was a fine attacking defender, quick in the tackle. Injury in the 1966-67 season robbed West Ham of what would probably have been his best years. In all he played 184 League and Cup games for the Hammers, 66 of them in the same team as Alan. His first-team career stretched throughout most of the 1960s, but he had come up through the club system in the late 1950s. He was capped for England at youth level and came very near to winning full international honours. Jack is currently working with the PFA Youth Training Scheme. Like all of the men paying homage to Alan here, Jack Burkett remains a true gentleman, and shining example to younger players. He is fine ambassador for his former club and the game in general.

"It was very sad news to hear of Alan's death. Lots of clubs have reunions, but it is not something that West Ham do as a rule, so it's sometimes difficult to stay in touch. Alan was always on the go. He is, of course, sadly missed."

## Malcolm Musgrove

Malcolm was one of the Second Division championship team of 1957-58. Malcolm was PFA chairman between 1963 and 1966 and was assistant manager to Frank O'Farrell at both Leicester and Manchester United. A generous and insightful man, at the time of writing, Malcolm was still very much involved with the game at Shrewsbury Town.

"I spent two seasons with Alan at Upton Park, starting with his debut game against Leicester in 1961 and ending in the 1962-63 season when I went to Orient, Alan's first club. Alan was a smashing lad, very jovial and I was very pleased to have known him and played 35 times in a West Ham team with him."

## Bill Lansdowne Senior

In the first game Bill and Alan played together, the victory against Cardiff City in April 1962, Alan scored the first of the Hammers' four goals.

"It doesn't seem fair that he had to leave us so soon."

## Eddie Presland

Eddie Presland played only once in the same team as Alan Sealey, at Blackburn in March 1965. However, he knew Alan when they were both teenagers. Eddie, being an East Ham boy, out of Strone Road, and a first-rate cricketer playing with Essex for some years, played with and against Alan before they finally joined forces under the Hammers banner.

Eddie has worked in the same East End school for well over 30 years. He is a credit to his football training, still giving great service to the community and the area he came from. A polite and modest man, Eddie is a person of quality, one of the unsung philosophers of the game. Meeting Eddie gives some rationale to supporting West Ham. While Upton Park continues to produce diamonds like him, it more than makes up for any lack of silverware.

"Alan was a lovely man. Like Bobby, he never forgot his roots."

## Harry Redknapp

Harry, the current manager of West Ham, joined the Irons in the early 1960s as a member of the ground staff. He broke into the Hammers' first team in the season Alan missed through injury, 1965-66. They played alongside each other just once, in the home game against West Brom late in 1966. Harry scored the first goal in this 3-0 win, from a cross by Brian Dear. This was the second of his eight-goal total for the club.

"Alan and I went back a long way. He had been at Upton Park ever since I returned and was with us on the Wednesday before he passed on, having a cup of tea and a chat. It was a tremendous shock and very sad. He was a real good character, a typical Londoner and we will miss him a lot. Alan's wife Barbara, son Anthony and mother Elsie loved him very much – just like we all did. God Bless Sammy."

## Martin Britt

A former England youth International, Martin was a talented centre-forward. West Ham had a prolific scoring front line while Martin was with the club, and if things had been different there is little doubt that he would have made a much bigger impact at Upton Park than he did before Blackburn splashed out a then huge £25,000 for him. However, his career was cut short following injury after only six games for Rovers. Martin is now a successful businessman. But he is also a good and kind person, who, as such, took the time out to talk and express his feelings about Alan.

> "Alan was a nice chap. We played only about seven games in the same team over a couple of seasons. The first was at home to Everton in 1963. We beat the then defending champions 4-2. Our final game together was the last match of that League season, this time at Goodison. A very sad loss."

## Sir Geoff Hurst MBE

Geoff Hurst, who was with West Ham when Alan Sealey arrived at the club, played 80 games alongside Sealey, including Alan's debut. In those matches the Hammers' forward line scored 149 goals, and Geoff got 38 of those. The final time they appeared together in the same team, in a competitive match, was the last game of the 1966-67 season at the Boleyn Ground against Manchester City.

> "I wish you every success with your forthcoming book, and I have no doubt, it will indeed, be a fitting tribute to Alan Sealey."

## Paul Heffer

Born within 'the sound of Upton Park', Paul was a tall, commanding and talented centre-half, who also carried the qualities of so many of the people of his area: determination and ability to work hard. This being the case, Paul achieved what young East Enders dream about in legion: to play for the Hammers. However, his promising career was cut short by injury just as he was starting to have an impact on the West Ham first team. Irons fans thus lost a fine, intelligent defender.

> "Alan was always cheerful and full of fun."

## Bill Kitchener

Bill was a tall, skilful full-back who played in the West Ham Youth Cup-winning side of 1963. After his playing career, like Alan Dickie, Bill translated his intelligent and cogent play into a distinguished career as a police officer.

> "I was very sorry to hear that Alan Sealey had passed away. I was unaware until I received your letter. 'Sammy' (the Seal) as he was affectionately known, was a good-hearted, happy character. I played alongside him in his final game for the club, that was the last game of the 1966-67 season against Manchester City at Upton Park. I will always remember Alan as a lively, likeable gent."

## Joe Kirkup

Joe Kirkup was the kind of player that made things possible; the pounding heart of football culture. He was a member of the Hammers team that lost to Manchester United in the 1956-57 FA Youth Cup and he won England youth honours. He went on to make the Under-23 side. Joe, an athletic and swift attacking full-back, and Alan Sealey were in the same West Ham side for the first time in the initial game of the 1961-62 season, a 1-1 draw against Manchester United at Upton Park. Alan laid on John Dick's goal for West Ham. In all they played together 84 times over six seasons, including four European appearances.

> "Alan was always an upbeat, cheerful character in the dressing-room, with a ready word and a smile for everyone. A pleasure knowing you, Alan."

## Alan Dickie

Trained by the immortal Ernie Gregory, Dickie was unlucky to be at the club while Jim Standen was in such good and consistent form. Dickie was a great servant of the Hammers, a solid squad player who had a devotion to club and team-mates hardly known in the game today. Even now he displays fidelity to West Ham that leaves one with great admiration for the man. He is a loyal and humane person.

"I was surprised to hear that Alan had passed on. The first I knew of it was when I got your letter. I'm very much a Charlton man, having been born overlooking the ground and not being one of the lads living that side of the river, I have lost touch. But my son is a season ticket holder at Upton Park and he hadn't heard anything. The last time I saw Alan was when he played in Wally St Pier's testimonial, when the 1964 Cup winning side played the 1975 winners. You tend not to say anything bad about people who have passed on, but in Alan's case there's not a bad word to say anyway."

## Trevor Hartley

When Trevor went to Bournemouth he became the youngest manager in the Football League at the age of 27. Trevor and Alan turned out for the Hammers together just twice, in 1967. Trevor represents the backbone of soccer history, the concrete between the bricks of the game. It is the likes of him of which football is made.

"When I joined the club, West Ham had just won the FA Cup. That season would see the team win European Cup-winners' Cup. This was followed by the achievements of our World Cup winning trio, Bobby Moore, Geoff Hurst and Martin Peters. As such, it was certainly a happy time for the Hammers. I thoroughly enjoyed my five years with West Ham, and Alan was very much a part of this. He made me feel welcome from the start. Fondest memories."

## Terry Connelly

Terry is one of the great lifetime West Ham supporters. He lives near the Sealey family home in Romford, and knew Alan well, not just as a footballer, but as a man.

"Alan was a wonderful guy. He was a real character."

## Ron Penn

Ron was a close friend of Alan Sealey for many years.

"I saw Alan about two weeks before he passed away. He told me that he was fine and that the hospital had sorted him out. It was such a shock when I heard he had died. There was no side to Alan, he was very modest about his achievements."

## Eddie Baily

Eddie was the assistant manager and coach at Leyton Orient when Alan arrived at the club. He went on to work for Tottenham and later West Ham. Eddie is recognised within the game as a ground-breaking coach from the 1950s and 1960s.

"Alan was such a nice lad."

And finally …

## Barbara Sealey
– Alan's widow

"All I can say is how much we all loved him and miss him dreadfully."

# Alan Sealey / West Ham United Chronology in the 1960s

**May 1959**          West Ham buy the Boleyn Ground for £30,000.

**March 1961**        Ted Fenton resigns. Alan Sealey joins West Ham from Orient.

**April 1961**        Ron Greenwood becomes manager.
                      Alan Sealey plays his first game for West Ham, away to Leicester (the Hammers lose 5-1). He scores his first goal for the Irons at Upton Park in a 1-1 draw with Manchester City.

**March 1962**        Johnny Byrne is transferred from Crystal Palace for £65,000, a record fee between English clubs.

**April 1963**        FA Youth Cup Final v Liverpool. West Ham won 6-5 on aggregate after extra-time.

| | |
|---|---|
| **July 1963** | West Ham become International Soccer League champions in the USA. |
| **February 1964** | West Ham reach the semi-final of the League Cup v Leicester City. West Ham lose 6-3 on aggregate. |
| **May 1964** | West Ham win the FA Cup (v Preston North End, 3-2). |
| **September 1964** | West Ham's first match in a European competition (v La Gantoise in the Cup-winners' Cup). |
| **February 1965** | Alan Sealey scores what is to be his final League goal for West Ham, in the 2-1 defeat at Sheffield United. |
| **May 1965** | West Ham win the European Cup-winners' Cup (v TSV Munich, 2-0). Alan Sealey scores both the Hammers' goals. These are the last goals he will score for the club in domestic or European football. |
| **July 1965** | Alan Sealey breaks his leg at the West Ham training ground in Chadwell Heath. |
| **August 1965** | West Ham's Peter Bennett becomes the first-ever substitute in First Division football (v Leeds at Upton Park – West Ham win 2-1). |
| **March 1966** | West Ham reach the Final of the League Cup (v West Brom, West Ham lose 5-3 on aggregate). |
| **April 1966** | West Ham reach the semi-final of the European Cup-winners' Cup (v Borussia Dortmund, West Ham lose 5-2 on aggregate). |
| **July 1966** | England win the World Cup. Bobby Moore, Martin |

Peters and Geoff Hurst, all West Ham players, take part. Hurst scores three and Peters one in the 4-2 win for England.

**January/February 1967** West Ham reach the semi-final of the League Cup lose 6-2 on aggregate to West Brom).

**May 1967** Bobby Ferguson is transferred from Kilmarnock for £65,000, a world record fee for a goalkeeper. Alan Sealey plays his final game for West Ham in English football. It is the last match of the 1966-67 season, a 1-1 draw with Manchester City at Upton Park.

**September 1967** Alan Sealey leaves West Ham for Plymouth Argyle.

**October 1968** Geoff Hurst scores six goals against Sunderland, equalling Vic Watson's club record for the most goals scored by an individual in one match.

**June 1970** Martin Peters, Bobby Moore and Geoff Hurst with the England squad in Mexico for the World Cup finals.

# Bibliography

Allison, M. *Colours of My Life* Everest 1975

Barber, D. *We Won the Cup* Pan 1981

Barrett, N. *The Daily Telegraph Football Chronicle* Carlton 1994

Blowers, S. *Arise, Sir Geoff* Hammers News August 1998

Butler, B. *The Official History of The Football Association* Queen Anne 1991

Campbell, D. & Shields, A. *Soccer City* Mandarin 1993

Churchill, R.C. *English League Football* Sportsmans 1962

Clavane, A. *'Arry talks a good game as Christian Soldiers on* Sunday Mirror (2/8/98)

Cook, C. and Stevenson, J. *Modern British History* Longman 1988

Edman, I. *John Dewet* Greenwood 1968

Francis, D. *West Ham United Official 1996-97 Handbook* Independent 1996

Gambaccini, P., Rice, J. & Rice, T. *Top 40 Charts* Guinness 1997

Green, G. *Soccer in the Fifties* Ian Allan 1974

Greenwood, R. *Yours Sincerely Ron Greenwood* Collins Willow 1984

Heatley, M.& Ford, D. *British Football Grounds Then and Now* Dial 1994

Hopcraft, A. *The Football Man* Collins 1970

Hogg, T. and McDonald, T. *Who's Who of West Ham United* Independent UK Sports 1996

Korr, C. *West Ham United* Duckworth 1986

Leatherdale, C. *England's Quest for the World Cup* Methuen 1984

Leatherdale, C. *West Ham United. From Greenwood to Redknapp* Desert Island 1998

Lyall, J. *Just Like My Dreams* Penguin 1989

Mason, T. *Association Football and English Society 1863-1915* Harvester 1980

Northcutt, J. & Shoesmith, R *West Ham United. A Complete Record* Breedon 1993

Pallot, J.(ed) *The Virgin Film Guide* Virgin 1996

# BIBLIOGRAPHY

Palmer, A.W. *Modern History* Penguin 1978

Pickering, D. *The Cassell Soccer Companion* Cassell 1994

Powell, J. *Bobby Moore* Robson 1993

Prole, D. *Football in London* Hale 1964

Oliver, G. *The Guinness Book of World Soccer (2nd Ed)* Guinness 1995

Rollin, G.*Rothmans Football Yearbook* Headline 1996

Wenborn, N. *The 20th Century* Hamlyn 1989

Young, P.M. *A History of British Football* Arrow 1968

# Index